THE GOLDEN BOOK OF
AMERICAN
WILDFLOWERS

THE GOLDEN BOOK OF
AMERICAN
WILDFLOWERS

Photographs by Farrell Grehan | Text by H. W. Rickett

Formerly Senior Botanist,
The New York Botanical Garden

GOLDEN PRESS • NEW YORK
Western Publishing Company, Inc.
Racine, Wisconsin

ACKNOWLEDGMENTS

The generous help of many botanists in identifying the plants shown in the photographs is gratefully acknowledged, particularly that of Dr. Mildred E. Mathias and her colleagues of the University of California, Dr. Robert K. Godfrey of Florida State University, Dr. Charles T. Mason Jr., of the University of Arizona, Dr. M. R. Birdsey of the Miami-Dade Junior College, and Miss Carol Beck of Highlands Hammock State Park, Florida.

FARRELL GREHAN
H. W. RICKETT

INTRODUCTION

There may be—it is difficult to estimate—some fifteen thousand species* of flowering plants growing wild in North America. There are, for instance, between four and five thousand in the northeastern quarter of the continent; four thousand in the Rocky Mountains; over three thousand in Arizona; about four thousand in California; over five thousand in the southeastern United States. Each of these regions has many species peculiar to itself: the cacti of the southwestern deserts, the violets and anemones of eastern woodlands, the Spanish-moss that hangs from southern trees. Each shares many species with other regions, so that we cannot simply add the figures for different parts of the continent to get the total; twenty per cent of all the flowering plants of Arizona, for instance, are introduced from elsewhere or are common to the whole continent. The figure I have given is little more than a guess; but it cannot be much too large. Moreover, these fifteen thousand species include many minor variants which are recognized and given names by botanists.

It is obvious that no person can know all these plants; and that a manual or guide to them would form a set of ponderous volumes. Yet, for the amateur naturalist or wildflower lover, things are not so bad as the figures may suggest. First, many of the supposed fifteeen thousand are trees and shrubs, most of which—oaks, elms, hickories, birches, alders, willows, pines, hemlocks, junipers, and others—have inconspicuous flowers (or cones) that are of interest only to the professional. Second, many other thousands of species are grasses and sedges and other plants with small greenish or brownish flowers hardly noticed by the amateur. Then there are many unlovely weeds—pigweeds, ragweeds, cockleburs, beggar-ticks, and such —that make us happiest

---

* Definitions of this and other botanical terms used in this book are given in the *Glossary of Terms* which follows this Introduction.

by their absence. When we eliminate all these plants, we have what are generally known as wildflowers, all of interest to the layman for their beauty and some perhaps for their rarity, as well as to the botanist for reasons of his own. Of these there are perhaps six or eight thousand.

To know all the wildflowers of North America even in this restricted sense is a formidable task even for a professional; and to describe and illustrate them all would still require a set of books—or one very large book. The present volume offers a selection from all this wealth of natural forms. The photographs and text embrace most of the colors and shapes and sizes of our wildflowers. They illustrate also the different types of plants that cover our varied landscape, and they represent the plant families by which the botanist creates some order in the apparently haphazard variety of nature.

THE VEGETATION OF NORTH AMERICA

Everyone knows that different parts of the country are clothed with different kinds of plants; yet few persons stop to consider why this should be so. Why do the redwoods grow along the coast of California and not along that of New England? Why are there no forests in western Kansas? Why do the high mountains support an evergreen forest of conifers, while the forests of Iowa are composed chiefly of maples, oaks, and hickories? Botanists cannot yet answer all such questions. But many of the problems of the geographic distribution of plants have been solved. The first step in the attack is to describe the various types of vegetation; these may then be correlated with differences in climate and soil. A further step is to investigate the history of various species. For species do have histories, just as the races of men have histories. They are wiped out by glaciers; they migrate to new lands; they become split into several portions by changes in the landscape, such portions perhaps subsequently developing into different varieties or even different species. All such events help to determine the present situation of particular species or groups of species.

Botanists have classified the vegetation of North America in a number of fairly obvious regional types, such as northern coniferous forest, northeastern deciduous forest, and so forth. Of course, man has interfered with these regions, replacing the original forests, in large part, by farm lands, highways, gardens, cities. But even in the most thickly populated parts of the country vestiges of the pristine vegetation persist, and it is in such relics of the forests and prairies that we most commonly seek for wildflowers. In this context, therefore, the botanical names of the regions may continue to be useful. And the principal differences of climate and other obvious factors may suggest, if they do not completely explain, why (for instance) the wildflowers found in New York are not common in Arizona. It is also worth noticing that the types of vegetation listed in the following pages are mostly characterized by and named for the trees that grow there. Trees are larger than shrubs and herbaceous plants and condition their lives. If the forest is removed, the whole vegetation changes; this has happened wherever man has intruded, substituting cultivated plants (which sometimes "escape" from cultivation) and cosmopolitan weeds for the original inhabitants.

In any one area, moreover, characterized by a certain type of vegetation, we find smaller areas that have their own conditions of temperature, precipitation, and so forth, different from those of the region as a whole. On exposed cliffs extremes of temperature run higher and lower than in the forest nearby, and the moisture is scantier. In the swamps, streams, and pools temperature may be more constant, and water, of course, almost too plentiful. So the type of vegetation called "northeastern deciduous forest" embraces many plants that are not deciduous trees and that form local communities —plant societies.

The account that follows is considerably simplified from that of the professional plant geographer. He would divide the large types of vegetation into more uniform ones, extending through smaller regions more homogeneous in their climatic conditions and in the other factors of plant distribution. The broadly sketched types of the following treatment will, however, suffice for the beginner who seeks to understand the elements of botanical science.

The Northeastern Deciduous Forest

A deciduous tree is one that loses its leaves periodically. The northeastern deciduous forest occupies (or once occupied) a vast area of the northeastern United States and adjacent Canada, with a climate marked by extremes of heat and cold, summer and winter dividing the year about equally. Most of the trees lose their leaves in winter. Over much of the area, however, evergreen (coniferous) trees are mingled with the deciduous species. This forest extends from New England westward to Minnesota and southward to Georgia, northern Alabama and Mississippi, and Arkansas. This is also the part of the country that has, in the main, proved most suitable for human enterprise, with a consequent density of population.

As one might expect of so large an area, conditions are not the same throughout. Rainfall (or more accurately, precipitation) decreases as one goes from east to west, from about 45 inches a year in New England to about 25 in Iowa. The spring comes in March in Missouri and Virginia, not until May in Maine and Minnesota. A traveler passing from east to west or from north to south finds corresponding differences in the plants he encounters: maples, beeches, oaks, ash, birches in the North Atlantic States and westward to Ontario and Minnesota, mixed with hemlock and white pine; oaks, spruce, and fir, with rhododendrons, along the mountain chains; oaks and hickories, mainly, in Iowa and Missouri, with shortleaf pine as one goes south; maple and basswood, with other species, in parts of Wisconsin and adjacent states; and so on. This is (or was) a region of summer shade; wildflowers enjoy their greatest glory in spring before many leaves appear on the trees (February to May). Here we find the trilliums and violets, anemones, dogtooth-violets, bloodroot, and many others. These species are perennial, sending up flowers and leaves together from bulbs, rhizomes, tubers, and other underground repositories of food. There are also shade-loving flowering plants and ferns that flourish through the summer and into autumn. And, as man opened the woods and made fields and roads, the annual weeds moved in, along with the perennial goldenrods, asters, and sunflowers, which put forth tall stems from a cluster of roots or a thin rhizome and take all summer to reach the flowering stage.

The Northern Coniferous Forest

North and northwest of the northeastern deciduous forest the northern coniferous forest stretches, in a relatively thin band, all across Canada and into Alaska, with fingers running down the mountains of New Hampshire and Vermont, and the Rocky Mountains—a wild terrain largely uninhabited by man. This is a forest of spruce, balsam fir, tamarack, white cedar, hemlock, and various pines, with a scattering of birches, aspens, and poplars. Many wildflowers are related to those of the deciduous forest. Much of the surface of the land was planed smooth by the great glaciers of thousands of years ago; when they retreated they left a landscape with low relief in which water moved sluggishly. In the resulting swamps and bogs and at the margins of the numerous shallow lakes grow many plants of the Shinleaf, Heath, and Blueberry families, many orchids, and other species adapted to cool, acid soils. This vegetation is the type fitted to a short growing season—only three or four months in the year, and none of these quite free from the threat of frost.

A northeastern meadow carpeted with
ox-eye daisies and viper's bugloss.

The Arctic and Subarctic Region

North of the northern coniferous forest is a vast region almost without trees, known as the tundra. The soil in much of this country never completely thaws; only the upper few inches support living plants, and beneath those few inches are many feet of ice. The growing season is only two or three months long; but in this season the sun shines for many hours. Such conditions conspire to create an environment for only very specially adapted plants. Many of these are low, their leaves lying flat on the soil; others have needlelike leaves. Here grow anemones, pinks, lupines, cinquefoils, and other herbs, related to those of less rigorous latitudes but not the same. There are also willows which reach heights of only a few inches. The tundra extends south on the highest summits of mountains, such as Mount Washington in the East and the peaks of the Rockies in the West. It has not been to any extent sampled by artists and photographers.

The Southeastern Evergreen Forest and Subtropical Peninsula

As one travels southward in the mountains of the eastern half of North America, one finds a forest of increasing richness. Mixed with the oaks, elms, and maples are more and more sweetgums and sourgums, magnolias, rhododendrons. Some of these are the "broadleaf evergreens," which combine with various conifers to form a permanent green mantle. In the high mountains the climate is still rigorous and the growing season no longer than in the lowlands farther north; many of the wildflowers of such altitudes are the same as those of the northeastern deciduous forest. Farther south, however, and nearer sea level, the growing season lengthens out to seven or eight months. Here are bogs, with the insect-catching plants in abundance. Here are many new species of irises, with lantanas, honeysuckles, some lovely relatives of the lilies, golden-club, lizard-tails, verbenas—a wealth of bright colors and graceful forms. Here are the spreading live-oaks (evergreen oaks), draped with Spanish-moss (a flowering plant). Along the coast itself, from New Jersey to Georgia and beyond, we find the "pine barrens," a stretch of sandy soil that supports not only pines but scrub oaks and many small, bright-flowered herbs.

Farther south all this gives way to the open pine forest of the southern coastal plain: tall yellow pines, longleaf pines, and loblolly pines, with an undergrowth of palmetto scrub and other low plants. Finally, in peninsular Florida, we reach the subtropical climate where palms and mangroves are abundant and the branches of the live-oaks and other trees support or-

Tillandsia, an air-plant,
growing on trees
in the Florida Everglades.

chids. Here many wildflowers bloom through the winter. Types are found that extend into tropical America: Venus' looking-glass, wild pineapple, seaside goldenrod; and intruders from the tropics, as water-hyacinth.

Grasslands

Going west, one is subject to a constantly decreasing precipitation; the western half of the great eastern deciduous forest is drier than the eastern. In Ohio, Indiana, and Illinois, the early settlers found openings in the everlasting woods, covered only with grasses and other low herbs: prairie openings. Large parts of northern Missouri and Iowa were prairies; and the western parts of Kansas and Nebraska are still almost without trees, except along streams. Here are the grasslands, extending southward into Texas and northward far into Canada:"tall-grass prairies" eastward, "short-grass prairies" farther west and higher above sea level. Precipitation in this vast expanse—the Great Plains—dwindles to twenty inches or less, and much of that arrives in the winter, as snow; droughts are frequent in summer. Temperatures are hotter and colder even than in the eastern states. An accurate description of the grasslands of North America would necessitate subdividing them according to differences in soil, climate, and other factors; but for present purposes they may be lumped together under one head. Vast herds of bison and other animals once roamed these plains; followed and hunted by the Indians who depended on them. In the course of their operations, the Indians often fired the grasses. The exact causes of treelessness are still somewhat controversial among plant geographers; but the conditions sketched above must have something to do with it. With the many species of grasses grow many herbs of the Bean family—prairie-clovers, loco-weeds, the well-known Texas bluebonnets; and many tall rosinweeds, compass-plants, tickseeds, and sunflowers of the Daisy family.

Forests of Western Mountains

Here we place, for convenience, a number of very different types of vegetation which extend southward along the Rocky Mountains and the Continental Divide, fingering out through the arid southwestern ranges, and there connecting with the parallel ranges of the Cascades and the Sierra Nevada. Along these mountain chains at high altitudes we find, as in the northern forests, short growing seasons separated by long periods of heavy snow. Here the coniferous trees find their proper place; their narrow leaves remain through the long winter and can carry on some activity when broader leaves have fallen; and their spirelike forms can better support weights of snow and ice than the broad-leafed trees. The mountains display, in different places, a wonderful assortment of conifers: pines, spruces, firs, hemlocks; piñon and junipers ("cedars") in the arid parts; and everywhere the great ponderosa pines and Douglas-firs. It is particularly among mountains that the histories of species exert an influence on their distribution. Mountain ranges, when they are folded upward, catch the masses of moist air coming from the oceans, catch the rain and snow, and throw a long shadow of dry air on the plains beyond. The big-trees (or giant sequoia) of the Sierra Nevada, thousands of years old, are the relics of a much larger population which once flourished in the western part of the continent. The mountain slopes above tree-line and below the snow in summer are adorned with thousands of bright flowers: bitter-root, blue and yellow columbines, larkspurs, gentians, lavender and yellow composites, monkey-flowers, beard-tongues, lupines, and many others.

The Southwestern Deserts (and the Great Basin)

Through much of Texas and across New Mexico, southern Colorado and Utah, and Arizona into southern California, rainfall is low and temperature high. Some parts of Arizona have as little as three inches of rain a year—none some years—and temperatures frequently above 100° F. in the shade —where there is no shade. But there are plants that can thrive in such an environment. Among them the cacti are conspicuous, with horrific armaments of spines and beautiful, large flowers: prickly-pears, cholla, barrel and pincushion and hedgehog cacti, saguaro and organ-pipes, and others. Mixed with these prickly plants are various wiry shrubs with small leaves: mesquite, palo verde, greasewood. Some of these lose their leaves between rains as trees in the East do in winter. The ground between plants is mostly bare of grass but springs into spectacular bloom after a rainy season; composites such as tidy-tips, desert-marigold, flannel-flower, golden-stars, groundsels, and many others carpet the ground with gold; prickly-poppies, evening-primroses, desert-mallows vary the pattern and the color.

Northward these deserts pass into the Great Basin of Nevada and Idaho, the vast semidesert of the "purple sage." This territory between the great mountain chains is a region of few streams, of salt seas and "sinks," and "alkali" that restricts the growth of plants much as does the arid heat farther south. The more attractive wildflowers, such as the larger cacti and many of the yellow composites mentioned above, do not reach into these parts; for

which reason we may combine many distinct types of vegetation. Prickly-poppies and evening-primroses and many other conspicuous flowers are to be seen; few from the Great Basin are illustrated in this book.

The Pacific Northwest

The transcontinental botanist finds the western limits of vegetation on the Pacific Coast. Here the steep mountains plunge into the sea, with room only for a narrow coastal flora between—and sometimes not even that. Rain and fog come in from the ocean and irrigate tall and lush forests of Douglas-fir, Sitka spruce, western hemlock, and many others, including, at the south, the beautiful tall redwoods. Behind the coastal mountains lie fertile valleys; and these are bounded on the east by the Cascade Mountains. The mountains shelter flowers much like those of the eastern forests, but in different species: violets, cinquefoils, spring beauty, trilliums, and many others. On the slopes of the great snow-capped extinct volcanoes—Hood, Rainier, Adams, Baker—one finds brilliant flower gardens extending above the tree-line to the edges of the eternal snow: valerians, lupines, monkey-flowers, painted-cups, cinquefoils, roses—and the avalanche-lilies (related to the eastern dogtooth-violets) even emerging through the snow itself. Here in the Pacific Northwest we find a great variety of different environments and a correspondingly rich vegetation.

California

California is a long, narrow state which embraces wide extremes of temperature and rainfall. At the north are the Siskiyou Mountains, which are connected with the Cascades already mentioned; and along the coast are the redwood groves and other fine coniferous forests belonging to the Pacific Northwest vegetation. At the south we find deserts and dry mountain ranges, closely connected with the southwestern deserts already described, and extending down into Baja California. In between these extremes we find a varied flora with many distinct environments. Along the coast there may be fog; on the cliffs grow the dudleyas and mesembryanthemums and other succulent plants; there is a beach vegetation of such things as *Franseria,* lupines, sand-verbena, and grasses. From the strand rise the coast ranges. Southward where the slopes are hot and dry the chaparral grows, composed of low broad-leafed shrubs, as chamise (greasewood), flannel-bush, yucca, woolly blue-curls, and many others. Farther south are various types of

The California coast near Monterey,
where a field of wild radish mixed with
California poppies nearly meets the sea.

greasewood, sage, and other plants of the desert or semidesert. ranges and the valleys between, the well-known California-pop- the dry slopes, with other colorful species called farewell-to- ..g, godetias, evening-primroses, larkspurs, saxifrages, blue-dicks, and the lovely mariposa-lilies. As in the southwestern deserts, a host of yellow-flowered species of the Daisy family bloom suddenly after a rainy season. At other times the land presents an aspect of slopes covered with yellow grasses and herbs.

THE NATURE OF FLOWERS

What is a flower? What is common to all flowering plants that enables us to apply this name to creatures so diverse as violets, grasses, oaks, cat-tails, ragweeds, roses, and sunflowers? How can we describe one flower so as to display the ways in which it differs from another flower?

Among flowers there is indeed an astonishing diversity—and an equally surprising uniformity. Their diversity is easily apparent; but the uniformity provides the clue to their essential nature. The differences among flowers are most obvious in their outer and generally larger and more brightly colored

The flower of a water-lily *(Nymphaea odorata)* opens; the green sepals which covered the inner parts have spread apart and downward, disclosing the erect crown of white petals.

parts, the sepals and petals, collectively called the perianth. The similarities are in the inner parts, the pistil and stamens, often called the "essential parts" of a flower, since they are directly concerned with the formation of fruit and seed.

A description of a flower must take account of both these sets of parts, the perianth and the essential parts. A certain technical vocabulary is necessary to a precise characterization of sepals, petals, stamens, pistil; recognition depends upon precision. In works that treat many thousands of species, this terminology is necessarily large and complex. In a book such as this, technical terms can be kept to a small number; but even here a certain amount of scientific jargon is necessary to deliver us from utter vagueness. The following exposition should be read with reference to the diagram on page 18 of a "typical" flower.

A fairly representative type of flower, then, consists essentially of a pistil (*pistillum*, "pestle" in modern English; from the resemblance of many pistils to a chemist's pestle) situated in the center, terminating the stalk that bears the flower; and several stamens standing around the pistil. The pistil consists of three parts: a lower hollow part, the ovary; a slender style (*stylus*, "column") rising from the ovary; a more or less sticky stigma at or near the

The perianth of an American lotus *(Nelumbo lutea)* opens to reveal the "essential parts," stamens and pistils. The pistils are in the hollows of the peculiar central body, which is found in no other plant.

summit of the style. The cavity or cavities of the ovary contain minute bodies called ovules ("little eggs"), the future seeds. A stamen is composed of a stalk, which may be threadlike or ribbonlike; and, at the summit of this stalk, an anther, generally divided by a lengthwise groove into two halves, each half containing two chambers side by side in which pollen is formed. The anther opens by a slit or a hole and discharges the pollen, which consists of thousands of microscopic grains, generally in a dusty or sticky mass. The pollen may cling to the outside of the anther for a time.

Around these essential parts, which vary in number, size, and proportions, is the envelope of more or less showy and beautiful petals; these are surrounded in turn by the usually green sepals; sepals and petals together compose the perianth. The petals are known collectively as the corolla ("little crown"); the sepals as the calyx ("covering"; they cover all the other parts in the bud).

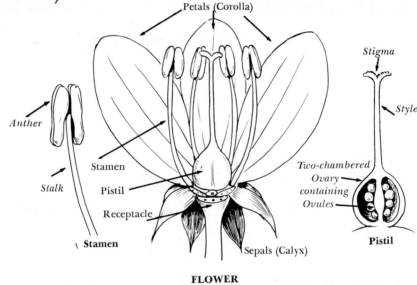

FLOWER

(ONE STAMEN, TWO PETALS, AND ONE SEPAL REMOVED)

The chief business of the flower—*from the plant's point of view*—is the production of fruit and seed; it is a reproductive organ. This is also the botanist's point of view; he interprets the flower as a means of producing more plants of the same kind, of furthering the survival of the species. All its beauty, its intricate structure, are understood in that light. The layman usually thinks of flowers as an adornment of his person, as an enhancement of his home, and as a comfort for his afflictions. The naturalist, whether professional or amateur, has the advantage, in his excursions, of appreciating flowers that are at the same time beautiful and functional in their natural environment: they satisfy their own needs as well as ours.

The reproductive processes in flowers are, in brief, the following. Pollen, a mass of minute living particles, is formed in the anthers of the stamens and is liberated by the opening of the anthers. From there it is transported, by one means or another, to the stigma of a pistil of the same or another flower. If certain conditions of compatibility are realized, each grain of pollen may send forth a slender living thread, which penetrates the stigma and finds its way down the style—inside it—into the ovary; there it enters an ovule. A single cell then passes from this living thread into the ovule and there unites with a single cell formed in the ovule. The result of this union is a new cell, which develops in due course into an embryo—the plantlet found in a seed. The surrounding parts of the ovule form the coat of the seed.

As the ovule becomes a seed, the ovary in whose cavity it lies undergoes vast changes in size, shape, color, and texture. In many flowers surrounding parts of the flower are joined with it and undergo a similar development. The result is that as the seed develops, it is still enclosed in another body, just as its first rudiment, the ovule, was enclosed in the ovary. The enclosing body, whatever its physical nature, is what the botanist calls the fruit.

THE DIVERSITY OF FLOWERS

The diversity of flowers is not only in their sizes and colors but extends also to every detail of their make-up. Any of the floral parts may be lacking—providing at least one of the essential parts is present. A stalk that corresponds in its anatomy to any other flower-stalk but bears only a single stamen must still be said to bear a flower; and flowers of such simplicity actually exist (in the Spurge family, for instance). Even if both stamens and pistil are present, the perianth may be lacking; many species have no such attractive colored envelope around the essential parts. Unfortunately the botanical concept of flowers leaves out many of our garden species and varieties, which were bred for petals and have lost, somewhere in their ancestry, both stamens and pistils. Many varieties of peonies, for instance, and most dahlias, are thus deficient. According to the botanical definition—which must evidently be taken with salt—these are not flowers. But in our present concern with flowers growing in the wild, we may agree with the scientist and leave the gardener to his own devices.

A further complication is that many kinds of flowers have a perianth that consists of only *one* circle of segments. These are generally and arbitrarily called sepals by the botanist, whether or not they are colored as petals usually are. A buttercup has two circles of perianth-parts, a calyx of green sepals and within these a corolla of usually yellow petals. A marsh-marigold (in the

19

same family) has one circle of bright yellow perianth-parts, which look like petals but are always called sepals, a distinction often confusing to the amateur naturalist. A further arbitrary distinction is made for flowers that have two circles of parts whose segments look all alike; in such flowers the words petals and sepals are not generally used; the whole envelope is simply the perianth.

Most commonly the sepals are green, like small leaves, and the petals larger and of another color (though green petals do exist). In the larkspurs the sepals are blue or purple or pink or white, the petals being small objects which cluster in the center to form the "bee" of the flower. Petals of many flowers are joined to form a tube which flares at the end into equal lobes (phlox), or a funnel (morning-glory), or a "two-lipped" corolla with upper and lower lobes clearly separated and often unlike (monkey-flower). The sepals also may be joined and the calyx two-lipped (salvia). Such facts are of diagnostic importance to persons who want to know the name and the family of a flower they find. And these different forms of corolla and calyx certainly contribute as much to the attractiveness of flowers as color does.

The form of the flower and the development of the fruit depend in part upon the shape of the tip of the flower-stalk and the manner in which the parts are disposed on it; it is called the receptacle. In a large number of wildflowers, the receptacle is nothing but a small knob or disc. But in others it is a column, the perianth attached at its base and the stamens and pistils on its sides; the receptacle thus seems to rise through the middle of the flower.

The flower of the clamshell orchid
has one petal, the uppermost, quite different from the
other two, which resemble the three sepals.

The flower of a western jimson-weed
shows the radial symmetry of its five petals,
which are joined to form a flaring funnel.

This is true in strawberries and cinquefoils and many anemones and buttercups. In still other species, as roses, the receptacle is hollow and forms a sort of cup or vase, the pistil or pistils situated on the inner surface and the perianth and stamens standing on the rim. This leads us to a type of structure which is often confusing but is nevertheless important in the identification of flowers and understanding of their development: the inferior ovary. The word "inferior" in Latin refers only to position, not to quality or efficiency; the inferior ovary is an ovary lower than the other parts. But, more important still, it has come to mean an ovary whose sides are joined to the surrounding sides of a cup-shaped receptacle so that the ovary cannot be lifted out as a unit, nor is there any definite boundary that separates the outside of the ovary from the inside of the receptacle-cup. This is the structure of an apple blossom, of all the flowers of the Cucumber, Blueberry, Bedstraw, Iris, Orchid, Lobelia, Bluebell, Evening-primrose, and many other families. Obviously as the ovary develops into a fruit (in the botanical sense) the surrounding receptacle will play some part in the finished product.

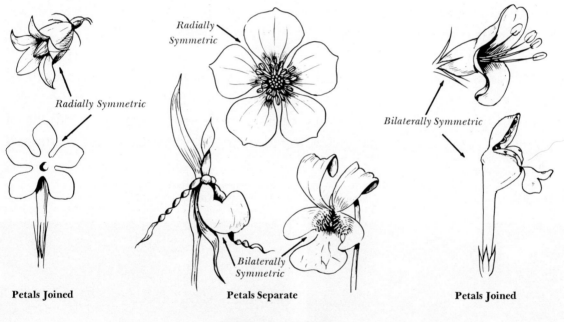

Petals Joined   Petals Separate   Petals Joined

TYPES OF COROLLA

FRUITS

The word has unfortunately several different meanings, among botanists as well as among housewives, merchants, and gourmets. To these, and others, it generally means succulent and delicious objects formed by plants, sometimes incorporated into salads but more often brought on as dessert: peaches, strawberries, pears, apples, melons. Other plant products *that have the same origin* are, according to our custom, served with the meat or as a salad: tomatoes, eggplant, cucumbers, peppers, avocado. These we are apt to call vegetables, classing them with potatoes, spinach, cabbage, and carrots. Yet a very slight acquaintance with botany reveals that the last-named objects are stems, roots, and leaves, while all the others, from peaches to avocado, are the product of flowers. We often use the word "fruit" also in wider senses, as equivalent to "product"; for the produce of any plant, for any part of a plant, or even for the result of reproduction in animals or the product of human actions.

Such vague usage finds no encouragement from botanists, who yearn for exact terms precisely defined. Considering the plant-parts commonly called fruits, such as peaches and strawberries, the botanist points out that they are derived from the ovary of the pistil of a flower, or from several ovaries, with or without other parts of the flower. But when we define "fruit" in this way, we find ourselves obliged to admit a large number of quite inedible objects to the group: pods of peas and beans and lilies, the hard shells of acorns, the grains of grasses, the "seeds" of strawberries and dandelions. All these are formed from the ovaries of flowers, from the same parts that give rise to grapes, cherries, tomatoes, bananas. So the botanist uses "fruit" in this all-inclusive sense; and this is the sense adopted in this book. (In the interest of precision, a more technical terminology may be desirable; but it becomes unpleasantly complicated.) Fruits, then, in this sense, are the products of flowers, comprising at least a developed ovary. And as the ovary contained

The berries of pokeweed are arranged in a raceme. Each fruit is the product of a single ovary which becomes succulent throughout.

Pods of common milkweed split open along one side (as do all follicles) to discharge the silky-hairy seeds.

one or more ovules, so the fruit contains one or more seeds (except for certain degenerate fruits, as bananas and seedless grapes, which we propagate by other means for our tables).

In the botanical sense fruits are of enormous variety; a satisfactory classification and naming of them has never been worked out. The term embraces *any* of the products of flowers; edible, inedible, even poisonous; succulent or hard and dry; pods that contain many seeds or complex bodies of several layers enclosing one seed; berries composed of many distinct fruits cohering or simple berries that develop from a single ovary.

In this book a few simple and common terms for fruits may be useful without being confusing.

A berry is defined as the succulent product of one ovary. It is unfortunate that this excludes strawberries, raspberries, and blackberries, which are formed of many ovaries on one receptacle; but this does not worry the botanist and will not concern the reader of the present volume. Examples of berries are blueberries, cranberries, grapes, tomatoes, bananas, and the fruits of Solomon's-seal, nightshades, and other wildflowers.

The fruit of cherry, plum, peach, olive, and dogwood is a stone-fruit. The outer parts of the ovary develop the more or less edible flesh; the inner parts become the stone. Within the stone is the seed (or two seeds in some).

There is a multitude of dry fruits, commonly known as "nuts," "grains," "pods"; the smaller ones are often miscalled seeds. The word "pod" may be used for any of these that open at maturity and discharge one or more seeds. To be slightly more technical, a pod that splits open along one vertical line is a follicle (larkspurs, meadow-rue). One that opens along several lines is a capsule (lily, evening-primrose); this is a very common type in the wild. The pods of the Bean family commonly split into two halves, and are called legumes; but some do not split open at all and are still called legumes, presumably because they belong to the Bean family; botanists are not always consistent! Many small dry fruits do not open at all. Most of these contain only one seed, and fruit and seed behave as a unit; they are called achenes; the buttercups and cinquefoils furnish examples.

THE ARRANGEMENT OF FLOWERS

This discussion is concerned not with the pleasant avocation of many persons, the creation of decorative syntheses of flowers and other objects, but with the ways in which flowers are arranged naturally on plants. For their disposition is not haphazard but precise and admits of exact classification and terminology. The subject, like that of fruits, is complex and not to be thoroughly expounded here; but a few elementary distinctions will aid in describing the species illustrated in the book, and—we hope—at the same time afford some insight into the manner in which plants grow and order their affairs.

One elementary type of flower cluster or inflorescence is the cyme. This is formed of a flower that terminates a branch with two flowers growing from the stalk below it and rising to its level or to a higher level. Such very simple cymes are not common in nature; usually the side flowers repeat the performance, each forming two side flowers, and so on, until a large and complex, usually flattish cluster may be formed. This is the sort of inflorescence we see in the Pink and Live-forever families, and many others.

Another type is the raceme. This is a more or less elongated cluster of flowers growing at different levels from a central stem. If the flowers have practically no stalks, the inflorescence is a spike. If the flowers have stalks that grow from or almost from the summit of the stem, the result is an umbel ("umbrella"); if the flowers grow from and near the summit on very short stalks, we call the cluster a head. The last term is used also in a special sense in the Daisy family (see the description of this family).

Many species arrange their flowers in a panicle, which is a rather loose inflorescence, often composed of irregular, small cymes arranged in a raceme (stick-tights, meadow-rue).

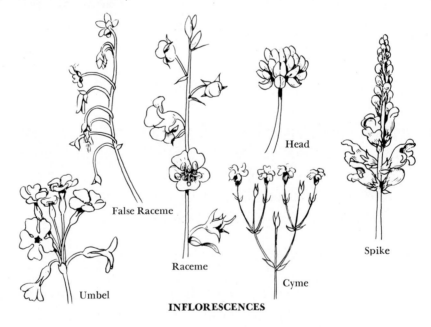

INFLORESCENCES

Of course flowers may grow at many points on a plant; how much of a plant should we call an inflorescence and designate by one of the above terms? The common test is the occurrence of foliage. If the flowers are mixed up with the leaves, each growing from the axil of a leaf (the upper angle between leaf-stalk and stem), we do not speak of an inflorescence; the flowers are said to be solitary (even if there are a thousand of them on the plant). But if a number of flowers occur together unmixed with foliage leaves, then we say they belong to an inflorescence. There are often small leaves in such a cluster, or leaves that differ in color from the foliage, or, sometimes, leaves that are larger than or of a different shape from the foliage leaves. These are called bracts. They take a great variety of forms, sometimes resembling sepals or petals and in some common flowers being easily mistaken for the flowers themselves (as in Indian paintbrushes or painted-cups). Accordingly some familiarity with this concept is necessary to any description of flowering plants.

Flowers, being a special form of branch, are generally found in the axils of bracts: growing in the angle made by the junction of bract and stem; this is true in many racemes and cymes. But in some families—the Forget-me-not family, the Waterleaf family, and others—flowers are found *opposite* bracts, on the other side of the stem. For inflorescences in which this occurs we use the terms *false* racemes, *false* heads, *false* umbels. They resemble those common types of clusters in general form; the actual differences are too technical to be treated here.

THE UNDERGROUND PARTS

Many wildflowers are perennial, displaying their foliage and blooms year after year from some part that lives through the dormant seasons. This is particularly true of the woodland flowers of early spring. The flowers and leaves appear usually together, growing from some underground part which endures the winter and which contains a reserve of food to start the new shoot in its early growth. The same is true of most of the species of high mountain slopes and of the tundra, which must be dormant most of the year and form foliage, flowers, fruit, and seeds in two or three months. Many fall-flowering species also are perennial, but spend the summer forming a tall stem and abundant foliage before coming into flower.

In understanding these habits of plants, it is useful to know something of their underground parts, little as these parts are seen or appreciated by most amateurs. The flowers of spring grow mostly from underground stems. These may be *horizontal* stems, often short and thick (violets), sometimes longer and more slender (Solomon's-seal, irises); they are called rhizomes. They are often miscalled roots ("bloodroot"), but have the buds and the anatomy of stems, and even vestiges of leaves. If they are very thick they are generally called tubers; a potato is a tuber.

Trilliums generally have a short, thick, *erect* stem; this is a corm. Some may call this a bulb, but the botanist reserves this term for the complex and beautiful bulb of a lily or onion or tulip: a body made up of circular, overlapping, succulent leaf-sheaths attached to a platelike or dome-shaped stem.

Roots also may become thick and filled with reserve food, as in dahlias; more frequently a cluster of moderately thick roots attached to a very short stem, a crown, may persist through the dormant season, as in some goldenrods and asters.

LEAVES AND STEMS

The visible parts of plants, the stems and branches with their foliage, are of enormous and baffling diversity; and, naturally, botanists have evolved an enormous—and baffling—vocabulary of descriptive terms, based chiefly on medieval Latin and nothing less than horrible to the beginning naturalist. A glance at any standard "flora" or "manual" generally leaves the amateur more bewildered and discouraged than informed. In the descriptions that follow, it has been possible to avoid almost all of these terms.

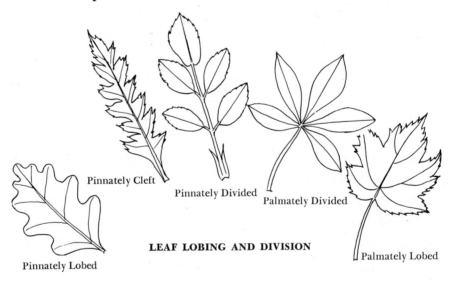

Pinnately Cleft

Pinnately Divided

Palmately Divided

Pinnately Lobed

LEAF LOBING AND DIVISION

Palmately Lobed

Many leaves are spoken of as "lance-shaped," "ovate," "elliptical," or "oblong." Lance-shaped of course refers to the *head* of a lance: narrow, broadest between the middle and the base, tapering to a point. Ovate refers to an egg (*ovum*); it designates the outline of an egg, with the broadest part near the base (the other end may be blunt or even pointed!). Elliptical means the geometrical figure, which is broadest in the middle and slopes off equally in

The leaves of thimbleberry are lobed
(the indentations not deep); the lobes are arranged palmately
(radiating from the central part).

The leaves of golden-flowers are divided
into many small blades on one stalk; the segments are
arranged pinnately, on two sides of a midrib.

both directions to rounded ends. Oblong is much the same but with the sides
more parallel.

Such terms as "toothed," "scalloped," "notched," or "plain" will do instead of their Latin equivalents and need no explanations. Leaves may
also be "divided," "cleft," or "lobed." A divided leaf consists of several
blades on one stalk (sometimes mistaken for several small leaves on one
stem, but it lacks the buds of a stem). The segments may be arranged palmately (radiating from the tip of the stalk) or pinnately (disposed along the
sides of a midrib). Cleft leaves are similar, but the indentations between
the lobes do not extend all the way to the stalk or midrib, so that one cannot
say that the leaf has separate segments. Lobed leaves are still more shallowly
indented. The lobes of cleft or lobed leaves may be palmately or pinnately
arranged.

On the stem leaves are attached singly, in pairs, or in circles. If the leaves
have lobes that project on either side of the stem, they are often said to
"clasp" it. Thin flanges that extend out from the surface of stems or leaf-
stalks (also from those of seeds and fruits) are often spoken of as "wings."
Stems and foliage may be "smooth," "rough," "downy," "woolly," "hairy,"
or "bristly"; such words have their ordinary significance in English.

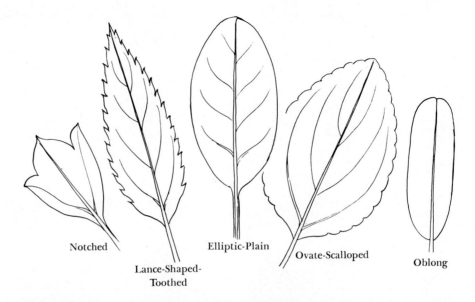

Notched

Lance-Shaped-
Toothed

Elliptic-Plain

Ovate-Scalloped

Oblong

LEAF SHAPES AND MARGINS

THE NAMES OF PLANTS

It is regrettable that many readers today are alarmed by foreign words, especially by the Latin words with which plants are named by botanists. The alarm is needless; the system of plant names is simple, easily assimilated by any person of average intelligence. A very little use will make them as familiar as—let us say—the language of baseball is to its fans.

The word "species" has been used many times in the preceding pages. It is almost impossible to give a precise definition for this useful word; but the idea is easily conveyed by a few examples. All the wood lilies are a species of lily; all the tiger lilies are another species. All the bloodroots make up a species; so do all the bunchberries, all the New England asters, all the marsh-marigolds. A species is a kind of plant that we recognize. Among the plants of a species there may be many small differences, some perhaps due to differences in soil, moisture, or light, but some caused by hereditary factors that reappear generation after generation. Plants with the latter kind of differences compose different forms or varieties within a species; many of these are the forms and varieties we cultivate in our fields and gardens.

Similar species form a genus. The various species of lilies form the Lily genus, the roses the Rose genus, and so on. If a species seems to have no close relatives, it forms a genus by itself; bloodroot is an example.

Many botanical names describe the leaves of the plants:
sheep-laurel, *Kalmia angustifolia* (A), has narrow leaves (*angustus* means "narrow");
Claytonia lanceolata (B) has lance-shaped leaves;
Penstemon centranthifolia (C) has leaves resembling in size, shape, and arrangement those of *Centranthus;*
Phacelia tanacetifolia (D) has leaves cut into many fine parts like those of tansy (*Tanacetum*).

A

B

C

D

Now for the names. Every genus is named by a single Latin word: *Lilium, Rosa, Aster, Sanguinaria*. Every species is named by two Latin words: *Lilium philadelphicum, Rosa virginiana, Aster novae-angliae*, Sanguinaria canadensis*. The first word of a species-name is obviously the name of the genus to which it belongs; the second is an adjective or other qualifying word which may recall the place where it was discovered or may designate some outstanding characteristic or even the name of the man who discovered it. That is all there is to it.

By this simple scheme we gain a precision that the users of common (vernacular) names can never attain. "Mayflower" means one thing in Long Island, something quite different in Wisconsin. "Bluebells" may mean any of half a dozen different kinds of plants. "Virginia-cowslips" are no relation to the cowslips of English poetry. "Primrose-willow" is neither a primrose nor a willow. And what about French and German and Swedish and Hebrew common names? Many vernacular names have a charm of their own—especially those that come down from ancient folklore. But if we want to know what we are talking about, we use the Latin "binomials."

Of course there is more to plant nomenclature than that; but further details are not essential to such descriptions of plants as those that follow. It is only necessary to mention that to avoid endless repetition of many characteristics, the plants in this book are arranged in their families; that is, genera with similar characteristics are grouped together under a family name; the family name usually ends in *aceae,* and is generally taken from the name of one of its genera: *Liliaceae, Rosaceae.*

The foregoing paragraphs contain a brief and elementary introduction to systematic botany—the branch of botany that is concerned with placing all the plants in a system, in a classification. While to pursue this branch of science into all its complications and ramifications might well demand more of the reader than he is prepared to give, yet it is to be hoped that this summary will increase his enjoyment of the natural world. The colors and forms of flowers are in themselves beautiful; to add some knowledge of their relationships, their structure, their place in nature is to enhance their elementary appeal. Let the reader, then, prepare to enjoy fully in the following pages what the art of the photographer and the science of the botanist, joined together, can provide.

---

* Three words here, but two joined by a hyphen so as to be equivalent to one.

H. W. RICKETT

GLOSSARY OF TERMS

The definitions below are intended to apply only to the terms as used in this book and for the plants herein described.

ACHENE: *a small seedlike fruit, containing one seed, and not opening at maturity.*

ANTHER: *the upper part of a stamen which forms the pollen.*

AXIL: *the upper angle formed by a leaf-stalk and the stem to which it is attached.*

BERRY: *a succulent fruit developed from a single ovary (with or without surrounding parts of the flower).*

BRACT: *a more or less leaflike part associated with a flower or an inflorescence and differing from an ordinary (foliage) leaf of the plant in size, shape, color, or any combination of these.*

BULB: *an underground part formed of circular, succulent leaf-bases growing on a small flat or domed stem, the outer leaves usually dry and hard.*

CALYX: *see Sepal.*

CAPSULE: *a dry fruit (pod) that splits open along several lines.*

CLEFT: *(of a leaf) indented at the margins so that distinct projecting portions appear. The indentations extend more than halfway to the stalk or midrib of the leaf.*

CORM: *an erect, approximately spherical underground stem.*

COROLLA: *see Petal.*

CROWN: *a small, erect, unelongated stem at the surface of the ground, bearing roots and leaves.*

CYME: *an inflorescence composed of a terminal flower, from the stalk of which spring two flowers on stalks; these lateral stalks may themselves bear lateral flowers, and so on.*

DIVIDED: *(of a leaf) composed of separate small blades, the divisions between them extending to the stalk or to the midrib.*

EMBRYO: *the small plant within a seed.*

EPIPHYTE: *a plant that grows attached to another plant without any connection of its own with the ground, but draws no nourishment from the supporting plant.*

FAMILY: *unit of classification above genus; commonly composed of a group of like genera.*

FOLLICLE: *a dry fruit (pod) that splits open lengthwise along one line.*

FRUIT: *the matured ovary or ovaries of a flower, normally containing seeds; other parts of the flower, or even of adjacent flowers, may adhere and take part in the development of the fruit.*

GENUS: (plural: *genera*): *unit of classification above a species; commonly composed of several or many like species.*

GLAND: *an organ that secretes some substance; in plants the nectary secretes sugar; other glands secrete essential oils which may be responsible for the odors and tastes of flowers and leaves. Glands are frequently small round bodies, often raised on stalks.*

HEAD: *an inflorescence composed of flowers with no stalks or very short stalks closely packed at the summit of a stem.*

INFERIOR OVARY: *an ovary whose sides are joined with the surrounding, cup-shaped receptacle.*

INFLORESCENCE: *a group of flowers not mixed with foliage leaves (bracts may be present).*

INVOLUCRE: *a circle of bracts or leaves beneath a flower or inflorescence.*

KEEL: *in the Bean family, the two lower joined petals; in general, a ridge or rib extending lengthwise in a leaf or other part.*

LANCE-SHAPED: *(of a leaf-blade) shaped like the head of a lance, the broader part between the middle and the base; much longer than broad and generally tapering to a sharp point.*

LATEX: *the milky or colored sap of certain plants.*

LEGUME: *a fruit (pod) of the Bean family, generally splitting lengthwise along two lines.*

32

LOBED: *(of a leaf) indented at the margins so that distinct projecting portions appear; the indentations do not extend more than halfway to the stalk or midrib of the leaf.*

NECTARY: *see Gland.*

OBLONG: *(of a leaf-blade) longer than wide, with approximately parallel sides.*

OFFSET: *a short branch extending sideways from the base of a plant and usually rooting and becoming a new plant.*

OVARY: *the lowest part of a pistil, containing an ovule or ovules in its interior chamber or chambers.*

OVATE: *(of a leaf-blade) shaped like the outline of an egg, the broader part between the middle and the base; not much longer than broad.*

OVULE: *a rudimentary seed.*

PALMATELY: *(of a leaf) so lobed or cleft or divided that the lobes or segments radiate from the end of the stalk or from a central portion.*

PANICLE: *a loose, much-branched inflorescence.*

PERIANTH: *the envelope of a flower which surrounds stamens and/or pistil(s); it may consist of sepals and petals or of sepals only.*

PETAL: *one part of the inner envelope of a flower that has two circles or parts around the stamens and/or pistil(s); the petals together form the corolla.*

PINNATELY: *(of a leaf) so lobed or cleft or divided that the lobes or segments are arranged along the sides of the midrib or a central part.*

PISTIL: *the part of a flower that contains the rudimentary seeds and receives the pollen which fertilizes them.*

POD: *any dry fruit that opens when mature.*

POLLEN: *the grains formed by stamens which develop the male fertilizing element.*

RACEME: *an inflorescence composed of stalked flowers arranged along one central stem.*

RECEPTACLE: *the end of the flower-stalk, variously elongated or distended, on which the parts of a flower are seated.*

RHIZOME: *a horizontal underground stem.*

SEPAL: *one part of the outer envelope of a flower; the sepals collectively form the calyx, which covers all other parts of the flower in the bud.*

SPADIX: *an inflorescence consisting of several or many small flowers without stalks all situated upon a thick, fleshy stem; a sort of spike.*

SPATHE: *a bract, or sometimes several bracts, that partly or wholly envelop a cluster of flowers (in the Arum family the spathe envelops or is associated with a spadix).*

SPECIES: *one of the kinds of plants (or animals) ordinarily recognized in the wild; generally reproducing itself but not interbreeding with other species to any extent.*

SPIKE: *an inflorescence composed of flowers arranged as in a raceme but with no stalks or very short stalks.*

SPUR: *a hollow backwards prolongation of a sepal or petal.*

STAMEN: *one of the organs of a flower that form pollen.*

STANDARD: *the upper petal of a papilionaceous flower in the Bean family; also a petal of an iris.*

STIGMA: *the part of a pistil, at or near the tip of the style, that receives the pollen.*

STIPULES: *paired organs at the base of a leaf, where the leaf is attached to the stem. They may be scalelike or they may resemble divisions of the leaf or even small leaves.*

STONE-FRUIT: *a fruit whose outer part is fleshy or sometimes fibrous, the inner part forming a hard stone around the seed or seeds.*

STYLE: *a slender column that rises from the ovary and bears the stigma.*

TEPAL: *one of the segments of the perianth of certain flowers, especially in the Lily family, in which sepals and petals are alike (or nearly so) in color, size, and form.*

TUBER: *a thickened underground stem.*

UMBEL: *an inflorescence composed of flowers on stalks that arise at or near the summit of a stem.*

WING: *as used in botany, a thin projecting membrane or flange; commonly found at the margins of a seed or dry fruit or extending lengthwise on a stem or leafstalk. Also a lateral petal of a papilionaceous flower of the Bean family.*

34

Pale dogtooth-violets, also known as
avalanche-lilies, blooming on the lower slopes of Mt. Rainier.

THE SEDGE FAMILY
CYPERACEAE

The Sedge family differs from the grasses (*Gramineae*) in the sheaths of its leaves, which completely enclose the stem; those of the grasses are split down one side. Many sedges have a triangular, solid stem; those of the grasses are generally round and often hollow. Both these families have minute flowers, without perianth, clustered in the axils of the scales of small spikes ("spikelets").

WHITE-TOPS
DICHROMENA COLORATA
Plate 1

White-tops sends up from a perennial rhizome a few leaves and a slender, leafless, unbranched stem, to a height of two or three feet. The stem is triangular; the leaves are long and very narrow except at the extreme base. The minute flowers are in small spikes clustered tightly at the tip of the stem. The decorative part of the plant is an involucre of several long, sharp, white bracts with narrow green tips; the older ones bend downward.

D. colorata grows in swamps and wet ground on the Atlantic coastal plain from Virginia to Florida and Texas. The flower-clusters sport their conspicuous bracts from January to August or later. White-tops is one of the few sedges that displays attractive colors. Mixed with it in the photograph are inflorescences of some species of panic grass (*Panicum*).

THE LILY FAMILY
LILIACEAE

Lilies have six perianth-parts in two circles, all shaped and colored nearly alike, so that the terms sepals and petals are not used; the term "tepals" has been coined for them. There are six stamens and a three-chambered ovary which forms a capsule. Besides these familiar plants, the family includes tulips, hyacinths, and other well-known inhabitants of our gardens; also onions, asparagus, and other food plants. Wild-flowers also are numerous. The floral plan of the lilies is quite general in the family. The fruit may be either a capsule or a berry. In some genera there is a well-marked distinction between green sepals and colored petals. In most species of the family the leaves have veins running unbranched from base to tip; but in some the veins form a network.

STAR-OF-BETHLEHEM
ORNITHOGALUM UMBELLATUM
Plate 2

The narrow, smooth, grasslike leaves grow from a bulb. In their midst rises the flowering stem, about eight inches tall. Each of the six pointed tepals has a broad green stripe on the outside; otherwise they are pure white.

Star-of-Bethlehem is a native of Europe, now very much at home along roadsides,

36

1
WHITE-TOPS
DICHROMENA COLORATA

2
STAR-OF-BETHLEHEM
ORNITHOGALUM UMBELLATUM

in parks and other grassy places from Newfoundland to Ontario and Nebraska and southward to North Carolina, Mississippi, and Kansas. It flowers from April to June.

Some beautiful species of *Ornithogalum* from South Africa are cultivated under the name chinkerichee.

The flower of *O. umbellatum* closes early in the day, whence the local English names eleven-o'clock-lady, Jack-go-to-bed-at-noon, sleepy Dick, and others. There seems to be no plausible explanation of the Latin name *Ornithogalum*, which means "bird-milk."

FIELD LILY
LILIUM CANADENSE   *Plate 3*

This wild yellow lily may have a stem six feet tall or even more. The leaves are lance-shaped, mostly attached in circles, sometimes as many as fifteen in one circle. At the summit of the stem there may be a single flower, but more commonly there is a cluster of several flowers; and many plants have flowers springing from the axils of leaves below the summit and even from the stem between the circles of leaves. Up to twenty-two flowers have been counted on a single plant. The flower-stalks are long, the flowers hanging from their ends. The perianth is commonly yellow, spotted with purple on the inside; forms are known with orange or even red perianth.

The field lily grows in meadows and along roadsides, especially where the ground is moist, from Quebec to Minnesota and southward to Virginia and Alabama. It flowers from June to August.

WESTERN LILY
LILIUM COLUMBIANUM   *Plate 16*

This lily has a slender stem which may attain a height of six feet. The leaves are lance-shaped, the narrow end toward the stem. The lower ones are in circles, the upper ones scattered. At the summit of the stem and in the axils of the upper leaves grow the flowers, each hanging from the curved tip of a long stalk. The six parts of the perianth curve sharply backward; they are orange, spotted with purplish-brown.

L. columbianum is common in moist open woods and meadows in the western mountains from British Columbia to Idaho and California. It flowers from June to August.

WOOD LILY
LILIUM PHILADELPHICUM   *Plate 17*

The wood lily grows to a height of three feet or more, with lance-shaped leaves, attached in circles or singly. At the summit of the stem is a single flower or a cluster of a few flowers, standing erect. The tepals are orange or orange-red, with purple spots inside; each narrows down to a slender stalklike portion. (There are yellow and scarlet varieties also.)

The plants grow in woods and thickets, in clearings and along brushy roadsides, from Maine to southern Ontario and southward to Maryland, and in the mountains to North Carolina and Kentucky. It blooms from June to August.

OSCEOLA'S-PLUME or CROW-POISON
ZYGADENUS DENSUS   · *Plate 4*

The flowering stem and leaves of Osceola's-plume grow from a rhizome. The leaves are long and narrow. The stem, with its dense cluster of white flowers, may reach a height of three feet or more.

Z. densus is conspicuous on the coastal plain in wet pinelands and edges of swamps from Virginia to Florida and Texas. It flowers in April and May. Probably all species of *Zygadenus* are poisonous. The more western species *Z. nuttallii* is called death camass (being easily mistaken for the true camass or quamash, *Camassia*, which has an edible bulb). It has caused deaths of many sheep.

SOAP-PLANT or AMOLE
CHLOROGALUM POMERIDIANUM   *Plate 5*

Soap-plant grows from a bulb several inches tall, coated with a thin, brown, fibrous skin. The narrow leaves with wavy margins rise about two feet above the ground. The gray-green, branched flowering stem may reach a height of eight feet, bearing many small white flowers.

Soap-plant is found in dry, open places or in woods from Oregon to southern California. The bulbs contain a substance (saponin) that forms a lather with water, and the early settlers in the West used it for soap. The Indians roasted and ate the bulbs, which are rich in starch. Crushed plants, thrown into water, stupefy fish and have been used by tribes that depended on fish as a means of catching them.

BELLWORT or MERRYBELLS
UVULARIA SESSILIFOLIA   *Plate 6*

From the rhizome an erect stem grows about a foot tall, forking at the tip. At flowering time most of the leaves are close together on the forks of the stem, and a pale yellow flower hangs from the end of each fork. The leaves are lance-shaped or oval. The yellow flower resembles that of a lily but is narrow, the tips of the perianth just curling outward. As the fruit matures, the stem lengthens, the forks arching and separating their leaves.

This bellwort grows in open woods and clearings from New Brunswick to North Dakota and southward (especially in mountains) to Georgia, Alabama, and Arkansas. It flowers in April and May. There are other species with larger flowers colored a brighter yellow, but having essentially the same form.

Sessilifolia means "with leaves" (*-folia*) "sitting" (*sessili-*)—that is, sitting on the stem without stalks.

39

3

OUR-LORD'S-CANDLE or QUIXOTE-PLANT
YUCCA WHIPPLEI   *Plate 7*

This yucca grows from a bulb which sends up a dense rosette of narrow, stiff, gray-green leaves up to three feet long, each ending in a sharp spine about half an inch long. From the midst of these rises the single flowering stem to a height of eight or ten feet. The white flowers are compactly arranged, each having a perianth of six ovate, pointed parts about an inch long, usually tinged with brownish purple on the outside. The whole plant dies after flowering and fruiting.

Our-Lord's-candle grows on dry, open slopes in the mountains of southern California and northern Baja California, flowering in April and May. Other species of *Yucca* are called Spanish-bayonets—a commentary on the early course of white men in the Southwest. The genus also includes the fantastic Joshua-tree, one of the few tree species of the Lily family.

BEAR-GRASS
XEROPHYLLUM TENAX   *Plate 8*

Bear-grass is not a grass; it has small but numerous flowers recognizable as of the lily kind. They grow in a large oval cluster which may reach a height of six feet above the ground. The numerous leaves are stiff, narrow, about three feet long, in a dense tuft from the base of the stem.

Bear-grass is a common and conspicuous plant of mountain meadows from Wyoming to British Columbia and southward to Idaho and California. It flowers from June to August (or earlier in some places). It is sometimes called squaw-grass; the Indian women used the leaves in their basketry. It is also known locally as turkey-beard.

FAIRY-LANTERN or GLOBE-LILY
CALOCHORTUS ALBUS   *Plate 9*

The "fairy-lanterns" hang from a slender stem perhaps two feet tall or even more. The plant grows from a bulb, with several long, narrow basal leaves. There are also leaves on the stem, successively shorter upward. There are three small, greenish sepals and three large, white petals, with yellowish base, forming a globe or round bell.

Fairy-lantern grows in open woodlands or chaparral in the foothills of the Sierra Nevada and in the coast ranges of California. It flowers from April to June.

MARIPOSA-LILY
CALOCHORTUS VENUSTUS   *Plate 15*

From a bulb grow erect, grasslike leaves six or eight inches tall and a stem which bears some small leaves and a single, large flower. The three narrow sepals are lance-shaped, with tips curled back. The three broad petals may be white, pink, purple, or yellow, usually with a red blotch on the inside of each.

This species of *Calochortus* grows in light soil in the Sierra Nevada and coast ranges of central California, often at high altitudes. It blooms from May to July. Many other species of *Calochortus* are called mariposa-lily, also butterfly-tulip (mariposa means

41

4

5

6

7

4

OSCEOLA'S-PLUME

ZYGADENUS DENSUS

5

SOAP-PLANT

CHLOROGALUM POMERIDIANUM

6

BELLWORT

UVULARIA SESSILIFOLIA

7

OUR-LORD'S-CANDLE

YUCCA WHIPPLEI

8

BEAR·GRASS

XEROPHYLLUM TENAX

9

FAIRY-LANTERN

CALOCHORTUS ALBUS

"butterfly") or star-tulip. *Calochortus* is from two Greek words meaning "beautiful grass." They are among the most colorful and striking of western wildflowers. Various species extend from western Canada to Mexico and eastward to the Dakotas. Thirty-seven are listed in California.

CANADA MAYFLOWER or WILD LILY-OF-THE-VALLEY
MAIANTHEMUM CANADENSE   *Plate 10*

Canada mayflower is a small plant which often forms a green carpet under trees. The stem is at most about five inches tall, growing from a slender, forking rhizome. On the stem are from one to three ovate leaves, with indented base and no stalk. In one variety the leaves are downy on the lower side; generally the plant is smooth. The white flowers grow in a raceme at the summit of the stem. They are exceptional for this family in having only four perianth-parts (tepals) and four stamens. The ovary contains two chambers, and the stigma is two-lobed. The fruit is a berry, containing only one or two seeds; it is at first gray and speckled, becoming red as it ripens.

Maianthemum is found in woods, often at high altitudes, from Labrador to British Columbia and southward to Delaware, Tennessee, and Iowa, and in the mountains to Georgia. It blooms in May and June.

CHIVES
ALLIUM SCHOENOPRASUM   *Plate 11*

This species grows in clumps from slender bulbs. The leaves, about a foot tall, are very narrow, round and hollow. The flowering stem is about as tall as the leaves; it bears none itself. Each flower has six lance-shaped perianth-parts, which taper to sharp points; they are rose-pink and marked by a strong vein.

Chives is a cultivated species which persists on the sites of old gardens. It flowers from June to August. The variety *sibiricum*, which is somewhat larger and coarser, grows across Canada and southward to New York, Minnesota, Colorado, and Washington; also in Europe and Asia.

LARGE-FLOWERED TRILLIUM
TRILLIUM GRANDIFLORUM   *Plate 12*

The stem of this trillium grows over a foot tall, bearing at its summit three leaves and a single flower. The leaves are without stalks, the blades broadly ovate and long-pointed; their veins form a network, which is exceptional in this family. The flower has three green sepals and three large white petals.

The large-flowered trillium is found in woods and thickets from Maine to southern Ontario and Minnesota and southward to Georgia and Arkansas. It flowers from April to June.

Trillium contains the Latin word for "three," the leaves and flower-parts being in threes. There are many species, all flowering in spring and in woods. *T. grandiflorum* is one of the handsomest. It is quite variable, forms having been found with green-striped or pink petals, with narrow leaves, with stalked leaves, even without leaves, and with other aberrant characteristics.

44

WOOD TRILLIUM
TRILLIUM VIRIDE

Plate 14

The wood trillium grows six or eight inches tall. The flower is seated without a stalk where the three leaves meet. The three green sepals and the three long, green (*viride*) or reddish petals stand erect.

T. viride grows in woods from Virginia to Alabama and westward to Kansas and Mississippi. It blooms from April to June, depending on latitude.

SOLOMON'S-SEAL
POLYGONATUM BIFLORUM

Plate 13

The thick rhizome forms the upright stem at one end every spring, then grows on beyond it. When, in the summer, the upright stem withers and dies, it leaves a circular scar on the rhizome, which may have suggested a seal to those who named it. The erect stem may grow to a length of three feet or more, but arches so that it does not stand that tall. The elliptical leaves are borne singly, and from the base of each hangs a stalk that bears one or two greenish-white flowers. The fruits are dark blue berries.

This species grows in woods from Connecticut to Nebraska and southward to Florida and Texas. The flowers appear in May and June.

John Gerard, in 1597, thought that the English name was perhaps derived from "the singular vertue that it hath in sealing, or healing up wounds. . . ." This seems a reasonable way to bring Solomon, the king learned in magic, into the picture, a detail not explained by the "seal" on the rhizome theory.

YELLOW DOGTOOTH-VIOLET
ERYTHRONIUM AMERICANUM

Plate 18

The dogtooth-violets are lilylike in many ways. From a deep-seated bulb grows, when the plant is young, a single, smooth, elliptical leaf, often mottled with brown; in a later year, two leaves appear, and between them a stem, six or eight inches tall, from whose tip hangs a single flower. The perianth of *E. americanum* is yellow, often spotted near the base inside, curving outward and upward.

The plants grow in colonies, in moist meadows and in woods from New Brunswick to Minnesota and southward to Georgia, Alabama, and Oklahoma; but they are more abundant eastward. The flowers appear from March to June. In the Midwest *E. albidum*, with white flowers, is commoner.

"Dogtooth" presumably refers to the white, pointed bulbs; "violet" was once the name of many wildflowers besides those we now call violets (*Viola*), especially of those with a blue or purple color. *Erythronium* comes from the Greek word for "red," the European species of this genus having a purplish-red flower.

AVALANCHE-LILY
ERYTHRONIUM MONTANUM

Plate 19

Avalanche-lily resembles the dogtooth-violets in manner of growth. The leaves have wavy edges; they are not mottled as the eastern *Erythroniums* usually are. The flower hangs about a foot above the surface. The perianth is white; the anthers yellow.

10

11

12

13

14

15

16

10 **CANADA MAYFLOWER** MAIANTHEMUM CANADENSE   *11* **CHIVES** ALLIUM SCHOENOPRASUM

12 **LARGE-FLOWERED TRILLIUM** TRILLIUM GRANDIFLORUM   *13* **SOLOMON'S-SEAL** POLYGONATUM BIFLORUM

14 **WOOD TRILLIUM** TRILLIUM VIRIDE   *15* **MARIPOSA-LILY** CALOCHORTUS VENUSTUS   *16* **WESTERN LILY** LILIUM COLUMBIANUM

46

Avalanche-lily often grows in wide fields of bloom; it is celebrated for flowering not only (with many other species) at the edges of snowbanks, but actually in the snow itself. It is a plant of high mountain meadows and woods in Washington and Oregon, flowering from June to August.

PALE DOGTOOTH-VIOLET
ERYTHRONIUM PALLIDUM   *Plate 20*

E. pallidum resembles *E. montanum* in its manner of growth and its size; as in that species, its leaves are not mottled. The flower reverses that of *E. montanum* in color: the perianth is yellow, the anthers white (this is the "pallid" part of the plant). The flower is fragrant.

E. pallidum grows in mountain meadows on the eastern slopes of the Cascade Mountains from British Columbia to Oregon (perhaps also in Montana). It flowers from April to July, depending on the altitude. It is closely related to *E. grandiflorum*, of which it has often been considered a variety.

THE DAFFODIL FAMILY
AMARYLLIDACEAE

The Daffodil family is closely related to the Lily family, the chief difference being that the ovary is inferior. There are six parts to the perianth and six stamens. Leaves and flowers grow from rhizomes, corms, or bulbs. Besides the attractive wildflowers described below (and many others) the family includes such favorite cultivated plants as the daffodils, amaryllis, snowdrops and many more, and the genus *Agave*, so important in Mexican agriculture.

SPIDER-LILY
HYMENOCALLIS OCCIDENTALIS   *Plate 21*

The spider-lilies have bulbs which produce a cluster of narrow leaves and a stem which bears at its summit one or a few conspicuous flowers. The perianth of *H. occidentalis* forms a long, narrow tube from which extend six narrow, pointed, yellowish segments. Within this is a funnel-shaped white crown with irregularly toothed margins. The six stamens are joined to this crown.

H. occidentalis grows in meadows and along streams from Georgia to Indiana and Missouri and southward, flowering from April to August. A number of other species occur in the South.

GOLDEN-STARS
BLOOMERIA CROCEA   *Plate 22*

The leaves of this plant grow from a corm underground. There are only a few leaves, very narrow, with a ridge or keel along one side, about a foot long, spreading

over the ground. In their midst rises a leafless stem up to two feet tall, which bears orange-yellow flowers at its summit.

Golden-stars is common in dry open places and in chaparral in the coast ranges of California. It flowers from April to June. The genus is named for H. G. Bloomer, a botanist of California. *Crocea* means "yellow."

BRODIAEA
BRODIAEA CORONARIA   *Plate 23*

The leaves of this *Brodiaea* are narrow and rounded, growing to six or eight inches tall. The leafless flowering stem is about the same height. The perianth is lavender or violet in color. Three of the stamens have no anthers but are simply flat stalks (the other three stamens also have flat stalks, wider at the base). In some forms these sterile stamens are folded around the fertile ones.

B. coronaria grows in dry places, including grassy and wooded slopes, in the coast ranges of Oregon and California and in the interior valley of California. It flowers from April to July.

BLUE-DICKS
BRODIAEA PULCHELLA   *Plate 24*

The leaves and flowering stem of the brodiaeas grow from a corm, the leaves erect and grasslike, those of *B. pulchella* ridged or keeled along one side. The flowering stem bears no leaves, only a group of flowers at the summit. Both leaves and stem of *B. pulchella* are about a foot tall. The perianth of blue-dicks is generally violet-blue. The six stamens are in two sets of three, those of one set having relatively wide, flat stalks.

Blue-dicks is common in open places, even in deserts, from Utah to Oregon and southward to northern Mexico and California. It flowers from March to May. Like many other plants, it is also called wild hyacinth; one variety is known as desert-hyacinth.

There are many other species of this western genus: Ithuriel's-spear (*B. laxa*), fire-cracker-flower (*B. ida-maia*), and pretty-face (*B. lutea*). The genus is named for a Scottish botanist, J. J. Brodie. *Pulchella* means "beautiful." The corms of several species were eaten by the Indians.

EASTER-LILY or ATAMASCO-LILY
ZEPHYRANTHES TREATIAE   *Plate 25*

The Easter-lily (which is not a true lily) grows from a bulb. This sends up a tuft of narrow, grasslike leaves up to a foot long and a leafless stem, about as tall, which bears one flower. The perianth is nearly three inches long. The outer parts are often streaked with pink on the back, and sometimes all of them turn pink inside.

Z. treatiae grows in the swamps and wet pinelands of Florida, flowering in spring. With other species of *Zephyranthes*, it may be known as Atamasco-lily, zephyr-lily, etc. One species, *Z. candida*, is commonly cultivated. *Zephyr*, in Greek, was the northwest

49

18 **YELLOW DOGTOOTH-VIOLET** ERYTHRONIUM AMERICANUM

19 **AVALANCHE-LILY** ERYTHRONIUM MONTANUM   *20* **PALE DOGTOOTH-VIOLET** ERYTHRONIUM PALLIDUM

21
SPIDER-LILY

HYMENOCALLIS
OCCIDENTALIS

wind, generally interpreted as bringing fair weather (though sometimes as stormy); *anthes* is from the word for flower; so *Zephyranthes* is the "flower of the northwest wind," or "flower of spring." *Treatiae* is named for Mary Lua Adelia Treat, a well-known American naturalist of the nineteenth century.

THE IRIS FAMILY
IRIDACEAE

The Iris family is distinguished by its six-parted perianth with three stamens and an inferior ovary. The leaves are generally arranged in the way fancifully called "equitant" by Linnaeus—riding horseback. In this arrangement each leaf is folded lengthwise and stands erect, the next younger leaf within the fold and itself enfolding the next, and so on.

BLUE FLAG
IRIS HEXAGONA
Plate 26

Iris hexagona has a somewhat zigzag stem up to four feet tall. The sepals and petals are violet, with greenish bases; the sepals have a yellow crest or ridge. The capsule is sharply six-angled (*hexagona*).

I. hexagona grows in swamps and other wet places on the coastal plain in Georgia and Florida. It blooms in March and April.

BLUE FLAG
IRIS VERSICOLOR
Plate 28

The narrow, swordlike leaves of blue flag grow up to three feet tall. The flowering stem about equals the leaves or overtops them slightly. At its summit grow several flowers from a spathe of two or more papery bracts, one flower opening at a time. Additional spathes may be seen in the axils of the upper leaves. The flower resembles that of a garden iris. The three sepals (the "falls" in gardeners' language) turn down; the three petals ("standards") turn up. Both are violet-blue, with darker veins, the sepals with a yellow region toward the base and crested with yellow hairs ("beard"). The style branches into three petal-like parts, which lie over the three sepals, the stigma being a narrow flap on the under surface of each of these branches. A stamen is hidden under each style-branch.

Blue flag grows in wet meadows, marshes, and other moist places from Labrador to Manitoba and southward to Virginia, Ohio, Michigan, and Wisconsin. The flowers appear from May to August.

The genus is named for the Greek goddess identified with the rainbow, presumably in reference to its many bright hues. It is a vast genus, with species all over the world. The garden varieties come mostly from European and Asiatic species.

SOUTHERN BLUE FLAG
IRIS VIRGINICA

Plate 29

Iris virginica has a stem about two feet tall, often zigzag. The flowers are slightly fragrant. The sepals vary in shades of violet to pink, with a yellow or orange blotch at the base. The petals also are violet or pink; both are tinged with yellowish-green at the bases.

I. virginica is the commonest southern iris, growing in roadside ditches, swamps, and other wet places on the coastal plain from Virginia to Florida and Texas. It flowers from March to June.

IRIS
IRIS MISSOURIENSIS

Plate 30

Iris missouriensis has rather light green leaves with a whitish bloom, reaching a height of eighteen inches. The flowering stem may be slightly taller. The sepals are lilac or whitish with lilac veins; the petals are similar in color.

I. missouriensis grows in meadows and flats that are wet up to flowering time, often at high altitudes (to 11,000 feet above sea level), from South Dakota to British Columbia and southward to Arizona, northern Mexico, and southern California. It flowers from May to September. The botanical name recalls the time when all North America west of the Mississippi was "Missouri territory."

BLUE-EYED-GRASS
SISYRINCHIUM BELLUM

Plate 27

Blue-eyed-grass is not a grass but has narrow, grasslike leaves that may reach two feet in height; they grow from a rhizome and are arranged like leaves of an iris. Among them rises the flat, sharp-edged flowering stem, at whose summit is a spathe of two bracts enclosing several flowers, one opening at a time. These vary greatly in color, from deep to pale blue, with a yellow "eye."

This is a highly variable species, growing in all sorts of places, generally grassy and open, in California and Baja California. The flowering period is from February to July (for all varieties). The photograph was made near the beach. There are many other species of *Sisyrinchium*, extending across North America.

THE SPIDERWORT FAMILY
COMMELINACEAE

The Spiderwort family is chiefly tropical. The leaves are marked by parallel veins. The uppermost leaves form a spathe from which the flowers emerge. The flowers have typically three often green sepals and three colored petals; but the plan varies greatly. The petals may be all alike, or they may differ in size and color.

22 **GOLDEN-STARS** BLOOMERIA CROCEA   23 **BRODIAEA** BRODIAEA CORONARIA

24 **BLUE-DICKS** BRODIAEA PULCHELLA   25 **EASTER-LILY** ZEPHYRANTHES TREATIAE

22

23

24

25

26
BLUE FLAG
IRIS HEXAGONA

SPIDERWORT
TRADESCANTIA OHIENSIS   *Plate 31*

The stem of this species is three feet tall or taller, sometimes branched. The leaves are long and narrow, and very smooth, with a whitish bloom. The flowers are clustered at the summit of the stem, just above a pair of unequal, leaflike bracts, which form a spathe. The species is identified partly by its three smooth, hairless sepals, which may have red tips or edges. The three petals are blue or sometimes rose or white. The six stamens bear blue hairs on their stalks.

T. ohiensis occurs in meadows, prairies, woods, pinelands, etc., from Massachusetts to Minnesota and southward to Florida and Texas. It flowers from April to June. This and other species are cultivated as garden flowers. Usually only one or two flowers open at once on a plant, withering in midday; numerous buds hang down beneath the open flowers. The hairs on the stamens are much used in teaching botany, since the cells of which they are composed are easily seen, alive, in a microscope.

DAYFLOWER
COMMELINA COMMUNIS   *Plate 32*

The dayflower is an annual weed, its stem mostly creeping on the ground, the tips curving up to produce the flowers. The leaves are rather succulent, lance-shaped or ovate, sheathing the stem at their base. At the tip of the stem is a folded bract or spathe, from which the flowers appear. Each flower opens only for one morning. The perianth consists of three green sepals and three petals; the two upper petals are stalked, bright blue or pale violet; the lower petal is much smaller and white, or nearly so. There are six stamens, three shorter and bearing cross-shaped anthers, the others of the usual form.

C. communis came from Asia and is now a troublesome weed in gardens, as well as growing in waste places and along roadsides, from Massachusetts to Wisconsin and southward to North Carolina, Alabama, Arkansas, and Kansas. It flowers from June to October. It is troublesome because it is hard to kill; stems uprooted and left lying on the soil, even in full sun, quickly put forth new roots and resume growth. Linnaeus named the genus after the three Dutchmen named Commelijn, two of whom were well-known botanists of the seventeenth century, while the third (the small petal) died young without accomplishing anything.

THE PINEAPPLE FAMILY
BROMELIACEAE

The Bromeliads are a large, almost entirely tropical family. Most are epiphytes, growing on the branches of trees but deriving no nourishment from them. The leaves are generally narrow, stiff, and crowded. The flowers are usually small, situated in the axils of bracts which may be bright-colored. The parts of the flowers are in threes. *Tillandsia usneoides*, Spanish-moss, belongs to this family, differing from most of the others in having small, scalelike leaves on its pendent branches.

56

27 **BLUE-EYED-GRASS** SISYRINCHIUM BELLUM   28 **BLUE FLAG** IRIS VERSICOLOR

29 **SOUTHERN BLUE FLAG** IRIS VIRGINICA   30 **IRIS** IRIS MISSOURIENSIS

27

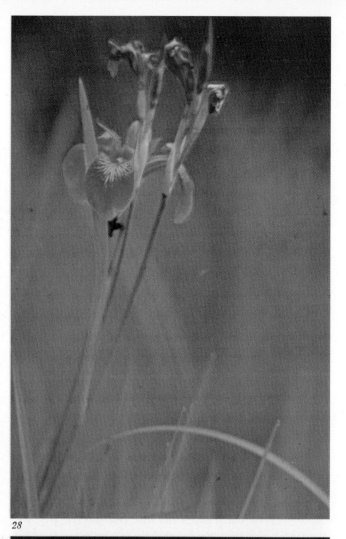

28

29

30

WILD PINEAPPLE or AIR-PLANT
TILLANDSIA FASCICULATA   *Plate 33*

Wild pineapple is an epiphyte. The long narrow leaves are mostly at the base; they have very slender, curved tips. They are grayish-green, becoming purplish. The flowers are inconspicuous, in the axils of red bracts. The petals are violet.

Wild pineapple grows on the branches of cypresses in the swamps and hammocks of southern Florida. The flowers are seen from January to July. It occurs also in Mexico and the West Indies.

THE ARROWLEAF FAMILY
ALISMATACEAE

The *Alismataceae* are plants of water or wet soil, the long-stalked leaves and flowering stems growing from submerged rhizomes or tubers. The flowers have three green sepals and three white or pink petals. In some genera stamens and pistils are in different flowers.

SWAMP-POTATO
SAGITTARIA GRAMINEA   *Plate 34*

This species grows to a height of two feet from a perennial base under water. Some of the leaves do not rise above the surface; they have no blades. Other leaves which emerge from the water have narrow, lance-shaped blades. The white or faintly pink flowers are in two or more circles on a leafless stem, the upper ones usually having stamens but no pistils, the lower ones pistils only.

S. graminea inhabits shallow water or wet mud from Labrador to Ontario and southward to Florida and Texas. It flowers at any time during the summer, from May to September. Many species of this genus have arrow-shaped leaves, whence the Latin name, and the English arrowleaf. Several species form tubers—the "potatoes" —which were used as food by the Indians.

THE PICKEREL-WEED FAMILY
PONTEDERIACEAE

The *Pontederiaceae* are all plants growing in water or very wet, marshy soil. There is a perianth of six parts colored alike but unlike in form, and six stamens, usually in two sizes.

WATER-HYACINTH
EICHHORNIA CRASSIPES   *Plate 35*

Water-hyacinth is a floating plant, its roots hanging in the water. The leaves have roundish blades on a stalk which is inflated and hollow. The flowers are in a spike about six inches long. The perianth consists of six parts which are not quite equal;

five are pale violet; the uppermost segment is deeper violet in the center, with a yellow spot. The three lower stamens are much the longest.

Water-hyacinth is a native of tropical America which was introduced into the United States and now occurs from Florida to Texas and north to Virginia and Missouri. In the southernmost parts of its range it grows in such abundance as to impede navigation in lakes and rivers. It has recently been destroyed by dusting from airplanes. It has sometimes been cultivated with the name water-orchid.

PICKEREL-WEED
PONTEDERIA CORDATA   *Plate 36*

Pickerel-weed grows in water, the rhizome at the bottom sending up long-stalked leaves and a branch that bears one leaf and a spike of flowers. The leaf-blades are deeply indented at the base, and the flowering branch commonly rises through the cleft of one of the leaves. The flowers are in a dense spike about five inches long, rising altogether some twelve or eighteen inches above the surface. The perianth has six parts: the three upper segments are joined, the three lower separate. The color is an intense blue, with two yellow spots on the upper lip. Each flower lasts for only a day.

The plants grow in slow-moving streams and shallow ponds, usually near shore, from Quebec to Ontario and southward to Florida and Oklahoma. The pickerel are supposed to lay their eggs on the underwater parts of this species in preference to others. The first flowers open in June, and others follow into November; but ponds and even streams dry up in late summer, and then the whole plant turns brown, everything dying except the rhizome.

THE ARUM FAMILY
ARACEAE

The Arum family is a very large family of mostly tropical plants. Many are grown as house-plants—the philodendrons—or in conservatories—anthuriums, monsteras, calla-lilies. They are characterized by small flowers, without petals, closely packed on a thick stem called a spadix. This is generally enveloped by a large bract, the spathe, in some species colored like a petal.

JACK-IN-THE-PULPIT or INDIAN TURNIP
ARISAEMA TRIPHYLLUM   *Plate 37*

Jack-in-the-pulpit is one of a few temperate members of the family. Each of the two (usually) leaves of Jack-in-the-pulpit has a long stalk, a foot or two tall, terminated by three segments (*triphyllum*—"three leaves," but the three compose one leaf). Between them rises the flowering stem, up to eight inches tall, bearing the spathe or "pulpit." The flowers are of two kinds, staminate and pistillate, both usually situated

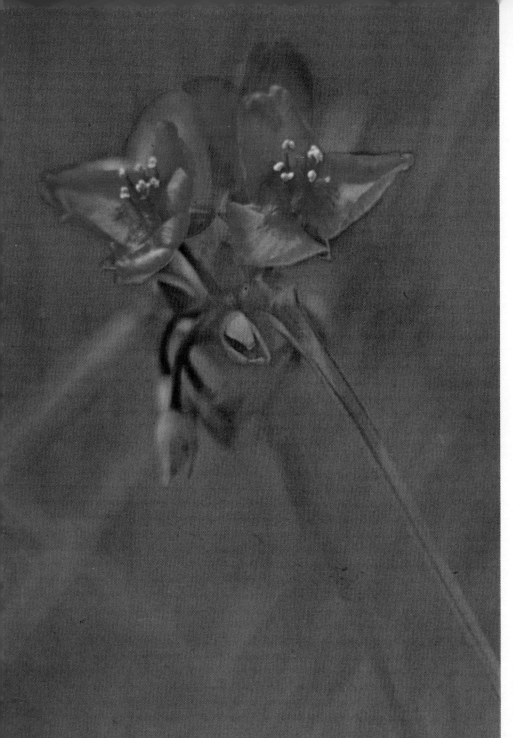

31

SPIDERWORT

TRADESCANTIA OHIENSIS

32

DAYFLOWER

COMMELINA COMMUNIS

33

WILD PINEAPPLE

TILLANDSIA FASCICULATA

34

SWAMP-POTATO

SAGITTARIA GRAMINEA

on the lower part of the spadix; the upper part of the spadix is visible, as "Jack," in the pulpit. The fruit is a cluster of bright red berries, above which may often be seen the withered remains of the spathe.

Jack grows in rich woods and in swamps and bogs from Nova Scotia to Manitoba and southward to Florida and Louisiana. It flowers from April to June.

The stem and leaves grow from a corm, which was eaten by the Indians—but only after careful cooking. If eaten raw it produces an intense burning sensation in the mouth, as many a schoolboy can remember.

GOLDEN-CLUB
ORONTIUM AQUATICUM *Plate 38*

Golden-club sends its pointed spadix up three or four inches above the water it grows in. The spathe is merely a sheath around the lower portion and is barely visible. From the same rhizome, in the mud on the bottom, grow leaves with narrow elliptic blades on long stalks up to a foot tall. The flowers are packed on the spadix, forming the "golden" part of the "club."

Golden-club grows in swamps and shallow water, mostly on the Atlantic coastal plain, from Massachusetts to Florida and Louisiana, and inland in New York, Virginia, and Kentucky. The yellow spadix is seen from April to June.

THE BUR-REED FAMILY
SPARGANIACEAE

This family contains only the genus *Sparganium,* a species of which is described below.

BUR-REED
SPARGANIUM ANDROCLADUM *Plate 39*

Most persons would hardly think of the bur-reeds as flowering plants. They grow in water (mostly shallow) or in mud, sending up from their rhizomes erect, narrow leaves from which emerges a zigzag stem; on this are more leaves and clusters of small greenish flowers. On the upper part of the stem the flowers are usually staminate (with no pistils); on the lower part pistillate (with no stamens). There are sepals but no petals. The staminate flowers disappear after they shed their pollen, leaving a bare length of stem. The pistillate flowers form achenes in tight, round balls, each achene with a sharp beak pointing outward: this is the bur.

S. androcladum grows in shallow water, swamps, and muddy shores from Quebec to Minnesota and southward to Virginia, Kentucky, and Oklahoma. The flowers appear in summer.

It is extremely difficult to identify a bur-reed without a mature bur in your hand. The species here named is a guess at the plant illustrated.

35

THE ORCHID FAMILY
ORCHIDACEAE

This, the "royal family" of plants, is distinguished by an extremely complex flower. There are three sepals and three petals; one petal, usually the lowest, differs from all other parts of the perianth in size, color, or form, or in all three. This is called the lip. The stamens and pistil are joined in a central structure called the column, in which an anther is generally to be found at the tip and a stigma just below; the column may be colored and decorated like another petal. The ovary is inferior. The family is characteristically tropical. The flowers of many tropical species are large and exhibit a striking array of forms and colors. Orchids native to North America are generally small plants, some with inconspicuous flowers (which are, however, just as complicated as the exotic ones).

Orchids are often miscalled parasites. A few perhaps are. Some of ours have no green color and live, with the help of certain fungi, on decaying organic material in the soil. But most of the tropical ones, though they live perched on the branches of trees, draw no nourishment from the trees but make their own food. They are called epiphytes. And most of our North American species grow in the soil and make their own food in much the same way as other plants do.

CORAL-ROOT
CORALLORHIZA MERTENSIANA
Plate 40

The coral-roots are among those flowering plants that lack green color and live (as fungi do) on organic matter in the soil. The "coral roots" are really rhizomes, divided into many small, round, pink branches. *C. mertensiana* is about a foot tall, with a brownish or pale purplish stem, bearing many short-stalked flowers. The perianth is purplish, the lip being marked with white; the column is yellowish. The base of the lip forms a small pouch or sac.

This species is fairly common in coniferous woods from Wyoming to Alaska and southward to California. It flowers from June to September.

DELICATE IONOPSIS
IONOPSIS UTRICULARIOIDES
Plate 41

Ionopsis is an epiphytic orchid. Its thick, narrow leaves grow from a rhizome, sheathing each other at the base of the flowering stem, which may be two feet tall. The lateral sepals are united at the base, forming a hollow sac or spur. The petals vary from lilac to white. The lip is large and two-lobed. The column is yellow.

Ionopsis is found chiefly in Big Cypress Swamp in peninsular Florida, flowering from December to March. It is widely distributed in tropical America.

COW-HORN ORCHID
CYRTOPODIUM PUNCTATUM
Plate 42

The cow-horn is one of the epiphytic orchids, the type common in many tropical and subtropical countries. The narrow, pointed leaves of this one grow from a bulb-

64

like part called a pseudobulb, found in many orchids. The flowers are in a loose cluster on a leafless stem, which grows from the same pseudobulb. The sepals are greenish, more or less spotted with brown. The lateral petals are pale yellow with brown markings. The lip is a deep yellow, with two wings extending upward at the sides and tending to conceal the column.

The cow-horn orchid grows on branches of trees in the hammocks of southern Florida and the keys. The flowers are seen in spring.

YELLOW LADY'S-SLIPPER
CYPRIPEDIUM CALCEOLUS   *Plate 47*

The stem of yellow lady's-slipper grows two feet or more tall, and has several ovate leaves which sheathe the stem at their bases. There may be one or two flowers at the summit of the stem. The lower two sepals are joined into one, so that there seem to be but two sepals in all. The two lateral petals are narrow and twisted; both they and the sepals are brownish, yellowish, or purplish. The lower petal, the lip, gives the plant its English name: it is a large, yellow sac shaped something like a very blunt (and unladylike) slipper, about two inches long. The column is bent over the opening of the slipper, with a mass of pollen on each side and a sort of shield in the middle; the stigma is beneath, projecting into the cavity of the slipper.

Two varieties are known; one, with somewhat smaller and fragrant flowers, growing in bogs from Newfoundland to British Columbia and southward to New Jersey, Georgia, Tennessee, Missouri, New Mexico, Utah, and Washington; the other, in woods from Nova Scotia to Minnesota and southward to Georgia, Tennessee, and Missouri. These were formerly considered distinct species. Flowers are seen from April to July.

The botanical name *Cypripedium* is derived from Cypris, a name of Aphrodite, who was born on the island of Cyprus; and the Greek word for sandal or shoe. This species grows also in Europe, and is known by the same name in England (where it is now extremely rare).

PINK LADY'S-SLIPPER or MOCCASIN-FLOWER
CYPRIPEDIUM ACAULE   *Plate 45*

Acaule means "without a stem," and is the epithet applied to this plant, since the leaves and the flower-stalk spring directly from the ground. However, they grow from a short rhizome, which *is* a stem. There are two broad leaves with conspicuous lengthwise ribs, the blades usually not quite opposite but at a slight angle with each other. The flower-stalk may reach a height of eighteen inches, but is usually about a foot tall. At its summit hangs a single flower, the petals and sepals greenish, yellowish, or purplish, the lip a rosy pink. The opening of the lip is a slit, the edges folded in, not an open hole as in other species of this genus.

The pink lady's-slipper grows in dry, acid soil in woods and in bogs, from Newfoundland to Alberta and southward to Georgia, Alabama, and Minnesota. It flowers in April, May, or June. Plants often grow in large colonies. There is also a white-flowered form.

36

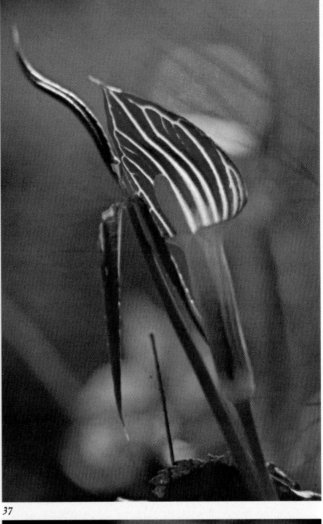

37

38

39

GRASS-PINK or SWAMP-PINK
CALOPOGON TUBEROSUS

Plate 44

The grass-pink (which is not in the Pink family) has but one narrow leaf, more or less lance-shaped, which grows from a tuber underground. From the same tuber grows the stem that bears the magenta-pink flowers. This is one of the few native North American orchids that does not twist as it develops: the lip stays in its "correct" position, that is, it is the uppermost petal. The lip has white hairs with yellow and magenta tips (*Calopogon* is from two Greek words that mean "beautiful beard"). The column, with two petal-like wings, curves upward from below.

Grass-pink grows in bogs and acid meadows from Newfoundland to Minnesota and southward to Florida and Texas. The flowers appear from May (in the south) to August (in the north).

BOG or REIN ORCHIS
HABENARIA DILATATA

Plate 46

Habenaria dilatata grows up to nearly three feet tall. The stem bears single lance-shaped leaves, which become smaller toward the top. The yellowish-white flowers are in a long, rather dense spike, about six inches in length. The lance-shaped upper sepal and the two lateral petals "connive" to form a hood over the column. The broader, lower sepals spread sideways. The narrow lip, which tapers to a blunt point, extends downward; it is usually slightly expanded ("dilated") at the base.

H. dilatata grows in bogs and other wet places from Greenland to Alaska and southward to New Jersey, Minnesota, New Mexico, and California. It flowers from April to September.

REIN ORCHIS
HABENARIA SACCATA

Plate 43

The stem of *H. saccata* is up to three feet tall. The lower leaves are elliptic and blunt; the upper ones, lance-shaped, smaller and grading into the bracts of the long flower-cluster. The lateral petals and the upper sepal form a hood; the narrow lip extends straight down, with a small hollow spur at its base. All these parts are green except the column, which is yellow.

H. saccata is quite common in wet ground in the mountains from Wyoming to British Columbia and southward to Arizona and Oregon. It flowers from June to August.

CLAMSHELL ORCHID
EPIDENDRUM COCHLEATUM

Plate 48

Clamshell orchid is an epiphyte on trees, its flowering stem and narrow leaves growing from pseudobulbs. The leaves may reach a length of over a foot, the flowering stem nearly two feet. The flowers are loosely arranged. This orchid is remarkable

36 PICKEREL-WEED PONTEDERIA CORDATA   *37* JACK-IN-THE-PULPIT ARISAEMA TRIPHYLLUM

38 GOLDEN-CLUB ORONTIUM AQUATICUM   *39* BUR-REED SPARGANIUM ANDROCLADUM

40
CORAL-ROOT
CORALLORHIZA MERTENSIANA

41
DELICATE IONOPSIS
IONOPSIS UTRICULARIOIDES

42
COW-HORN ORCHID
CYRTOPODIUM PUNCTATUM

in having (like *Calopogon*) the lip uppermost. The sepals and the lateral petals are nearly alike, narrow and greenish. The lip is the "clamshell," colored brown or purplish with green markings. The column (marked with brown or purplish) is also remarkable in having three anthers instead of the usual one.

Clamshell orchid is found in the hammocks and cypress swamps of southern Florida, flowering all the year.

THE LIZARD-TAIL FAMILY
SAURURACEAE

This small family has only two species in North America. The flowers are in dense spikes or racemes and lack a perianth. There are several stamens and pistils.

LIZARD-TAIL
SAURURUS CERNUUS
Plate 49

The lizard-tail has a branched stem several feet tall, growing from a rhizome, in shallow water. The leaves have heart-shaped blades on long stalks. The small white flowers are in a long spike which terminates a branch; the end of the spike droops characteristically.

Lizard-tail is a plant of swamps and shallow water, occurring from Quebec to Minnesota and southward to Florida and Texas. It flowers from June to September. It is related to the vast tropical family which yields commercial pepper.

THE WHITE-ALDER FAMILY
CLETHRACEAE

The *Clethraceae* are shrubs or small trees, with undivided leaves attached singly. The very fragrant flowers have five sepals, five petals, usually ten stamens, and a pistil containing three chambers and a three-lobed stigma.

SWEET-PEPPER-BUSH or WHITE-ALDER
CLETHRA ALNIFOLIA
Plate 50

Sweet-pepper-bush, a branching shrub, grows to a height of ten feet. The leaves are oblong, very finely toothed toward the tip, with short stalks. The sweetly fragrant white flowers are densely clustered along the stems.

Sweet-pepper-bush grows along streams, in swamps, and in moist woods from Maine to New York and Pennsylvania and southward and southwestward to Florida and Texas. The flowering season is from July to September. This native American has been brought into cultivation in our gardens.

THE SMARTWEED FAMILY
POLYGONACEAE

The most conspicuous characteristic of the Smartweed family is the sheath that encircles the stem at every point where a leaf is attached. The flowers have no petals but several sepals which may be petal-like. The stamens vary in number. The pistil becomes a small, flat or triangular grain containing one seed.

DOCK
RUMEX HASTATULUS   *Plate 51*

There are many species of docks. This one grows up to four feet tall, with the lower leaves six inches long; the stem grows from a rhizome. The epithet *hastatulus* refers to the shape of many of the leaves, which have pointed lobes spreading sideways at the base as in an ancient spear (*hasta*). The yellowish or pinkish flowers are in a tall, narrow but loose cluster. The sepals remain attached and enlarge as the fruit develops; the outer three have thin membranes or "wings" growing from their midribs, which form the little pendent blades of the photograph.

R. hastatulus grows in fields, along roadsides, in sandy places, etc., from Massachusetts to Oklahoma and southward to Florida and Texas. It flowers from February to June. Another species of this genus, *R. acetosella*, common sorrel, is a bad weed of fields and lawns.

DESERT-BUCKWHEAT or SKELETON-WEED
ERIOGONUM DEFLEXUM   *Plate 52*

Desert-buckwheat is a branching annual about a foot tall, the branches green, smooth, and leafless. The leaves are at the base, with round woolly blades on relatively long stalks. The flowers grow one or several from a small funnel-shaped, five-toothed involucre; these are scattered up and down the stems on short stalks which often bend downward. The perianth of each flower has six white petal-like sepals.

Desert-buckwheat is common in the deserts of Nevada and southern California; and southward to Arizona and Baja California. It flowers from May to October. There are about 150 species of *Eriogonum* in the West, with 76 species listed in California alone.

WILD BUCKWHEAT
ERIOGONUM CROCATUM   *Plate 55*

This species of *Eriogonum* is perennial, growing from a woody base clothed with old leaves which are woolly with white hairs. The flowering stems grow about eight inches tall, forming flowers on right-angle forks (the flowers in the photograph are seen from above). The flowers are in small, dense clusters, each cluster surrounded by joined, woolly bracts—an involucre. The sepals are yellow.

43

45

46

47

48

43
REIN ORCHIS
HABENARIA SACCATA

44
GRASS-PINK
CALOPOGON TUBEROSUS

45
PINK LADY'S-SLIPPER
CYPRIPEDIUM ACAULE

46
BOG OR REIN ORCHIS
HABENARIA DILATATA

47
YELLOW LADY'S-SLIPPER
CYPRIPEDIUM CALCEOLUS

48
CLAMSHELL ORCHID
EPIDENDRUM COCHLEATUM

This wild buckwheat grows in rocky places near the coast in southern California. It flowers from April to July.

SMARTWEED or PINKWEED
POLYGONUM PENSYLVANICUM   *Plate 53*

This annual grows to be three feet tall or more. It is distinguished from many other species of *Polygonum* by the numerous glands on the stem and the lack of hairs at the edge of the sheaths. The leaves are mostly lance-shaped. The flowers are in dense spikes at the ends of the branches. There are about five pink sepals.

P. pensylvanicum is found from Quebec to Minnesota and South Dakota and southward to Florida and Texas. It flowers throughout the summer, from May to October. It is an exceptionally variable species, the varieties differing in size of calyx, presence or absence of hairs and glands, and size and shape of leaves. Other species of smartweed deserve the name more than this one, which is not particularly peppery. There are many species, practically cosmopolitan weeds. A few have handsome spikes of red flowers, and one, *P. orientale* or prince's-feather, is cultivated as an ornamental plant. Other local names for some that resemble *P. pensylvanicum* are ladies'-thumb and Adam's-plaster.

CLIMBING or FALSE BUCKWHEAT
POLYGONUM SCANDENS   *Plate 54*

This is a common weed which climbs by twining around other plants (or any support that offers). The stems, leaf-stalks, and flower-stalks are rough on their angles. The leaves have ovate or heart-shaped blades, with veins that are often rough on the lower side. The small, white flowers grow on erect branches about six inches tall, which rise from the leaf-axils. The sepals enlarge as the fruit, a glossy black grain, is formed, and three of them bear broad flanges or "wings."

Climbing-buckwheat forms tangles among other plants in various situations, wet and dry, in meadows and along roadsides, in thickets and waste places, from Quebec to Manitoba and southward to Florida and Texas. It flowers from August to November.

CHORIZANTHE
CHORIZANTHE FIMBRIATA   *Plate 56*

The stem of this annual may reach a height of a foot. The leaves are all at the base; they are about two inches long, wider near the tip than at the base. The inflorescence is repeatedly forked, with most of the flowers in tight clusters at the tips of the branches. The flowers are enclosed in small tubes composed of joined bracts; when only one flower occupies this tube, the latter may be mistaken for a calyx. Actually the six pink parts that compose the perianth are sepals; there are no petals. Each sepal is beautifully fringed (*fimbriata*).

This chorizanthe grows on dry slopes in southern California and Baja California. It flowers from April to June.

49

50

51

52

49

LIZARD-TAIL

SAURURUS CERNUUS

50

SWEET-PEPPER-BUSH

CLETHRA ALNIFOLIA

51

DOCK

RUMEX HASTATULUS

52

DESERT-BUCKWHEAT

ERIOGONUM DEFLEXUM

53

SMARTWEED

POLYGONUM PENSYLVANICUM

54

CLIMBING or FALSE BUCKWHEAT

POLYGONUM SCANDENS

The genus is a large one (thirty-five species are listed for California), and most species seem to have acquired no English names.

THE FOUR-O'CLOCK FAMILY
NYCTAGINACEAE

The Four-o'clock family consists largely of tropical or semitropical herbs and vines. The flowers have no petals but a tubular calyx colored like petals. Many have, in addition, an involucre—an envelope formed from joined bracts. In *Bougainvillea* the involucre provides most of the gorgeous color.

FOUR-O'CLOCK
MIRABILIS FROEBELII
Plate 57

The branching stem grows from a tuberous root to a height of nearly three feet; it is hairy and sticky (smooth in one variety). The ovate leaves are in pairs. The flowers grow from three to ten together in a narrow, five-toothed involucre. In each involucre one flower at a time blooms and projects. The calyx is funnel-shaped and rose-pink or rose-purplish.

This is a plant of stony places and deserts, from Nevada to California and southward to Arizona and northern Mexico. It blooms from April to August. Most species of *Mirabilis* grow in warm and tropical parts of the Americas. The garden four-o'clock or marvel-of-Peru is *M. jalapa*, from tropical America.

SAND-VERBENA
ABRONIA UMBELLATA
Plate 58

This sand-verbena has stems (three feet long or longer) that lie on the ground, only the branches that bear the rose-pink flowers standing erect. The leaf-blades are mostly oval, about two inches long. The whole plant is often sticky. The calyx is a tube flaring at the rim into five flat lobes, each cleft into two.

A. umbellata is a plant of the California seashore from Los Angeles southward into Baja California. It flowers from June to September. There are other species of *Abronia*, some inhabiting deserts, some the slopes of the mountains. Though the flowers bear a superficial resemblance, in color and in arrangement, to those of *Verbena*, they are not in the Vervain family.

THE BUTTERCUP FAMILY
RANUNCULACEAE

This is a common family in temperate lands. It includes besides buttercups such plants as columbines, larkspurs, and aconites; also anemones and a number of other spring-flowering plants. All species are herbaceous except some slightly woody vines. A distinguishing feature of most species is a large number of stamens in the flower;

pistils also are several or numerous in many species. In many genera petals are lacking, the sepals generally having a petal-like appearance.

TALL BUTTERCUP
RANUNCULUS ACRIS   *Plate 59*

There are many species of *Ranunculus*, mostly much alike. *R. acris* grows from a short underground stem; the erect stem rises to four or even five feet, with several branches and leaves; it is more or less hairy. The leaves are round in outline but cleft into narrow, pointed, and toothed parts; the lower ones are on long stalks. Each flower has usually five green, hairy sepals and five butter-yellow, shining petals. There are many stamens and pistils, the latter on the dome-shaped receptacle in the center of the flower. They develop into rather flat achenes, a small hook marking the position of the style.

Tall buttercups are natives of Europe that have invaded roadsides, fields, and meadows from Labrador to Alaska and southward to North Carolina, Illinois, Missouri, Kansas, and Oregon. The flowers bloom in May and continue through the summer.

This is the species that carpets English fields with gold. It is also called goldcups and kingcups. Cattle avoid eating the bitter-tasting stems and leaves (*acris* means "sharp" or "bitter").

Ranunculus means "little frog"; the genus is so named because many of its species grow in wet places, with the frogs. They are also often called crowfoot, because of the radiating narrow lobes or divisions of the leaves found in many species.

SWAMP BUTTERCUP
RANUNCULUS SEPTENTRIONALIS   *Plate 70*

The swamp buttercup has long stems that generally trail on the ground; the flowering branches turn upward. Each leaf is divided into three, the segments being irregularly cleft, lobed, and toothed. The plant is more or less hairy or sometimes smooth. The yellow flowers are much like those of the tall buttercup. The achenes are distinctive, being edged with a relatively broad flange and provided with a strong, flat, pointed beak.

The swamp buttercup grows in various sorts of situations other than swamps—meadows, moist woods, streamsides—from Labrador to Manitoba and southward to Virginia, Kentucky, Arkansas, and Texas. It flowers from April to July.

COLUMBINE
AQUILEGIA CANADENSIS   *Plate 74*

The delicate flowers of this columbine hang from the branches of a leafy stem which may reach a height of three feet but is usually about half that tall. Each leaf is divided into three segments, the segments again into three, and these perhaps again divided; the ultimate segments are small, three-lobed blades. The whole plant is smooth. Each flower has five pointed sepals, colored reddish, and five blunt petals,

55
WILD BUCKWHEAT
ERIOGONUM CROCATUM

56
CHORIZANTHE
CHORIZANTHE FIMBRIATA

57 **FOUR-O'CLOCK** MIRABILIS FROEBELII

58 **SAND-VERBENA** ABRONIA UMBELLATA

59 **TALL BUTTERCUP** RANUNCULUS ACRIS

red outside and yellow inside; each petal is extended backward (upward because the flower droops) into a hollow tube called a spur. Nectar is formed in the spurs. There are numerous stamens and usually five pistils. Each pistil develops into a follicle.

A. canadensis grows in rocky places in woods (one local name is rock-bells) from Nova Scotia to Saskatchewan and southward to Florida and Texas. It flowers from April to June.

The English name is derived from the Latin word for "dove"; perhaps the five petals have some fancied resemblance to five doves clustered together. The older form of the Latin name was *Aquilina*, "eaglelike."

CALIFORNIA COLUMBINE
AQUILEGIA PUBESCENS

Plate 60

The California columbine has downy stems about eighteen inches tall. The basal leaves are divided into three, the round segments being deeply cleft. Besides these there are smaller leaves on the stems. The flowers are distinctive among columbines in being erect on their stalks, the spurs of the petals pointing downward. The color varies from creamy to yellow and pink.

Aquilegia pubescens grows in rocky places at high altitudes in the Sierra Nevada of California. It flowers from June to August.

BLUE COLUMBINE
AQUILEGIA CAERULEA

Plate 67

Blue columbine grows about two feet tall. The leaves are divided only twice by threes—less than those of other species. The flowers are large, with bright blue, spreading sepals and white petals.

The species occurs in moist meadows, in open woods, and in various other situations at fairly high altitudes from Colorado to Idaho and California and southward to New Mexico. It flowers from June to August. This is the state flower of Colorado.

GOLDEN COLUMBINE
AQUILEGIA CHRYSANTHA

Plate 73

This western columbine is a graceful, much-branched plant reaching a height of three feet or more. The leaves and the flowers have much the same characteristics as *A. canadensis* of the eastern states, but the sepals are pale yellow, and the petals bright yellow, only the long spurs being tinged with pink.

A. chrysantha grows in moist soil, generally in light shade under pines, at the elevations where desert gives way to forest, from southern Colorado to Arizona and southward to Texas and northern Mexico. It flowers from April to September.

MOUNTAIN COLUMBINE
AQUILEGIA FORMOSA

Plate 71

Mountain columbine has a branched stem which lifts the hanging blossoms two feet or more above the ground. The leaves are divided much as in the common eastern

80

60
CALIFORNIA COLUMBINE
AQUILEGIA PUBESCENS

61
LIVERLEAF
HEPATICA NOBILIS

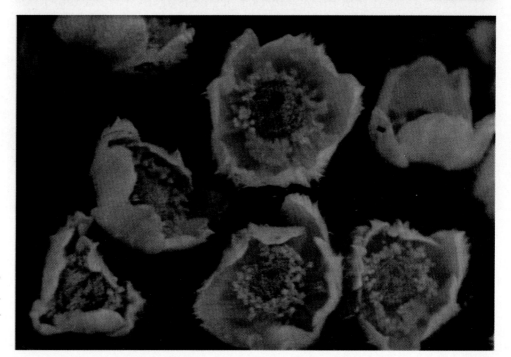

62
PASQUE-FLOWER
ANEMONE HUDSONIANA

columbine (*A. canadensis*). The flowers also resemble those of their eastern relative in structure and color; but the spurs of the petals are shorter and the sepals curve outward.

Mountain columbine is found in western mountain woodlands from Montana to Alaska and southward to Utah and California. It blooms from April to August.

PASQUE-FLOWER
ANEMONE HUDSONIANA   *Plate 62*

This pasque-flower has stems between one and two feet tall growing from a woody crown; they are densely hairy, as are the leaves. The leaves are divided into three, these segments again divided, and often still again divided, the final segments being very narrow and sharp. There are a stalkless leaf and from one to three flowers at the summit of each stem. The sepals are hairy and bluish on the outer surface, creamy-white inside. (There are no petals.) There are numerous stamens and many pistils with long styles; the ovaries become silky achenes, with the styles as "tails."

A. hudsoniana is a mountain species, occurring on alpine slopes from Labrador to Alaska and southward to Maine, Nebraska, Arizona, and Oregon. It flowers from April to August, depending on latitude and altitude. Some botanists regard it, with several other similar species, as merely varieties of one species, *A. patens*. Others would put all these plants in a genus of their own, *Pulsatilla*; they certainly differ in many ways from other anemones. The name pasque-flower comes from England, where one of these species grows, and refers to its blooming at Easter. That species, *A. pulsatilla*, is also known as Danes'-blood, apparently by association with certain dikes built by the Danes when they occupied England.

RUE-ANEMONE
ANEMONELLA THALICTROIDES   *Plate 66*

The slender stem of rue-anemone rises from a cluster of root-tubers to a height of about a foot. There are a few long-stalked leaves from the base of the stem, each divided into three, and each segment again divided into three small rounded blades notched at the outer edge. The effect is much like a leaf of columbine or meadow-rue. Just below the cluster of flowers are what seem to be six or nine stalked leaves; they are really two or three leaves, each divided into three, the main stalk of each leaf being very short. Several flowers are at the tip of the stem. Each has several white (or occasionally pink) petal-like sepals, numerous stamens, and a few pistils. "Double" flowers, in which many stamens are replaced by sepals, are not uncommon. The pistils become achenes.

This dainty plant grows in open woods and meadows from Maine to Minnesota and southward to Florida and Oklahoma, opening its flowers in April and May. It is named in Latin for the likeness of its flowers to those of an anemone and of its foliage to the meadow-rue (*Thalictrum*). The English name refers to the foliage of rue (*Ruta graveolens*).

82

LIVERLEAF
HEPATICA NOBILIS   *Plate 61*

The leaves and flowers grow in spring from a short perennial stem. The flowers appear first, each on a hairy stem. At this time the old leaves, usually brown and withered, lie limp on the ground. New leaves appear as the flowers are passing. The leaves have three-lobed blades on long stalks. Each flower has several petal-like sepals, colored white, pink, lavender, or pale blue, and no petals; but an involucre of three bracts a short distance below the flower may be mistaken for a calyx, and the sepals will then be miscalled petals. The stamens and pistils are numerous.

Liverleaf (or liverwort) is found in woods, usually in moist places, from Quebec to Minnesota and southward to Georgia, Alabama, and Missouri. Its flowers open in March and April. Our plants, which have been given various Latin names, seem to be merely varieties of the same species that grows in Europe. Because of the shape of the leaf and the "doctrine of signatures" (see *Saxifraga virginiensis*), the plant was in medieval times thought to provide a remedy for diseases of the liver.

EARLY MEADOW-RUE
THALICTRUM DIOICUM   *Plate 63*

This meadow-rue grows to a height of nearly three feet. The leaves have long stalks, at the end of which are three segments, these again divided and redivided; the ultimate segments are small oval blades, usually with two notches in the outer edge; they are not generally fully developed at flowering time. The general effect of the pale green foliage is very graceful and feathery. The numerous flowers grow loosely in a wide cluster. There are four or five narrow, greenish, yellowish, or purple sepals, which soon fall; and no petals. The stamens and pistils are not only in separate flowers but on separate plants (this is the meaning of *dioicum*: "two households"). The stamens hang from the end of the flower-stalks, lending a further airy effect. On the female plant the pistils become narrow, ribbed achenes pointed at each end.

T. dioicum grows in moist woods from Quebec to North Dakota and southward to Georgia, Alabama, and Missouri. The flowers open in April.

The foliage may be compared with that of *Anemonella* and *Aquilegia*; like the rue-anemone, this plant receives its English name from a resemblance to the cultivated herb *Ruta graveolens* (rue).

TALL MEADOW-RUE
THALICTRUM POLYGAMUM   *Plate 69*

Tall meadow-rue may grow to a height of eight feet. The leaves at the base are long-stalked and pinnately divided, the segments again divided, much as in *T. dio-icum*. The ultimate small blades are oblong and mostly three-lobed at the end, each lobe usually tipped with a sharp point. There are some stalkless leaves on the stem, the divisions being like those on the basal leaves. The white flowers are in a large loose cluster. They are of two kinds: staminate (shown in the photograph) and pistil-

63

64

65

66

late; the pistillate flowers may have a few stamens, and are then "perfect." ("Polyg-amous" is the botanical term used to describe the separation of the flowers into staminate and perfect, instead of staminate and pistillate.) The sepals soon fall (there are no petals). The stamens of the staminate flowers spread upward and sideways; they are not pendent as in *T. dioicum*.

Tall meadow-rue is common in meadows and roadsides from Newfoundland to Ontario and southward to Georgia and Tennessee. It flowers from June to August.

LARKSPUR
DELPHINIUM GLAREOSUM   *Plate 64*

D. glareosum has delicate stems up to three feet tall, usually somewhat sticky. The leaves, which grow singly on the lower parts of the stems, are cleft into narrow lobes. The blue parts of the flowers are the sepals; the upper sepal is prolonged back into a long hollow spur. The petals are small and white, with blue veins, forming the "bee" in the center of the flower. The pistils become small pods (a cluster of three is shown in the center of the photograph).

This larkspur is found usually in rocky places high in the mountains of Washington and Oregon. It flowers in July and August.

MARSH CLEMATIS or LEATHER-FLOWER
CLEMATIS CRISPA   *Plate 65*

Marsh clematis is a vine, climbing by its prehensile leaf-stalks. The leaves are pin-nately divided into four, six, or eight lance-shaped or ovate segments, the lower pair much larger than the others. The flowers are on rather long, leafless stalks. The perianth consists of four sepals; there are no petals. Each sepal is rather thick, pinkish-lavender, with a thin band of light blue on each side, the margins being crisped. There are numerous stamens and pistils. The pistils become achenes, the styles developing into long, feathery tails.

Marsh clematis grows in wet woods and swamps on the Atlantic coastal plain from Virginia to Florida and Texas. It flowers from April to August. Many handsome species and varieties of *Clematis* are known in cultivation; most have blue or purple sepals.

WHITE MARSH-MARIGOLD
CALTHA LEPTOSEPALA   *Plate 68*

White marsh-marigold is the western counterpart of the golden marsh-marigold of eastern swamps. The leaves are ovate, and slightly toothed. The flowers have white sepals instead of yellow (and no petals).

C. leptosepala grows along streams in the Rocky Mountains from Canada to Arizona and westward to Alaska, Washington, Oregon, and California. It flowers in July and August.

63 **EARLY MEADOW-RUE** THALICTRUM DIOICUM   *64* **LARKSPUR** DELPHINIUM GLAREOSUM

65 **MARSH CLEMATIS** CLEMATIS CRISPA   *66* **RUE-ANEMONE** ANEMONELLA THALICTROIDES

67
**BLUE
COLUMBINE**
AQUILEGIA
CAERULEA

68

69

70

71

72

73

74

68 WHITE MARSH-MARIGOLD
CALTHA LEPTOSEPALA

69 TALL MEADOW-RUE
THALICTRUM POLYGAMUM

70 SWAMP BUTTERCUP
RANUNCULUS SEPTENTRIONALIS

71 MOUNTAIN COLUMBINE
AQUILEGIA FORMOSA

72 MARSH-MARIGOLD
CALTHA PALUSTRIS

73 GOLDEN COLUMBINE
AQUILEGIA CHRYSANTHA

74 COLUMBINE
AQUILEGIA CANADENSIS

MARSH-MARIGOLD
CALTHA PALUSTRIS

Plate 72

Marsh-marigold has a branching hollow stem which bears numerous leaves and flowers, the plant forming a mound of foliage and flowers usually a foot or two high. The leaves are round or kidney-shaped, the margins bluntly toothed. The whole plant is smooth and shining. The flower has from five to nine bright yellow sepals, no petals, numerous stamens, and several or many pistils. The pistils form follicles.

This species is found in marshes and swamps (*palustris*), in the open or in woods, from Labrador to Alaska and southward to South Carolina, Tennessee, Iowa, and Nebraska; also in the northern parts of Europe and Asia. The flowers appear in April and May.

This is no relation to the true marigolds of our gardens, which are in the Daisy family. It is sometimes called cowslip, but the English cowslips are primroses—again no relation. The name "marigold" seems to be a corruption of the Anglo-Saxon *meargalla*, the name of a marsh plant. Most dictionaries derive it from "Mary" and "gold"; but why? It is, however, called maybuds or mayflower in various parts of England. In Ireland it is associated with May Day, having power, when hung in the window, to keep ill-natured fairies away. Be that as it may, the leaves make palatable greens when cooked; the flower-buds also have been eaten.

THE PAW-PAW FAMILY
ANNONACEAE

This is a large family of trees and shrubs, almost entirely tropical. The flowers have three sepals and two circles of three petals each. Most species have many stamens, and there may be a number of pistils. The fruit is generally fleshy and soft. Well-known fruits of the family, besides pawpaw, are cherimoya, soursop, and custard-apple.

PAWPAW or DOG-APPLE
ASIMINA RETICULATA

Plate 76

This species of *Asimina* is a shrub only about three feet tall. It has elliptic leaves. The purplish-brown flowers grow singly in the axils of leaves of the preceding season, which have fallen. The fruit is an elliptical soft berry two or three inches long; it is edible but tasteless.

A. reticulata grows in pinelands and scrub in Florida, flowering in March. The Seminole Indians are said to use a tea made from the flowers, as medicine.

FLAG-PAWPAW
ASIMINA SPECIOSA

Plate 75

Flag-pawpaw is a shrub about five feet tall. The young branches are covered with matted tawny hair. The leaves, which grow singly on the branches, are somewhat leathery, more or less elliptic, with short stalks; when young they are densely woolly.

88

75
FLAG-PAWPAW
ASIMINA SPECIOSA

76
PAWPAW
ASIMINA RETICULATA

The flowers droop singly or in pairs at the nodes of the stem, appearing before the leaves. The petals are cream-colored. The fruit is a soft berry.

Flag-pawpaw grows in the pinelands of the coastal plain of Georgia and Florida. It flowers in March and April. In the same genus is the pawpaw familiar in the central states, *A. triloba*, sometimes called poor-man's-banana. The large, oblong, soft fruit is edible but nearly tasteless.

THE WATER-LILY FAMILY
NYMPHAEACEAE

This small family is entirely aquatic. Some species have leaves under the surface; these are divided into almost hairlike segments. Others have more or less round leaf-blades floating on the surface or raised above it. Sepals, petals, and stamens vary from three to an indefinite number. The pistil also varies, as is evident in the descriptions that follow.

LOTUS or SACRED-BEAN
NELUMBO LUTEA
Plate 77

The leaf-blades of the lotus are circular, with their long stalks attached at the center and raising them out of the water. The flowers also are raised above the surface. The green sepals pass gradually into the pale yellow (*lutea*) petals; there are many stamens. In the center of the flower is an unusual structure, an extension of the receptacle which is narrow at the bottom and grows broader upward. In its flat top are holes, and in each hole there is a pistil, or, later, a one-seeded nut developed from a pistil.

This lotus is found rather rarely growing in scattered bodies of quiet water through most of the eastern United States; in the Illinois River and in parts of the Mississippi it forms extensive colonies. The flowers open from July to September. This striking plant is related to the sacred lotus of ancient Egypt, which was used as a model for the capitals of columns and for various decorative designs, lasting even down to our own times. Another name for it is water chinquapin.

WATER-LILY
NYMPHAEA ODORATA
Plate 78

The leaves of the common water-lily have almost round blades, with a notch extending to the center, where the long stalk is attached. The fragrant white or pink flowers are borne singly on long stems. There are four sepals and many petals; the petals become narrower toward the center of the flower, where many of them bear anthers; there is thus a transition from petals to stamens. The many-chambered ovary is crowned with a number of narrow, radiating stigmas.

N. odorata inhabits quiet waters from Newfoundland to Manitoba and southward to Florida and Texas. It flowers from June to September. Most of the species of *Nymphaea* are tropical; they have flowers of many colors. Many have been brought into cultivation, and have yielded numerous hybrids.

YELLOW POND-LILY or SPATTERDOCK
NUPHAR ADVENA   *Plate 79*

From the rhizome rise the long leaf-stalks, which usually carry the notched, round blades above the surface of the water. The flower-stalks also rise above the surface. There are several sepals, greenish on the outside, yellow inside. The numerous small petals are scarcely visible. Many stamens rise around a central disc, which is the stigma of the pistil.

The yellow pond-lilies are familiar in quiet waters throughout the eastern half of the United States, flowering from May to October. There are several other, less common species, some of which have floating leaf-blades.

THE POKEWEED FAMILY
PHYTOLACCACEAE

The plants of this family are related to the pigweeds, having flowers without petals. The distinguishing feature is the pistil and fruit described below.

POKEWEED
PHYTOLACCA AMERICANA   *Plate 80*

The straggling, untidy green bushes of pokeweed may be six or eight feet tall; they grow each year from large perennial roots. The stem often becomes crimson. The leaves are singly attached, lance-shaped or ovate. The small flowers are borne in erect clusters, which appear at the tips of the branches but are pushed to one side by the growth of a bud just beneath, and so come to be opposite the leaves. Each flower has five round, white, petal-like sepals and no petals. The pistil is formed of several parts joined in a ring, each with its own style and stigma. The whole mass becomes a dark purple—almost black—berry; and the stems that carry the berries now hang down.

Pokeweed grows in moist woods, in clearings and disturbed soil, and in roadside ditches, from Quebec to Minnesota and southward to Florida and Texas. It flowers from July to October, new racemes appearing when the earlier ones are already in fruit. The root and the mature foliage are poisonous, but the young shoots may be boiled and eaten as greens; they are more palatable than many plants cultivated for the purpose. The berries also have been called poisonous but this is doubtful. They are eaten by birds and formed one of the foods of the now extinct passenger pigeon, whence they are still sometimes called pigeon-berries. The crimson juice was used as a dye by Indians and as a pigment for painting by the Missouri artist Bingham.

CARPET-WEED FAMILY
AIZOACEAE

Most of the *Aizoaceae* are South African, but a few are weeds in America. They are somewhat succulent plants, with many petals and stamens.

77 **LOTUS** NELUMBO LUTEA

78 **WATER-LILY** NYMPHAEA ODORATA

ICE-PLANT
MESEMBRYANTHEMUM CRYSTALLINUM

Plate 81

Ice-plant owes this name to the many tiny glistening projections on the surface of leaves and stem. This is a succulent plant which grows prostrate on the ground, the stem much branched, with more or less ovate leaves, either paired or single, all somewhat reddish-tinged. The flowers grow in the axils of leaves and at the tips of stems. The corolla is white or reddish and nearly an inch across.

This is apparently a native of Africa which has become naturalized in California. It grows along the coast from Monterey south and into Baja California. It blooms from March to October. Several other species of *Mesembryanthemum* from Africa have settled in California, some making a brave show. The low, succulent plants may be entirely covered by magenta, white, or yellow flowers. These, however, open only in bright weather and during the bright part of the day. The tongue-twisting name of the genus is derived from two Greek words that mean "midday" and "flower."

THE PURSLANE FAMILY
PORTULACACEAE

Perhaps the best-known member of the family is purslane or pussley, a common weed in gardens, succulent and hard to kill, and edible when cooked as greens. The flowers have two sepals and five petals (or none). The number of stamens varies.

SPRING BEAUTY
CLAYTONIA VIRGINICA

Plate 83

This graceful small plant whitens open grassy places in early spring. The underground stem, which is a corm, sends up several erect stems about a foot tall. Each of these bears a pair of narrow, pointed, rather thick leaves about halfway up. The inflorescence begins just above these leaves, bearing flowers to right and left along one side, the end curled over and the buds drooping close together. The petals are white veined with pink or pink veined with red. The stamens have pink anthers.

Spring beauty grows under trees in open woods, and on lawns and roadsides, forming large colonies, from Quebec to Minnesota and southward to Georgia and Texas. It flowers from March to May.

SPRING BEAUTY
CLAYTONIA LANCEOLATA

Plate 82

This western spring beauty grows about six inches tall, the stem coming from a corm underground. On the stem is a pair of dark green, lance-shaped, rather thick leaves an inch or two long. Above these are the white-and-pink blossoms arranged as in *C. virginica*.

C. lanceolata is found in high mountain meadows, often at the edge of snowbanks, from Wyoming to British Columbia and southward to California. Flowering time is from April to June.

79
YELLOW POND-LILY
NUPHAR ADVENA

80
POKEWEED
PHYTOLACCA AMERICANA

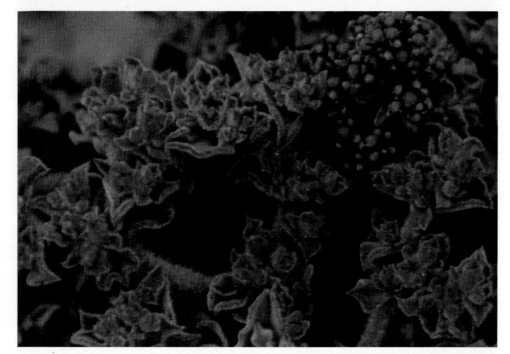

81
ICE-PLANT
MESEMBRYANTHEMUM CRYSTALLÍNUM

82
SPRING BEAUTY
CLAYTONIA LANCEOLATA

83
SPRING BEAUTY
CLAYTONIA VIRGINICA

84
BLADDER CAMPION
SILENE CUCUBALUS

85
CALIFORNIA CAMPION
SILENE LACINIATA

82

83

84

85

THE PINK FAMILY
CARYOPHYLLACEAE

The Pink family is composed of herbaceous plants largely of temperate regions. There are four or five sepals, the same number of petals or none, stamens often twice as many as the sepals, and a single pistil with from two to five styles.

BLADDER CAMPION
SILENE CUCUBALUS
Plate 84

Several stems rise from the same root to a height of two or three feet. The rather thick leaves are paired, lance-shaped to ovate. The whole plant is very smooth, with a slight bloom. The flowers are in a forking inflorescence. The five sepals join to form the papery "bladder," which becomes larger in fruit. The five white petals stand on narrow stalks, their spreading blades two-lobed. Each flower lasts two or three days but is open only from evening until morning (in dull weather it may remain open through the morning). The stamens mature first, then the stigmas; pollination is by moths.

Bladder campion, a native of Europe, now adorns roadsides, fields, and waste places throughout the United States (except in the south and southwest) and adjacent Canada. It comes into flower in April and continues through summer and into autumn.

Among other English names for the plant are Billy-busters, cow-rattle, fat-bellies, kiss-me-quick, rattle-bags, spattling-poppy, thunderbolt, white riding-hood. The herbalist Gerard says it is good against venomous bites—even if you just hold it. The young shoots, boiled, are said to be delicious.

CALIFORNIA CAMPION
SILENE LACINIATA
Plate 85

This campion is perennial, the weak stems growing from a large root; they reach a length of about two feet. The leaves are narrow, about four inches long. The petals are pink or scarlet, each deeply cleft ("laciniate") into four narrow lobes.

S. laciniata is common on grassy or brushy slopes in the coast ranges of the southern half of California and southward into Mexico. It blooms from May to July.

MOUNTAIN CHICKWEED
CERASTIUM OREOPHILUM
Plate 86

This relative of the chickweeds of our lawns and borders has stems growing in a tuft, lying down at the base, then rising to a height of about eight inches. The stem is downy with small stalked glands. The paired leaves are hairy and very narrow. The sepals have white, translucent margins and tips. The white petals are deeply cleft.

Mountain chickweed grows in wet places in the mountains from Colorado to New Mexico. It flowers from May to July.

86

MOUNTAIN CHICKWEED

CERASTIUM OREOPHILUM

87

GREAT CHICKWEED

STELLARIA PUBERA

88

89

90

91

GREAT CHICKWEED
STELLARIA PUBERA

Plate 87

Stellaria pubera is about a foot tall, a perennial with paired elliptic leaves. Each white petal has a narrow, erect, stalklike part and spreading blade, deeply two-lobed, so that at first glance there may seem to be ten petals instead of five.

This chickweed grows in shady places from New Jersey to Illinois and southward to Florida and Alabama. It flowers from March to June. The chickweeds embrace two genera, *Stellaria* and *Cerastium,* usually having respectively three and five styles. Some species are common weeds in lawns.

THE CAPER FAMILY
CAPPARIDACEAE

The Caper family is much like the Mustard family, the chief differences being that there are generally only four stamens, and that the pistil is raised on a stalk. The capers of commerce are the dried buds of *Capparis spinosa* from the Mediterranean. The spider-flower, *Cleome*, is a favorite in old-fashioned gardens.

CLAMMYWEED
POLANISIA TRACHYSPERMA

Plate 88

Clammyweed, as the name suggests, is sticky and has a rather heavy, disagreeable odor. The stem grows about two feet tall, bearing leaves which are palmately divided into three mostly ovate segments. Each flower has four sepals which soon fall; and four white petals which stand at one side of the flower, each having a notched blade on a narrow stalk. The stamens vary from few to many.

Clammyweed inhabits sandy and gravelly places from North Dakota to British Columbia and southward into Mexico. It flowers in July and August.

THE POPPY FAMILY
PAPAVERACEAE

The plants of the Poppy family are mostly herbaceous, many of them with milky or colored juice. There are generally two or four sepals, several petals, and often many stamens. The fruit is usually a capsule with seeds attached in rows to the walls. There are two subfamilies (sometimes considered distinct families): the Poppy subfamily (*Papaver, Sanguinaria, Platystemon, Argemone*), and the Bleeding-heart subfamily (*Corydalis*).

PINK CORYDALIS or ROCK-HARLEQUIN
CORYDALIS SEMPERVIRENS

Plate 90

This delicate plant rises to three or four feet, a branching stem clothed in gray-green, feathery foliage. The lower leaves have long stalks; all are pinnately divided

99

88 CLAMMYWEED POLANISIA TRACHYSPERMA   89 CREAM-CUPS PLATYSTEMON CALIFORNICUS

90 PINK CORYDALIS CORYDALIS SEMPERVIRENS   91 BLOODROOT SANGUINARIA CANADENSIS

92 **CAROLINA-POPPY** ARGEMONE ALBA

93 **RED POPPY** PAPAVER CALIFORNICUM

and subdivided, the ultimate segments rather wedge-shaped and toothed. Each flower has four pink petals with yellow tips, of which the upper one is the largest and is prolonged backward into a "spur" (hollow saclike portion), so that the flower-stalk, with two tiny sepals, seems to be attached about one-fourth of the way from the end of the flower. The tips of the upper and lower petals spread apart, and those of the lateral petals come together, hiding the six stamens and the pistil.

Pink corydalis grows in rocky woods, usually in the shade, from Newfoundland to Alaska and southward to New York, Georgia (in the mountains), Tennessee, Montana, and British Columbia. The flowers appear from May to September.

CREAM-CUPS
PLATYSTEMON CALIFORNICUS   *Plate 89*

Cream-cups is a small, hairy annual up to a foot tall. Many stems grow from one base, with lance-shaped or grasslike leaves on their lower parts. There is one flower at the tip of each stem. The perianth is composed of three sepals and six petals; there are many stamens. The petals vary from white to cream-color or even yellow.

Cream-cups grows with grasses in open ground from Utah to California and southward to Arizona and Baja California. It flowers from March to May. There are many varieties, forms, etc., the plants varying in degree of hairiness, color and shape of petals, and other characteristics.

BLOODROOT
SANGUINARIA CANADENSIS   *Plate 91*

The underground part with the orange-red sap, from which the plant takes its name, is not a root but a rhizome. From the growing end of this rises in spring a single flower on a stalk up to six inches tall, which is enveloped by the folded blade of the single leaf. The leaf-blade is round, deeply lobed, and prominently veined. There are two sepals, which fall as the flower opens, and, typically, eight white petals, alternately broad and narrow; the number, however, varies. A crowd of stamens surrounds the pistil.

Bloodroot grows in moist meadows and streamsides, especially at the margins of woods, and on open wooded slopes, from Nova Scotia to Manitoba and southward to Florida and Texas. The flowers appear from March to May.

The red juice was used as a dye by the Indians.

RED POPPY
PAPAVER CALIFORNICUM   *Plate 93*

Red poppy is a slender annual about two feet tall. The leaves grow at or near the base of the flowering stems, each pinnately lobed. Each stem bears a single flower, whose buds droop at first, the flower-stalks straightening as the flowers open. There are two sepals, four brick-red petals, and many stamens. The radiating stigmas form a flat disc on top of the ovary, and this lasts to the mature stage of the capsule. The capsule opens by pores under the edge of this disc.

95

96

97

98

The red poppy grows on burned-over land and in other disturbed ground in the coast ranges of California. The orange-red wind poppy (*Stylomecon heterophylla*) is often found growing with it; it has a distinct style atop the capsule, with a small stigma.

CAROLINA-POPPY
ARGEMONE ALBA   *Plate 92*

The stem of Carolina-poppy is a foot or more tall. The leaves, which are singly attached, are pinnately lobed, the margins with spine-tipped teeth and the midrib also prickly. The flowers grow singly from the axils of leaves. Each has two or three spine-tipped sepals which fall as the flower opens, and usually six broad, overlapping white petals.

Carolina-poppy is found in waste places and on roadsides from South Carolina to Missouri and southward to Florida and Texas. It flowers from March to September, or all the year in the southernmost parts of the range.

PRICKLY-POPPY
ARGEMONE PLATYCERAS   *Plate 94*

Prickly-poppy is a perennial with prickly leaves covered with a whitish bloom. The large flowers terminate the branches. Each has three sepals, from four to six white petals, and very numerous yellow stamens. The sepals fall as the flower opens; each is tipped with a stout spine.

A. platyceras is common in dry places from Nebraska and Wyoming to Arizona, California, and northern Mexico. It may be found in flower at almost any time of the year, but flowers are most abundant in spring and summer. In parts of the Mojave Desert it may form fields of white and yellow bloom. The herbage contains an orange latex. The seeds are strongly narcotic. Some species of *Argemone* have found favor in eastern gardens, and escape from cultivation and grow wild, especially from Illinois westward and southward, and even occasionally in New England.

THE MUSTARD FAMILY
CRUCIFERAE

They are called "cross-bearers," because their four petals form a cross. There are also four sepals. Most species of the family are recognized by their (usually) six stamens, two shorter than the other four; for this condition Linnaeus coined the amusing term "tetradynamous" (four-powered). The fruit is a two-chambered pod, mostly either long and narrow or round and flat. This is a large family which includes familiar vegetables and condiments (cabbage, turnip, mustard) and equally familiar weeds (wild mustard, yellow rocket, shepherd's-purse), as well as some attractive wild and garden flowers (candy-tuft).

95 **RADISH** RAPHANUS SATIVUS   96 **BITTER CRESS** CARDAMINE CORDIFOLIA

97 **WILD WALLFLOWER** ERYSIMUM CHEIRANTHOIDES   98 **BLADDER-POD** LESQUERELLA KINGII

RADISH
RAPHANUS SATIVUS

Plate 95

One does not expect to discover an ordinary radish under a pretty wildflower; but radishes do "escape," as the botanists have it. Radish is annual or biennial, first forming leaves at the ground level, then a flowering stem, which may be as much as four feet tall. The lowest leaves are pinnately lobed, the upper merely toothed. The flowers are rose-purple or white. The pod is two- or three-seeded, about an inch long, with a conspicuous beak.

Radish grows as a weed in waste places throughout North America, flowering from February to July. The tap-root which we eat becomes tough and inedible as the plant reaches the flowering stage; various forms of the species are cultivated.

BITTER CRESS
CARDAMINE CORDIFOLIA

Plate 96

This cress is perennial. The erect stem springs from a rhizome to a height of nearly two feet. The leaves have round blades on fairly long stalks; the blades are indented (or "heart-shaped"—*cordifolia*) at the base, and shallowly toothed around the margins. The flowers are white. The pod is narrow, flattish, short-beaked, held erect on stalks that point upward.

C. cordifolia grows in wet places, even in water, along streams in the mountains from Montana to Oregon and southward to New Mexico and Arizona. It flowers from May to August.

WILD WALLFLOWER or WORMSEED-MUSTARD
ERYSIMUM CHEIRANTHOIDES

Plate 97

The wild wallflower grows about two feet tall, bearing leaves with elliptic or lance-shaped blades without teeth. The pod is long and narrow.

Wild wallflower is found mostly in sandy soil from Newfoundland to Alaska and southward to North Carolina, Tennessee, and Washington. The yellow flowers appear from March to October, depending on latitude.

BLADDER-POD
LESQUERELLA KINGII

Plate 98

The stems of bladder-pod are weak, reclining or sprawling, up to six inches long. The basal leaves are ovate, stalked, and about an inch long. There are a few smaller leaves on the stems. The plant is silvery with star-shaped hairs. The small yellow flowers are in long, often curved clusters. The most distinctive feature is the pod, of a globular shape unusual in the mustard family.

Bladder-pod occurs on rocky slopes at high altitudes, on desert mountains and with pines and junipers, from Nevada to California and southward to Arizona. The flowers open from March to July. The genus-name commemorates Leo Charles Lesquereux, a well-known American botanist of the nineteenth century.

99
YELLOW CRESS
RORIPPA ISLANDICA

100
CRINKLEROOT
DENTARIA DIPHYLLA

101
BLACK MUSTARD
BRASSICA NIGRA

102
PITCHER-PLANT
SARRACENIA PURPUREA

YELLOW CRESS
RORIPPA ISLANDICA

Plate 99

Rorippa islandica has a stem that sometimes reaches four feet in height but usually forms a bushy plant half that tall. The leaves are singly attached, more or less lance-shaped, often pinnately lobed or divided, or merely toothed. The yellow flowers are small.

This cress is found on shores of lakes and streams and in damp places generally throughout North America; also in Greenland, Europe, and Asia. It flowers from May to September. It is a variable species, the several varieties differing in the degree of lobing or division of the leaves, shape and size of pods, presence or absence of hairs.

CRINKLEROOT
DENTARIA DIPHYLLA

Plate 100

Crinkleroot grows from a long, wrinkled rhizome, the erect stem reaching a height of a foot or so. There is usually a pair of leaves (*diphylla*) on the stem about halfway up. Each has a stalk at the end of which the blade is divided palmately into three segments; the segments are ovate and coarsely toothed. There are also leaves at the base of the stem, similarly divided. The white flowers are at the summit of the stem.

Crinkleroot grows in the loam of rich woods from Quebec to Minnesota and southward to Georgia (in the mountains), Alabama, and Kentucky. It flowers from April to June. The name derives from the rhizome (generally mistaken for a root), which is crisp and palatable. Another species of *Dentaria* is *D. laciniata*, commonly called toothwort or pepper-root. The leaves are divided into narrow, toothed segments, and the rhizome is constricted into a series of tubers (perhaps the "teeth"?).

BLACK MUSTARD
BRASSICA NIGRA

Plate 101

Black mustard has a branching stem up to eight feet tall, often weak and curved. The lower leaves are pinnately cleft, with a large lobe at the end; the upper leaves are much smaller. The whole plant is either smooth or more or less bristly. The petals are yellow. The seed-pod stands erect against the main stem; it ends in a round beak; the seeds within cause slight bulges in the wall of the pod. The color of the seeds is responsible for the "black" (*nigra*) part of the name.

Black mustard is cultivated as the source of the condiment. It also runs wild as a weed in waste places throughout North America, flowering from April to October, depending on the climate.

THE PITCHER-PLANT FAMILY
SARRACENIACEAE

This small family consists entirely of plants with pitcherlike leaves which trap and digest insects.

103 **MOSSY STONECROP** SEDUM ACRE

104 **STONECROP** SEDUM DIVERGENS

105 **LIVE-FOREVER** DUDLEYA SAXOSA

PITCHER-PLANT or INDIAN-JUG
SARRACENIA PURPUREA   *Plate 102*

The pitcher-plants derive their name from their curious leaves. These stand erect or nearly so and are shaped like pitchers or vases. Water collects in the cavities of the leaves; insects, lured by a sweet secretion, crawl into the pitcher and are prevented from leaving by down-pointing hairs. Continuing downward, they drown in the water and decay; the products of their decomposition may be absorbed by the walls of the pitcher and contribute to the nourishment of the plant. The pitchers of *S. purpurea* are six or eight inches tall. They grow in a circle at the ground level. The single flower hangs from the bent tip of a leafless stem between one and two feet tall. There are five petals of a dark purplish-red color and numerous stamens. The most striking aspect of the flower is the style, which expands into a five-angled, umbrella-like body, the minute stigmas being underneath.

S. purpurea is a plant of bogs and peat, found from Labrador to Mackenzie and southward to Florida, Louisiana, and Saskatchewan. It flowers from May to August. It is the official flower of Newfoundland.

THE LIVE-FOREVER FAMILY
CRASSULACEAE

The *Crassulaceae* are succulents, embracing such well-known plants as live-forever, hen-and-chickens, and the large genus *Sedum*. The number of flower-parts varies, the stamens being generally twice as numerous as the petals, and the pistils usually of the same number as the petals.

MOSSY STONECROP or WALLPEPPER
SEDUM ACRE   *Plate 103*

Some species of *Sedum* are handsome native wildflowers; some are valued garden flowers; this species is a common and troublesome weed, forming mats in rocky and open places. The creeping stems are covered with small, thick, succulent leaves about a quarter-inch long. The flowering branches rise erect, bearing small yellow flowers.

Sedum acre is a native of Europe, now a weed from Nova Scotia to Washington and southward to North Carolina and Illinois. It flowers in June and July.

Like most succulent plants, it is hard to get rid of; the plant does not die quickly when uprooted and exposed to the sun. The name wallpepper refers to its ability to grow on stone walls and to its pungent taste; *acre* also refers to the taste. In England it is also known as creeping-jenny, wall-ginger, wall-moss, golden stonecrop, and, in certain southern counties, as welcome-home-husband-though-never-so-drunk!

STONECROP
SEDUM DIVERGENS   *Plate 104*

It is perhaps impossible to put a scientific name to a species of *Sedum* from a photograph only; there are many species, subspecies, and varieties, and the differences between them are often slight. The plant illustrated answers to the description of *S. divergens* in its paired, succulent leaves, its lance-shaped, narrow, yellow petals, and the five spreading follicles that form its fruit.

S. divergens grows on rocky alpine slopes from British Columbia to northern California, flowering in July and August.

LIVE-FOREVER
DUDLEYA SAXOSA   *Plate 105*

The very short, thick stem at the surface of the ground bears from ten to twenty-five leaves in a rosette. These leaves are gray-green, lance-shaped, thick, three or four inches long. From the axils of the leaves rise several erect stems, bearing small succulent, ovate leaves (they may be called bracts) and broad terminal, curving clusters of flowers. The stem, leaves, and sepals are reddish, purplish, or blue. The five petals, which are joined near the base, are yellow.

This is a species found in dry, rocky places in southern California, blooming from April to June. There are some forty species of *Dudleya* in southwestern North America, mostly plants of dry places, cliffs, and the like. Many are extremely variable and difficult to name, perhaps because of hybridizing. The particular plant illustrated belongs to subspecies *aloides* of *D. saxosa*. The genus is named for W. R. Dudley, professor of botany at Stanford University.

SAXIFRAGE FAMILY
SAXIFRAGACEAE

The saxifrages have usually five sepals, five petals, and two pistils which are often partly joined by their ovaries. Many of them have a cup-shaped receptacle with which the bases of the ovaries are united.

FOAM-FLOWER
TIARELLA UNIFOLIATA   *Plate 106*

The stem of this foam-flower rises about a foot, bearing a loose cluster of delicate small flowers, which hang from curved stalks. There are leaves both at the base and on the stem, with the blades divided into three or more segments; those at the base have long stalks. There are five sepals, forming a tiny white bell, and five narrow white petals, which curve slightly outward and upward.

T. unifoliata is found in woods in mountains from Alberta to Alaska and southward to Montana and California. It flowers from June to August.

FOAM-FLOWER
TIARELLA CORDIFOLIA   *Plate 109*

The rhizome—or the runner that it generally emits—usually forms two leaves, rising from the ground, each with an ovate or nearly round, irregularly toothed blade

111

106
FOAM-FLOWER
TIARELLA UNIFOLIATA

107
TREE-ANEMONE
CARPENTERIA CALIFORNICA

108
MOUNTAIN SAXIFRAGE
SAXIFRAGA GREENEI

109
FOAM-FLOWER
TIARELLA CORDIFOLIA

110
CORAL-BELLS
HEUCHERA SANGUINEA

111
EARLY SAXIFRAGE
SAXIFRAGA VIRGINIENSIS

112
MITERWORT
MITELLA DIPHYLLA

109

110

111

112

on a long stalk. From the same point rises the flowering stem, a foot or more tall. The small flowers are arranged along the stem on short stalks. The white petals are less than one-fourth of an inch long. The two pistils, which are joined at the base, form two follicles of unequal size—a lopsided, two-horned fruit.

Foam-flower grows in rich woods from Nova Scotia to Michigan and southward to Georgia and Alabama. Flowers appear from April to July.

TREE-ANEMONE
CARPENTERIA CALIFORNICA   *Plate 107*

Tree-anemone belies its name by being a spreading shrub, usually about six feet tall (the branches sometimes much longer). The leaves are paired, rather thick and tough, and lance-shaped or oblong, the upper surface green and the lower gray with a fine down. The white flowers grow singly in the leaf axils, or a few clustered together at the ends of the branches.

Tree-anemone grows on dry slopes and ridges in central California. It flowers from May to July. It is also cultivated. It is no relative of the true anemones, which are in the Buttercup family, and does not even resemble them; but there is no accounting for common names. The genus-name commemorates a professor of botany.

MOUNTAIN SAXIFRAGE
SAXIFRAGA GREENEI   *Plate 108*

The flowers of mountain saxifrage are in a delicate cluster which rises from a tuft of leaves close to the ground. The leaves are oblong or ovate with hairs along the edges. The flowering stem is beset with minute gland-tipped hairs. The five white petals have a round blade on a narrow stalk.

Mountain saxifrage is found among the rocks of high mountain slopes from Montana to Nevada and southward to Utah. It flowers in June and July.

EARLY SAXIFRAGE
SAXIFRAGA VIRGINIENSIS   *Plate 111*

The main stem of this saxifrage is very short and thick, bearing a compact rosette of small leaves. From this rises the flowering stem, reaching a height of about a foot when mature, and bearing several tight clusters of small white flowers at the summit. This stem is usually downy and often the leaves are also.

The early saxifrage grows mostly on rock ledges and rocky slopes, in the open or in light woods, from New Brunswick to Manitoba and southward to Georgia, Tennessee, and Oklahoma.

The name means "stone-breaker," which is said to refer not to the common habitat of rocks but to the supposed powers of certain European species to dissolve bladder-stones. This reputation was derived from the "doctrine of signatures," which held that each plant bore the likeness of the part it was divinely ordained to heal in sickness, or, as in this case, the likeness of the abnormal growth to be dispelled. The species so named in medieval times bore small tubers—"stones"—on their roots.

113 **THREE-TOOTHED CINQUEFOIL** POTENTILLA TRIDENTATA   *114* **WILD ROSE** ROSA GYMNOCARPA

115 **MEADOWSWEET** SPIRAEA LATIFOLIA   *116* **POTENTILLA** POTENTILLA FLABELLIFOLIA

113

114

115

116

CORAL-BELLS or ALUM-ROOT
HEUCHERA SANGUINEA *Plate 110*

Coral-bells lifts its slender flowering stems only a few inches from the scaly rhizome. The leaves are at the base of the stems; they have round, toothed blades on long stalks. The flowers are in narrow clusters. Each has five sepals and five pink petals.

Coral-bells grows on moist rocks in shady places through Arizona and northern Mexico, flowering from March to September. It is often cultivated in other parts of the United States. The rhizome (not the "root") is astringent, like alum, and has been used medicinally in the desert.

MITERWORT
MITELLA DIPHYLLA *Plate 112*

Miterwort resembles foam-flower in several ways, having a basal cluster of long-stalked leaves growing from a rhizome and a slender flowering stalk (or several) rising from the same point to a height of a foot or more. The basal leaves have ovate or heart-shaped blades, more or less three-lobed; there is also a pair of leaves (*diphylla*), without stalks, on the flowering stem. The tiny white flowers are in a raceme. Each has five sepals and five petals; the petals, only about one-tenth of an inch long, are deeply cut pinnately into a number of narrow lobes, so that the flower viewed through a magnifier has a very delicately complex, almost crystalline appearance. The ovaries together form a follicle which opens across the top, displaying the black seeds as if in a minute basket. The two horns on this fruit, suggesting a bishop's miter, give the plant its name.

Miterwort grows in the loam of rich woods from Quebec to Minnesota and southward to South Carolina, Tennessee, Mississippi, and Missouri.

THE ROSE FAMILY
ROSACEAE

This large and important family includes not only roses, but strawberries, blackberries, raspberries, cherries, peaches, plums, almonds, and, in its widest sense, apples, pears, and hawthorns. It has usually singly attached, often divided leaves with stipules. The sepals and petals are generally in fives, the stamens numerous, the pistils from one to many. The receptacle takes the form of a disc or cup, sometimes with a hump in the middle. The type of fruit varies greatly, as is evident from those mentioned above.

MEADOWSWEET
SPIRAEA LATIFOLIA *Plate 115*

This is a shrub with reddish stems up to four feet tall. The leaves are numerous, undivided, ovate (or *obovate*, that is, with the broadest part away from the stalk), and toothed. The plant is smooth or nearly so. At the top is a tall cluster of many crowded

116

small flowers, forming a pyramid of white or pale pink. The pistils, usually about five, form small follicles.

Meadowsweet grows in meadows and on rocky slopes from Newfoundland to Michigan and southward to New York and in the mountains to North Carolina. It shows its flowers from June to September.

A very similar species, *S. alba*, is distinguished by its yellowish-brown stems, which are downy in the flowering part. It grows westward to Alberta and southward to North Carolina, Indiana, Missouri, and North Dakota.

SHRUBBY CINQUEFOIL
POTENTILLA FRUTICOSA   *Plate 122*

Potentilla may at first sight look like a buttercup, with its five-parted yellow flowers; but the divided leaves with conspicuous stipules, and the disclike receptacle, are obvious differences. This species is one of the few that are woody. It grows three or four feet tall. The leaves are smooth or silky, pinnately divided into narrow segments. The flower is about an inch across. There are about twenty stamens, and a number of pistils on a hump (part of the receptacle) in the center.

Shrubby cinquefoil is widespread in North America, growing in meadows and on hillsides from Labrador to Alaska and southward to New Jersey, Pennsylvania, Indiana, Iowa, South Dakota, New Mexico, Arizona, and California. It is in flower—somewhere—from June to October. It is often cultivated, and a number of varieties are known in gardens.

THREE-TOOTHED CINQUEFOIL
POTENTILLA TRIDENTATA   *Plate 113*

This little cinquefoil is woody at the base but scarcely a shrub. The visible parts grow from numerous creeping stems, both underground and on the surface. The leaves are evergreen; each is palmately divided into three segments, which broaden toward the three-toothed (*tridentata*) end. The flowering stem rises to a height of not more than a foot, bearing a cluster of several white flowers. In structure the flowers are like those of *P. fruticosa*, but the receptacle and achenes are very hairy.

P. tridentata grows in open rocky or peaty places, from Greenland to Mackenzie and southward to Connecticut and New York; to Georgia in the mountains; and to Michigan, Iowa, and North Dakota.

Potentilla was so named by the medieval herbalists because it was supposed to be "potent" in medicine. Modern research has not confirmed this reputation.

POTENTILLA
POTENTILLA FLABELLIFOLIA   *Plate 116*

Potentilla flabellifolia is perennial, the stems spreading from a short rhizome. The leaf-blade is divided into three wedge-shaped segments, only about an inch long,

117

117
NOOTKA ROSE
ROSA NUTKANA

118
WILD STRAWBERRY
FRAGARIA VIRGINIANA

119
WILD ROSE
ROSA CAROLINA

and toothed at the end. The yellow flowers (in the photograph seen from above) grow in a loose cluster.

This species is common in moist alpine meadows above 4,500 feet in altitude, from Alaska to Oregon. It blooms from June to August.

WILD ROSE
ROSA GYMNOCARPA   *Plate 114*

This wild rose has bristly stems up to six feet tall. The leaves are divided pinnately into five, seven, or nine segments which are sharply toothed; the teeth are tipped with small round glands; the stalk and midrib bear bristles and glands. The flowers are red.

R. gymnocarpa is common in mountain woodlands from Western Montana to British Columbia and southward into California. It flowers from June to August.

NOOTKA ROSE
ROSA NUTKANA   *Plate 117*

Nootka rose reaches a height of six feet or more. The stems usually bear straight, strong prickles a third of an inch long. Each leaf is divided into from five to nine elliptic, sharply toothed segments. The pink flowers are mostly borne singly at the tips of the branches. The petals are broad and indented on the outer margin.

Rosa nutkana grows in moist places among coniferous trees from the Rocky Mountains to Alaska and southward to California. It flowers from May to July. It takes its name from Nootka Island, off the west coast of Vancouver Island, where the Mexican botanist José Mociño discovered it in 1792.

WILD ROSE
ROSA CAROLINA   *Plate 119*

This wild rose is a low bush, with prickly canes up to three feet tall; the prickles are in pairs just beneath the leaf-stalks, and are straight or nearly so. The leaf is pinnately divided into from five to nine segments. Usually the flowers grow singly, at the tips of branches. There are five green sepals, five pink petals. The receptacle is a cup, with numerous stamens on the rim with the perianth, numerous pistils lining the inner surface. The entire cup becomes the red, berrylike fruit, the hip; within are the small, nutlike fruits (commonly mistaken for seeds).

R. carolina is quite common in dry open places or light shade from Maine to Minnesota and Nebraska and southward to Florida and Texas. The flowers are seen from May to July. There are many wild species of *Rosa*, some very difficult to identify. This species may be distinguished from another common species of eastern North America by its straight prickles; *R. virginiana* has hooked prickles beneath the leaf-stalks.

The hips of roses are used for making jams. They are rich in vitamin C.

120

APACHE-PLUME

FALLUGIA PARADOXA

121 **GREASEWOOD** ADENOSTOMA FASCICULATUM

122 **SHRUBBY CINQUEFOIL** POTENTILLA FRUTICOSA

123 **CLIFF-ROSE** COWANIA MEXICANA

WILD STRAWBERRY
FRAGARIA VIRGINIANA   *Plate 118*

The wild strawberry closely resembles its cultivated relatives except in the size (and taste) of the fruit. The leaves and flowering stem grow from a short crown, which also emits slender stolons (runners). The stolons root at their tips, forming new clusters of leaves and flowers. Each leaf is palmately divided, having three sharply toothed segments at the end of a long stalk. The white flowers may be perfect or pistillate; they grow in clusters on a leafless stem. There are many pistils on a hump in the middle. The hump becomes the edible fruit. The things on its surface commonly called the seeds are really fruits, each developed from an ovary and each containing a seed.

Wild strawberry grows in open places from Labrador to Alberta and southward to Georgia, Alabama, Louisiana, and Oklahoma. It flowers from April to July. The species is quite variable in hairiness, size of leaf-segments, etc. The cultivated straw-berries are all hybrids, one of the original parents having been this species. Dr. Boteler, as quoted by Izaak Walton in *The Compleat Angler*, said, "Doubtless God could have made a better berry, but doubtless God never did."

APACHE-PLUME or PONIL
FALLUGIA PARADOXA   *Plate 120*

Apache-plume is an evergreen bush about three feet tall. The branches bear leaves which are deeply cleft into narrow lobes. The flowers are at the ends of long leafless stalks. There are five sepals and five broad white petals, numerous stamens, and several pistils. Each ovary becomes a small nut, the style growing into a long, silvery, slightly purplish tail (illustrated).

Apache-plume grows on rocky slopes from southern Colorado to California and southward to Mexico. It flowers in May and June, and perhaps again in September. The English name is derived from the fruits, the long tails of which suggested the feathered headdress of the Apache Indians. Because of the evergreen habit, the species has some value as a forage plant; it is useful also in controlling erosion. The Hopi Indians are said to use an infusion of the leaves as a hair tonic.

GREASEWOOD or CHAMISE
ADENOSTOMA FASCICULATUM   *Plate 121*

Greasewood is a shrub that grows up to ten feet tall, with reddish bark that shreds with age and small evergreen leaves in bunches. The white flowers are borne in a loose cluster. Each has five sepals and five petals on a green receptacle.

Greasewood grows on dry slopes everywhere in the coast ranges and the Sierra Nevada foothills in California, up to 5,000 feet above sea level, forming the dominant element in the chaparral. It flowers in May and June; the dried, brown flowers last through the rest of the summer.

This species should not be confused with the greasewood of the Great Basin, the deserts, and the prairies, which is *Sarcobatus*, related to the pigweeds, in the Goosefoot family.

CLIFF-ROSE
COWANIA MEXICANA

Plate 123

Cliff-rose is a shrub which reaches ten feet in height, with reddish twigs. The leaves are divided and redivided pinnately into narrow segments whitened with wool on the lower surface. The creamy flowers are about two-thirds of an inch across. There are from five to ten pistils with styles that remain attached to the ovaries as these develop into small nutlike fruits. These styles form feathery tails, up to two inches long, on the fruits.

Cliff-rose is a member of the Rose family but is not a true rose (*Rosa*). It grows on mesas, in canyons, and in other dry places from Colorado to California and southward into Mexico. It flowers from April to July. The plant illustrated belongs to the variety *stansburiana*, which occurs in the dry mountains of southern California.

THE BEAN FAMILY
LEGUMINOSAE

The flowers of the Bean family are mostly on the order of a sweet-pea. The two lower petals are joined, forming the "keel," which encloses stamens and pistil. There are two lateral petals, "wings," at the sides of the keel, and a "standard" which may be erect or folded over the other petals. There are commonly ten stamens, of which several may be joined by their stalks. The pistil has a single chamber, which contains one or several ovules.

This is a large family of temperate and tropical regions, embracing herbs, trees, and shrubs. The leaves of most species are divided pinnately or palmately. Many climb by twining or with tendrils.

CARDINAL-SPEAR or CORAL-BEAN
ERYTHRINA HERBACEA

Plate 124

Cardinal-spear is a herb up to four feet tall. The leaves are divided into three segments, each somewhat triangular or spear-shaped. The flowers are in a long, narrow cluster. Each has a cup-shaped calyx and a long red corolla. The seeds are bright scarlet.

E. herbacea occurs in pinelands and thickets from North Carolina to Florida and thence westward to Texas. It flowers from January to June. The seeds are often used as beads.

CAT-CLAW or SENSITIVE-BRIER
SCHRANKIA NUTTALLII

Plate 125

Cat-claw has stems that run horizontally, sending up branches which bear leaves and flowers; all are armed with sharp, backward-curved thorns. The leaves are divided pinnately, each having from four to six pairs of segments rather distantly spaced, and each segment itself divided into from eight to fifteen pairs of small, crowded, lopsided

segments. The flowers are in spherical heads. This species belongs to the subfamily of the Bean family (considered a distinct family by some botanists) whose flowers have a perianth of four or five equal parts and numerous stamens. Cat-claw has very long pink stamens, those of a head of flowers together forming a sort of "powder-puff." Some flowers have stamens only, some have both stamens and pistil. The pod is long, narrow, tough, and thorny.

Cat-claw is a plant of dry, open places from Illinois to South Dakota and southward to Alabama and Texas; occasionally farther eastward. The flowers appear from June to September. This subfamily includes the mimosas, the mesquite of the Southwest, and the vast genus *Acacia*, characteristic of Australia, South Africa, and the savannas of the American tropics. *Mimosa pudica* is the sensitive-plant which folds its leaf-segments together at a touch; and several other species of the subfamily have this peculiarity to some extent.

PARTRIDGE-PEA or DWARF SENNA
CASSIA ASPERA   *Plate 126*

Many species of *Cassia* go by the name of partridge-pea. The genus belongs to a subfamily of the Bean family in which the flowers are not like those of a sweet-pea but have almost equal spreading petals. The leaves are generally divided pinnately, and the fruit is a legume much like those of peas and beans. (The subfamily is considered by some authors a distinct family.) *C. aspera* has a stem up to two feet tall bearing singly attached leaves pinnately divided into from fifteen to twenty-seven pairs of segments, each only about half an inch long. There are five sepals and five yellow petals, the lowest petals being the largest; the two upper ones have red spots at the base. Of the stamens, which number from seven to ten, the upper ones are shorter and form no pollen.

C. aspera grows in hammocks, sand dunes, and pinelands on the Atlantic coastal plain from South Carolina to Florida. It flowers in summer and autumn. With other species of this subfamily, it has the habit of folding up the two rows of leaf-segments at night—whence the name sensitive-plant.

PARTRIDGE-PEA
CASSIA FASCICULATA   *Plate 141*

C. fasciculata in general characteristics resembles *C. aspera* but is taller—up to three feet in height—and has larger flowers—more than an inch across. The segments of the pinnately divided leaves are in fewer pairs (from six to twelve) but are somewhat longer (up to nearly an inch).

This partridge-pea is a common roadside flower, found also in fields and open woods from Massachusetts to Minnesota and southward to Florida and Texas. It blooms from June to November, depending on latitude.

125
CAT-CLAW
SCHRANKIA NUTTALLII

126
PARTRIDGE-PEA
CASSIA ASPERA

127
INDIGO-BUSH
DALEA WISLIZENII

128
PALO VERDE
CERCIDIUM MICROPHYLLUM

129
STICKTIGHT
DESMODIUM CANADENSE

130
VETCHLING
LATHRYUS LATIFOLIUS

131
BUSH LUPINE
LUPINUS ARBOREUS

128

129

130

131

INDIGO-BUSH
DALEA WISLIZENII   *Plate 127*

Indigo-bush is a shrub about a foot tall. The leaves, singly attached and more or less hairy, are pinnately divided into from eleven to seventeen segments. The flowers are in spikes which terminate branches. The petals are magenta with purple tints.

Indigo-bush grows in canyons and on dry slopes in southern Arizona and northern Mexico. The strange name is derived from an early collector.

PALO VERDE
CERCIDIUM MICROPHYLLUM   *Plate 128*

Palo verde ("green plant") is a tall, much-branched, spiny shrub or small tree, reaching a height of about twenty-five feet. The bark of young branches is smooth and green, so that the plant is green even when leaves are lacking, as they are during the dry seasons of the Southwest, where it grows. The leaves are twice pinnate; that is, the segments, pinnately disposed, are themselves divided pinnately into from four to eight pairs of very small segments. The yellow flowers are numerous in short clusters which grow from the axils of leaves.

Palo verde is a common shrub in the deserts of Arizona, southern California, and Baja California—a striking sight in full flower, during April and May.

STICKTIGHT
DESMODIUM CANADENSE   *Plate 129*

The sticktights are not loved wildflowers, for their small jointed pods may adorn one's clothes by the hundreds after a walk through woods and fields and are hard to remove. They are in general weedy and straggling plants. Some, however, make a handsome show of flowers, and *D. canadense* is one of these. The leaves, borne on a branching stem up to six feet tall, are pinnately divided into three lance-shaped, blunt segments on a very short stalk. The flowers are in a loose cluster. Each has the papilionaceous form and is colored a bright lavender-pink. The pod is composed of from three to five oval joints. Their surface is covered with minute hooked hairs, which are responsible for their affinity to clothing and hair.

D. canadense is one of the commonest sticktights, growing in various situations—commonly along roadsides—from Quebec to Alberta and southward to South Carolina and Arkansas. It flowers in July and August.

VETCHLING or EVERLASTING-PEA
LATHYRUS LATIFOLIUS   *Plate 130*

The vetchlings are herbaceous vines, many with handsome flowers (*L. odoratus* is the sweet-pea). Some are difficult to identify without specimens in hand. *L. latifolius* has flat, sharp-edged stems a quarter-inch wide or more. The stipules are characteristic: they have two lobes, one pointing up and the other down, both lance-shaped. Each leaf is pinnately divided, all but the two lowest segments being tendrils. The flower has crimson, veiny petals, except the keel, which is a pale greenish-white.

Everlasting-pea is a cultivated plant from Europe which has escaped in a few places (roadsides, waste places, etc.) from New England to Kansas and southward to Virginia. It flowers from June to September.

BUSH LUPINE
LUPINUS ARBOREUS   *Plate 131*

This species of lupine grows as a shrub, mostly about six feet tall with many short branches. Each leaf is palmately divided into from five to twelve segments on a stalk about two inches long. The plants vary from almost smooth to silky and silvery. The flowers, of the usual structure for the family, vary from yellow to lavender.

L. arboreus is a plant of the California coast, growing in sandy places. It blooms from March to June. The name suggests a tree, but it is scarcely treelike in form. The lupines form a vast genus; eighty-two species are listed in California alone, and many more grow in the mountain states. Many species are difficult to identify. The blue-bonnet, state flower of Texas, is *L. texensis*. Our cultivated lupines are mostly hybrids, many of unknown parentage; but native species are also grown in gardens.

SKY-BLUE LUPINE
LUPINUS CUMULICOLA   *Plate 140*

This lupine may reach a height of four feet or even more. The leaves are exceptional for lupines in not being divided; each has a single elliptic blade on a long stalk. The flowers are in a branched cluster. The two-lipped calyx ends in very unequal lobes, the lower ones being much longer. The petals are blue except for a white streak in the center of the standard. The pod is silky.

Sky-blue lupine is found in Florida on sand-dunes and in scrub, flowering through the winter and into spring.

WHITE SWEET-CLOVER
MELILOTUS ALBA   *Plate 132*

White sweet-clover has a branching stem usually about six inches tall, bearing small leaves divided pinnately into three narrow segments (like the leaves of a true clover). The flowers are on numerous narrow branches, which grow from the axils of the leaves and terminate the main stems. The white flowers are of the typical Bean family form. The pods are very short, almost round.

This is an immigrant from Europe, now a very common weed in waste places and roadsides throughout North America. It flowers from May to October. The name is derived from the sweet, haylike fragrance of the herbage when it is crushed or dried. There is also a yellow-flowered species, *M. officinalis*. These species are much visited by honey-bees. The weight of such an insect on the keel bends this part down, so that the stigma and the stamens spring up, one receiving pollen from a flower previously visited, the others dusting the body with pollen to be carried to another flower or rubbed off on the neighboring stigma.

132

133

134

135

135 A

136

137

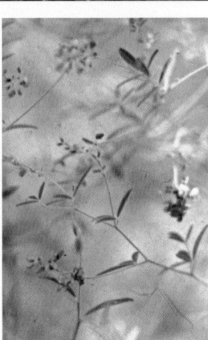

138

132 **WHITE SWEET-CLOVER**
MELILOTUS ALBA

133 **BIRD'S-FOOT TREFOIL**
LOTUS SCOPARIUS

134 **SPURRED-BUTTERFLY-PEA**
CENTROSEMA VIRGINIANUM

135 **HAIRY or WINTER VETCH**
VICIA VILLOSA

135 A **RABBIT-FOOT CLOVER**
TRIFOLIUM ARVENSE

136 **RED CLOVER**
TRIFOLIUM PRATENSE

137 **SMOKE-TREE**
DALEA SPINOSA

138 **MILK-PEA**
GALACTIA WRIGHTII

BIRD'S-FOOT TREFOIL
LOTUS SCOPARIUS   *Plate 133*

This is a bushy plant sometimes six feet tall. The leaves are pinnately divided into from three to five segments, each barely half an inch long. The flowers are in heads on stalks which arise from the axils of leaves. The corolla is red in the bud, yellow when mature, and red again as it withers.

The plant illustrated belongs to the variety *dendroideus*, which grows in the coastal ranges of southern California. It flowers from February to August. Other varieties of *L. scoparius*, widely distributed in California, are distinguished from this by the lack of a stalk for the flower-head; the flowers grow clustered in the axils of leaves. This trefoil ("three-leaves") is not well named, since the segments of the leaves often number five. The name comes from England, where three-leaved species of *Lotus* carpet the ground. Like many American wildflowers, our numerous species have apparently acquired no English names of their own. Lotus was a classical Greek name given to various plants besides the well-known water-lilies.

SPURRED-BUTTERFLY-PEA
CENTROSEMA VIRGINIANUM   *Plate 134*

The spurred-butterfly-pea is a vine, climbing over other plants, bearing leaves pinnately divided into a few very narrow or ovate segments. The violet-colored flowers grow in short clusters on stems that rise from the axils of leaves. The standard of the flower is an inch broad and distinguished by being "spurred" on the back near the base—that is, provided with a narrow, hollow extension.

C. virginianum is a conspicuous plant of open places and light woodlands on the coastal plain, and inland, from New Jersey to Florida and Texas and northward to Arkansas. It flowers from March to September (or to December in the extreme south). Butterfly-pea is *Clitoria mariana*, similar to *Centrosema* but without the spur.

HAIRY or WINTER VETCH
VICIA VILLOSA   *Plate 135*

The vetches climb with their tendrils, which are segments of the leaves. *V. villosa* has a hairy stem. Its leaves are pinnately divided into from eight to twelve pairs of ordinary segments, with several tendrils at the end. The calyx is bordered by very narrow, unequal teeth; the flower-stalk is attached at one side so that the calyx projects backward on the upper side. The corolla is violet or red-purple, with the wings and inside of the standard usually white.

Hairy vetch is a native of Europe, cultivated for forage and now growing along roadsides and in fields and waste places almost throughout North America. (The photograph was made in California.) The blooming period is from April to October in various places. The tares of the New Testament were vetches.

132

139 **SPANISH BROOM** SPARTIUM JUNCEUM

140
SKY-BLUE LUPINE
LUPINUS CUMULICOLA

141
PARTRIDGE-PEA
CASSIA FASCICULATA

RABBIT-FOOT CLOVER
TRIFOLIUM ARVENSE   *Plate 135 A*

This clover has branching stems growing more than a foot tall. The leaves are divided into three narrow segments on a short stalk. The whole plant is hairy. The head of flowers is cylindrical or oblong, up to nearly two inches long, noticeably hairy; the long gray hairs of the calyx project beyond the corollas. The petals are pale pink.

This is a European plant which has become a roadside wildflower from Quebec to Ontario and southward to Florida.

RED CLOVER
TRIFOLIUM PRATENSE   *Plate 136*

Red clover may reach a height of eighteen inches or even more, several stems usually growing in a clump. Each leaf is compound, having three oval segments on a long stalk; each segment usually bears a V-mark midway. The plant may be smooth or hairy. The flowers are in a dense round head about an inch in diameter; the corolla is pink.

Red clover is a native of Europe and a valuable cultivated plant. It is important, like other legumes, for its contribution of nitrogen to the soil and is often planted with hay in dairy country. It is also valuable as a nectar source for honey-bees. A field of red clover on a bright, warm day is fragrant, giving off the scent of grapes. As a wildflower *T. pratense* generally grows in roadsides and grassy places, practically throughout North America.

SMOKE-TREE
DALEA SPINOSA   *Plate 137*

Smoke-tree may be only a shrub; in any form it does not exceed twenty feet in height. The leaves soon fall, leaving the bare branches beset with stout, sharp spines. The flowers are in short, dense clusters. The calyx is reddish; the corolla, bright blue.

Smoke-tree is common in sandy deserts from Colorado to California and southward through Arizona into northern Mexico. Flowers appear in June and July.

MILK-PEA
GALACTIA WRIGHTII   *Plate 138*

Milk-pea is a vine, twining around other plants or any other supports. The leaves are divided pinnately into three elliptic or lance-shaped segments. The flowers are on branches that grow from the axils of the leaves. The corolla is pale purple and greenish-yellow, with wings joined to the keel, and standard folded over both. The halves of the narrow pod twist into a spiral as they separate.

Milk-pea occurs on high, dry slopes from western Texas to southern Arizona and northern Mexico. It flowers from July to September.

SPANISH BROOM
SPARTIUM JUNCEUM   *Plate 139*

The nearly leafless, rushlike stems of Spanish broom may reach ten feet in height. The leaves are narrow and only about an inch long. The bright yellow flowers grow in a narrow cluster.

Spanish broom comes from the Mediterranean and is naturalized in various places in California, growing in dry soil. It flowers from April to June. The plants generally known in English as broom or Scottish broom are a species of *Cytisus* in the same family and with similar appearance. The generic name is derived from the Greek word *sparton,* meaning "broom."

LOCO-WEED
OXYTROPIS SPLENDENS   *Plate 142*

This loco-weed is a silky-haired plant about a foot tall, with leaves divided pinnately into numerous small segments. The blue flowers grow in a dense hairy spike, opening from the base of the cluster upward. Each flower is only about half an inch long.

O. splendens grows on prairies and mountain slopes from Manitoba to British Columbia and southward to Minnesota, Colorado, and Montana. It begins to flower in July.

In calling this loco-weed we are applying a general name used for many species of *Astragalus* and *Oxytropis.* The name refers to their poisonous properties. Horses and cattle that browse them undergo convulsions followed by coma and death. Because of the antics displayed in the first stages of poisoning, the word *loco,* Spanish for "crazy," was applied.

THE FLAX FAMILY
LINACEAE

The flowers of the Flax family are very regular, with sepals, petals, and stamens all in fives. The stamens are wide at the base so that they partly cover the ovary. The ovary has from two to ten chambers, and as many styles. Several species of *Linum* are cultivated, for flax (from which *linen* is made), *lin*seed oil, and ornament.

WILD FLAX
LINUM LEWISII   *Plate 143*

The numerous species of flax that grow wild are mostly slender plants with narrow leaves. *L. lewisii* usually has several stems from one base, reaching a height of about two feet. The leaves are numerous, narrow, less than an inch long. The petals are blue.

This species has a wide range from Alaska to Texas and Mexico by way of California, growing on dry slopes at fairly high altitudes. It flowers from May to September.

THE OXALIS FAMILY
OXALIDACEAE

The Oxalis family has flowers with parts in fives and tens: five sepals, five petals, ten or fifteen stamens, and an ovary with five chambers and often five styles.

VIOLET WOOD-SORREL
OXALIS VIOLACEA   *Plate 144*

Violet wood-sorrel sends up its leaves and flowers from a cormlike base. The leaves have stalks usually four or five inches tall, each bearing at the summit three (or sometimes more) segments palmately disposed; each segment is pointed where it is attached and broadens fanlike to an indented margin. They frequently droop on the stalk so as to bring their edges together. The light violet under surface is revealed only when the wind ruffles them. The flowers are in a cluster at the tip of a leafless stem from six to twelve inches tall.

Violet wood-sorrel occurs on prairies, banks, and in meadows, etc., often in solid carpets, from Massachusetts to North Dakota and Colorado and southward to Florida, Texas, and New Mexico. The flowers open from April to July.

YELLOW WOOD-SORREL or SOUR-GRASS
OXALIS STRICTA   *Plate 145*

It is difficult to identify the yellow wood-sorrels because of their great variability; it is practically impossible without the pods. This is *O. stricta*, one of the commonest species. The form of leaves and the parts of the flowers are much as in *O. violacea*; the color, of course, is different. *O. stricta* is generally a foot or two tall, the leaf-segments about half an inch wide. The photograph shows clearly the two alternating sizes of stamens.

O. stricta grows in all sorts of situations practically throughout North America, flowering in spring and summer. The name *Oxalis* is derived from a Greek word meaning "sharp" or "sour," and, like the English names, refers to the sour taste from oxalic acid in the cells. In various countries the leaves are used in salads and soups.

THE GERANIUM FAMILY
GERANIACEAE

The *Geraniaceae* are mostly herbaceous plants of temperate regions. The flowers are typically on a plan of five: five sepals, five petals, stamens in from one to three circles of five each, and a pistil composed of from three to five parts. The style is like the long beak of a crane (*Geranium* is derived from the Greek word for "crane" or "heron"). When the fruit is mature it splits into several parts (five in our wild geraniums) which become detached from the bottom up, the tips remaining attached to the central fiber of the style; these parts then curl up, spilling their seeds.

143

144

145

146

143
WILD FLAX
LINUM LEWISII

144
VIOLET WOOD-SORREL
OXALIS VIOLACEA

145
YELLOW WOOD-SORREL
OXALIS STRICTA

146
CRANE'S-BILL
GERANIUM COWENII

147
WILD GERANIUM
GERANIUM MACULATUM

148
FIRE-ON-THE-MOUNTAIN
EUPHORBIA HETEROPHYLLA

149
JEWELWEED
IMPATIENS CAPENSIS

CRANE'S-BILL or WILD GERANIUM
GERANIUM COWENII   *Plate 146*

G. *cowenii* is a foot or more tall. The stems and leaf-stalks are covered with hairs that point downward. The leaves are lobed, with from three to five toothed lobes. The five petals are purplish-pink with darker veins.

This wild geranium inhabits mountain meadows in Wyoming and Colorado, flowering in June and July.

WILD GERANIUM or CRANE'S-BILL
GERANIUM MACULATUM   *Plate 147*

Wild geranium grows up to two feet tall. The flowering stem and the long-stalked leaves grow from a rhizome; the stem has a pair of short-stalked leaves. All the leaves are palmately cleft into from five to seven toothed lobes. The rose-purple flowers are in a forking inflorescence, usually one open at a time.

Wild geranium grows frequently in woods, sometimes in open fields, from Maine to Manitoba and southward to Georgia, Arkansas, and Kansas. It is in flower from April to June.

The house-plant known as geranium is in another genus, *Pelargonium*, of this family. The flowers have essentially the same plan, with the irregularities often found in cultivated plants. A European species of *Geranium* has the distinction of having been the first to draw the attention of a botanist to the relation between insects and flowers.

THE SPURGE FAMILY
EUPHORBIACEAE

The *Euphorbiaceae* form a large family, mainly tropical but with many species in temperate regions. The flowers have stamens or pistils, not both, and may or may not have sepals and petals. In some species (particularly in the genus *Euphorbia*) each flower is reduced to a single stamen or a single pistil. The pistil has three chambers, three styles (often forked), and three or six stigmas. Usually such flowers are in a close group surrounded by bracts which may simulate petals (as in the cultivated poinsettia and crown-of-thorns). The juice of many *Euphorbiaceae* is milky and often poisonous. Rubber is obtained from a tree in this family, also castor oil, tung oil, and other important products.

FIRE-ON-THE-MOUNTAIN or FIDDLER'S SPURGE
EUPHORBIA HETEROPHYLLA   *Plate 148*

Fire-on-the-mountain recalls the poinsettia grown at Christmas-time—a more tropical species of *Euphorbia*. It is a perennial herb up to four feet tall (but usually about a foot or two). The leaves vary greatly in shape (this is the meaning of *heterophylla*), from ovate with the broad end either outward or inward to elliptic or very narrow and

grasslike; they may be sharply toothed or lobed. The upper leaves are partly or entirely colored bright pink (usually with green tips), simulating petals. The flowers are tiny, without perianth.

Fire-on-the-mountain is found in woods, usually in wet soil, from Wisconsin to North Dakota and southward to Florida and Arizona. It flowers from February to November, depending on the locality.

THE TOUCH-ME-NOT FAMILY
BALSAMINACEAE

This relatively small family is mainly tropical. It is characterized by one peculiar sepal, which is petal-like in color and prolonged backward into a hollow spur; also by the stamens, which have flat stalks covering the ovary. The fruit is a pod which opens explosively when touched, whence the name of the family.

JEWELWEED or TOUCH-ME-NOT
IMPATIENS CAPENSIS

Plate 149

This is a smooth, much-branched plant with leaves attached singly and orange flowers dangling from slender curved stems. The leaves are light green and so well waxed that they shed water. The plants may attain a height of six feet. The remarkable, jewel-like flower is composed of three sepals and three petals. Two sepals are very small; the third forms most of the flower, a large orange sac open at one end and protruding backward so that the flower seems to hang by its middle. A short, hollow tube or "spur," bent forward, prolongs the sac and makes the nectar inaccessible to visitors with short tongues (it is visited by hummingbirds). The petals emerge from the opening of the large sepal, the upper one broadest.

Jewelweed grows in moist woods and bottomlands from Newfoundland to Alaska and southward to Georgia, Alabama, and Oklahoma. It is an annual, the light green, oval pairs of seed-leaves appearing in crowds on moist soil in May or June and the plant flowering from July to September. The juice is reputed to heal the blisters and rash caused by poison-ivy; also to cause warts to disappear; the present author has no evidence for these properties. The color of the flower varies greatly. There is also a species with pale yellow flowers, *I. pallida*.

I. capensis (so named because it was erroneously thought to have come from the Cape of Good Hope) was introduced into England as a garden flower and now grows wild there along streams.

THE MALLOW FAMILY
MALVACEAE

The Mallow family is characterized by the numerous stamens whose stalks are joined in a hollow column through which the style emerges. In some genera the

142

anthers are all at the rim of this column (*Sphaeralcea, Abutilon, Malva*); in others they are along the sides of the column, the rim of which is toothed (*Kosteletzkya*). There are five sepals and five petals; the sepals are often surrounded by several bracts. The single pistil consists of several parts, from each of which a threadlike stigma may arise. The ovary develops into a dry fruit which separates into segments.

TREE-MALLOW or MALVA-ROSA
LAVATERA ASSURGENTIFLORA   *Plate 150*

Tree-mallow grows up to twelve feet tall, but is a shrub rather than a tree. The leaves are attached singly; the blades, borne on long stalks, are round, with from five to seven lobes. The rose-colored flowers are in the axils and clustered toward the tip of the stem.

The tree-mallow is a native of the Santa Barbara Islands of California, growing in sandy and rocky places; it was early introduced into gardens on the mainland and now grows wild there long the coast. It flowers from March to November.

VELVET-LEAF or PIE-MARKER
ABUTILON THEOPHRASTI   *Plate 151*

The annual stem rises four feet or more above the ground, bearing large, softly downy, singly attached leaves with long stalks and heart-shaped blades. The small flowers (up to an inch across, often less) are borne in the axils. The corolla is yellow. The ovary becomes the decorative seed-pod shown in the photograph (mixed with various grasses). The parts of the pod curve out into horns, and split open on top.

Velvet-leaf comes from India and has now become a common and sometimes troublesome weed in fields and waste places from New England westward and southward through most of the United States. It flowers from July to October. In India some species of *Abutilon* are cultivated for fiber. This species is named for Theophrastus, a pupil of Aristotle, who wrote the first known work on botany.

MUSK MALLOW
MALVA MOSCHATA   *Plate 152*

Musk mallow grows up to three feet tall. The stems bear leaves singly attached, each cleft palmately into three or five lobes which are themselves pinnately toothed or lobed. The leaves at the base of the stem are round and often not lobed. The pink or lavender flowers are in short clusters at the ends of the branches.

Musk mallow was brought from Europe as a garden flower and is now found growing wild in fields and roadsides and around abandoned dwellings from Newfoundland to British Columbia and southward to Maryland, Tennessee, and Nebraska. It flowers in June and July. All our true mallows (*Malva*) came from Europe. They differ from the native poppy-mallows (*Callirhoë*) in having notched petals.

143

151

152

153

154

SEASHORE-MALLOW
KOSTELETZKYA VIRGINICA

Plate 153

Seashore-mallow grows up to four feet tall. The lower leaves are heart-shaped, often with coarse teeth; the upper leaves have more or less spear-shaped blades, the lobes at the base extending outward. The flowers grow singly on slender stalks arising from the axils of leaves. The five pink petals are fan-shaped.

Kosteletzkya grows near the shore in brackish marshes from Long Island to Florida and Texas. The flowers appear from July to September. In most characteristics it resembles the genus *Hibiscus*.

GLOBE-MALLOW or DESERT-MALLOW
SPHAERALCEA AMBIGUA

Plate 154

Globe-mallow is a shrubby perennial which grows in clumps of a hundred or more stems; these may reach three feet in height. The leaves, attached singly, are roundish and slightly lobed. The plants are generally covered with grayish or yellowish scurfy hairs. The pink flowers grow from the axils of leaves and at the summits of the stems.

Globe-mallow grows in the deserts from Nevada and Arizona to California and Baja California. It flowers from March to June. Since the juice is irritating to the eyes, it is known locally as sore-eye-poppy; in Mexico as mal-de-ojos or plantas-muy-malas. But an Indian name signifies "cure for sore eyes"; perhaps this was not the same species.

THE COCOA FAMILY
STERCULIACEAE

This is a small, mainly tropical family which resembles the Mallow family in many ways. The stamens may be separate but are usually joined in a tube. The petals are small, or there may be none. Cocoa is derived from the seeds of *Theobroma cacao*, a native of the American tropics.

FLANNEL-BUSH
FREMONTIA CALIFORNICA

Plate 155

This is a spreading shrub up to twelve feet tall or even more, with three-lobed leaves singly attached on short side-branches. The showy flowers, often two inches across or more, also grow on these branches. Each has five large, bright yellow sepals that resemble petals; there are no petals. The five stamens are joined by the lower parts of their broad stalks; this joined part forms a cover for the four- or five-chambered ovary.

Flannel-bush adorns dry slopes in the Sierra Nevada and coast ranges of California and in Arizona. It flowers from April to June, its brilliant flowers covering the bushes in a striking display.

151 **VELVET-LEAF** ABUTILON THEOPHRASTI   *152* **MUSK MALLOW** MALVA MOSCHATA

153 **SEASHORE-MALLOW** KOSTELETZKYA VIRGINICA   *154* **GLOBE-MALLOW** SPHAERALCEA AMBIGUA

155

156

157

158

THE ST.-JOHN'S-WORT FAMILY
HYPERICACEAE

The St.-John's-wort family is distinguished by having mostly paired leaves marked with black or translucent dots, flowers with petals and sepals in fours or fives, numerous stamens usually joined in from three to five bundles, and a pistil with from three to five styles.

ST.-JOHN'S-WORT
HYPERICUM PERFORATUM

Plate 156

Most of the numerous species of *Hypericum* have yellow petals. The petals of *H. perforatum* have black dots on the margin. The leaves are marked by dots seen as translucent spots when held to the light. The plant grows up to three feet tall and is much branched; the flowers are in clusters at the tips of the branches. There are five sepals and five petals.

This St.-John's-wort is a native of Europe which has become a common weed in our roadsides, fields, and waste places, practically throughout North America. It flowers from June to September.

The plant is the subject of a host of superstitions. For instance, the dew that fell on it on the eve of St. John's day (June 24) was believed to protect the eyes from disease. The plant, if gathered on St. John's day and hung in the window, was supposed to avert devils, witches, and the evil eye.

ST.-PETER'S-WORT or ST.-ANDREW'S-CROSS
ASCYRUM TETRAPETALUM

Plate 157

Ascyrum tetrapetalum is a shrubby plant which may become three feet tall. The leaves are in pairs, elliptical or ovate, without stalks and indented at the base so that they "clasp" the stem. A striking characteristic is the presence of small pits evenly distributed over the leaves and sepals (easily seen with a hand magnifier); these contain dark-colored glands. The flowers terminate the short branches. Each has four sepals in two sizes, the larger ones much like the leaves, the smaller ones lance-shaped. The four yellow petals form "St. Andrew's cross."

A. tetrapetalum grows in swamps and moist pinelands on the coastal plain in Georgia and Florida. It flowers from spring to autumn; or, in the extreme south, all the year.

THE ROCKROSE FAMILY
CISTACEAE

The plants of the Rockrose family (no relation of the roses) are low herbs or shrubs mostly of temperate regions. There are five sepals, of which two are much smaller (or sometimes lacking), and three or five petals. The stamens are numerous. The pistil forms a capsule with many seeds in one chamber.

147

155 **FLANNEL-BUSH** FREMONTIA CALIFORNICA   156 **ST.-JOHN'S-WORT** HYPERICUM PERFORATUM

157 **ST.-PETER'S-WORT** ASCYRUM TETRAPETALUM   158 **ROCKROSE** HELIANTHEMUM CORYMBOSUM

ROCKROSE
HELIANTHEMUM CORYMBOSUM

Plate 158

Rockrose is a slender plant, usually six or eight inches tall, with small, dark green, elliptical leaves scattered along the stem. The flowers are in a small cluster at the summit. Sepals and petals vary from three to five; the petals are bright yellow. These flowers last for only a day. The later flowers lack petals and have fewer stamens.

Rockrose grows in pinelands and dunes and in the hammocks on the Atlantic coastal plain from South Carolina to Florida, flowering all the year in the southern part of this range.

ROCKROSE
HELIANTHEMUM SCOPARIUM var. ALDERSONII

Plate 159

This rockrose is a somewhat shrubby plant, growing sometimes to a height of three feet. The very narrow leaves are singly attached; they soon fall. The flowers are in a narrow cluster. Each is about half an inch across. The five broad petals are yellow. The stamens are numerous.

This variety grows in the chaparral in California and Baja California. Other plants of the species are more widely distributed in California. The flowers are seen from March to July. There are other American species of *Helianthemum* (not to be confused with *Helianthus*, the sunflowers). *H. canadense* is a species of the eastern United States.

THE OCOTILLO FAMILY
FOUQUIERIACEAE

This small family consists entirely of thorny shrubs native in southwestern North America. There are five sepals, five petals, and ten or more stamens.

OCOTILLO, COACHWHIP, or CANDLEWOOD
FOUQUIERIA SPLENDENS

Plate 160

Ocotillo lifts its slender, prickly stems sometimes to a height of twenty feet; they are unbranched except at the summit. The spines are derived from the stalks of leaves whose blades are soon lost. In the axils of the spines tufts of leaves appear during and after the rains; these also soon fall, so that the plant is leafless most of the time. The brilliant red flowers are in dense spikes grouped at the summit of the stems. Each has reddish sepals, and a tubular, bright red corolla.

Ocotillo grows only in dry regions from western Texas to southeastern California and northern Mexico. The flowers appear from April to May. This odd-looking desert plant has been used in many ways by the Indians: the stems for building and for making living fences (they root easily); the wax on the stems to dress leather; the capsules as food; the root to ease pain and (as a decoction) to relieve fatigue.

159 **ROCKROSE** HELIANTHEMUM SCOPARIUM *var.* ALDERSONII

160 **OCOTILLO** FOUQUIERIA SPLENDENS

161 **COMMON BLUE VIOLET** VIOLA PAPILIONACEA

162
WHITE VIOLET
VIOLA PRIMULIFOLIA

163
SWEET WHITE VIOLET
VIOLA BLANDA

THE VIOLET FAMILY
VIOLACEAE

The Violet family is represented in this country chiefly by the genus *Viola*, described below. There are also tropical species, some of them shrubby, united with the violets by certain technical characteristics.

The flowers of violets (genus *Viola*) are complex in structure. The lower petal has an expanded tip which serves as a landing-place for insects, and a hollow prolongation at the other end, the so-called "spur." The ovary is closely invested by the five anthers of the stamens (they have almost no stalks); these open to the inside. From the lower two stamens hang succulent nectaries, which curve backward into the spur of the corolla. When an insect penetrates the flower and chances to push against these nectaries, the corresponding stamens are moved and pollen falls out between them onto the back of the intruder. In the next flower visited the pollen is scraped off onto the stigma, which faces outward in the entrance to the flower. In this intricate (and not always successful) manner pollen can only be transferred to the stigma of another flower. There are also, in many species, flowers that do not open but nevertheless form fruit and seed—by pollinating themselves.

There are two groups of violets. One group bears leaves on an erect stem, the flowers springing from the axils of leaves. In the other group both leaves and flowers rise from a rhizome underground. There are many species, and those of the second group hybridize with each other in nature, yielding forms that are impossible to identify.

COMMON BLUE VIOLET
VIOLA PAPILIONACEA
Plate 161

This is the most familiar blue violet of spring in the eastern United States. The leaves are heart-shaped, scalloped on the edges and more or less downy or smooth. They and the flowers grow from a thick rhizome. The flowers are on stalks about the same height as the leaves, three or four inches. The corolla is blue or purplish with a white center; the two lateral petals wear white "beards"—dense masses of hairs. These lateral petals spread like a pair of wings (*papilionacea* means "butterflylike").

The common blue violet grows along streams, in moist woods and meadows, and generally in damp, shady places, from Maine to Wyoming and southward. There are numerous varieties and hybrids, some of which are cultivated. One of the best-known varieties has white petals with blue veins.

WHITE VIOLET
VIOLA PRIMULIFOLIA
Plate 162

This white violet (there are others) has a threadlike rhizome from which rise smooth leaves four or five inches tall; the leaf-blades are ovate, indented at the base. Later there are slender runners that form more leaves. The flowers have white petals veined with purple; they rise to about the same height as the leaves.

151

164 **YELLOW VIOLET** VIOLA PENSYLVANICA

165 **SWAMP VIOLET** VIOLA PALUSTRIS

166 **WESTERN BLUE VIOLET** VIOLA ADUNCA

V. primulifolia grows in meadows, open woods, and on streamsides, from New Jersey to Oklahoma and southward to Florida and Texas. It flowers from April to June. There is a variety with hairy leaves.

SWEET WHITE VIOLET
VIOLA BLANDA   *Plate 163*

The sweet white violet has slender runners coming from its rhizome, besides the leaves and flowers. The leaves are heart-shaped. The small, sweetly fragrant flowers are on stems that rise above the leaves. The lateral petals are narrow, without "beards" (this, with the fragrance, distinguishes them from *V. pallens*, of more northern distribution).

Sweet white violet grows in the cool shade of moist woods from Quebec to Minnesota and southward to Georgia, Tennessee, and Illinois. Its flowers appear in April and May.

YELLOW VIOLET
VIOLA PENSYLVANICA   *Plate 164*

This yellow violet is one of the group of violets characterized by an erect stem bearing both leaves and flowers. The stem, which comes from a rhizome, is about a foot tall. There are from one to three leaves at the base with long stalks and round blades. The leaves on the stem have lance-shaped or ovate stipules. The lower petal is small compared with the others, and veined with brown-purple. The seed-pod is in one variety covered with white wool; in another, it is smooth.

V. pensylvanica is common in wooded bottomlands and other shady places from Quebec to Manitoba and southward to Georgia and Texas. It flowers in April and May. A similar species, *V. pubescens*, is distinguished by having downy stems and leaves, and by having not more than one basal leaf and frequently none. It grows over a similar range but in drier places.

SWAMP VIOLET
VIOLA PALUSTRIS   *Plate 165*

The swamp violet grows from a slender rhizome, both leaves and flower-stalks growing from the ground. The leaf-blades are round, about an inch across. The flower-stalks overtop the leaves. The petals are white with dark purple veins.

This violet is common in swamps, in wet meadows, and on stream-banks, from Labrador to Alaska and southward to New England, Montana, and Oregon. It flowers from April to July.

WESTERN BLUE VIOLET
VIOLA ADUNCA   *Plate 166*

V. adunca has a stem that rises above ground, but this is sometimes so short as to be barely visible. The leaves are over an inch long. The flowers, here seen in a somewhat withered condition, are blue or violet, about half an inch long.

167
BLAZING-STAR
MENTZELIA INVOLUCRATA

168
CHOLLA
OPUNTIA TETRACANTHA

169 **PRICKLY-PEAR** OPUNTIA ENGELMANNII

170 **SAGUARO** CARNEGIEA GIGANTEA

V. adunca is common in sandy soil from Nova Scotia to British Columbia and southward to New York, Ontario, Minnesota, New Mexico, and California. It flowers from May to August in some part of this vast range.

THE LOASA FAMILY
LOASACEAE

The family is characterized by peculiar rough hairs, which in some species sting. The parts of the perianth are in fours or fives. The stamens are numerous. The ovary is inferior.

BLAZING-STAR
MENTZELIA INVOLUCRATA *Plate 167*

This blazing-star grows about a foot tall. The stems are white with stiff hairs. The leaves, attached singly, are either narrow with parallel sides or lance-shaped, and coarsely toothed, with rough hairs that cause them to adhere to clothing. The pale yellow, reddish-veined flowers are borne singly at the tips of stems, with a pair of broad, white, green-tipped bracts.

M. involucrata grows commonly in dry sandy and rocky places, including deserts, from southern California to northern Mexico. It flowers from January to April. There are many other species of *Mentzelia*, most of them known as blazing-star, some ranging east to Iowa, Missouri, and Texas; others from British Columbia to Nebraska and Mexico; still others limited to California. In the eastern states a quite different genus, *Liatris* in the Daisy family, is called blazing-star; its flowers are blue or purple.

THE CACTUS FAMILY
CACTACEAE

The spiny, prickly, or woolly bodies of the Cactus family are well known. These are stems—though they sometimes have the appearance of leaves. In general the cacti lack leaves. They have strikingly beautiful flowers. These have many sepals and petals, between which there is often no sharp distinction. The receptacle forms usually a sort of funnel, lined with the numerous stamens. The ovary is inferior; the fruit is either dry or a berry, with many seeds.

PRICKLY-PEAR
OPUNTIA ENGELMANNII *Plate 169*

The pear-shaped "joints" of prickly-pear are not the leaves they suggest but the stem of the plant. Leaves appear briefly at the summit of each branch of this stem; they are only an inch or two long, narrow, succulent; they fall almost at once. In the axils of these leaves are small structures from which spines and short barbed bristles may grow. The flowers have many yellow petals (not distinctly separate from the sepals) and the usual crowd of stamens. The fruit (*tuna*) is red, juicy, and sweet.

This prickly-pear grows in large clumps, often five feet high, in dry soil from Texas to Arizona and Mexico, flowering from April to July. The spines can inflict a painful wound, but the minute barbed bristles are a worse danger to the incautious; they become detached, work into the skin, and cause a painful rash. The fruits are eaten by many animals, including human ones; they are also made into candy. Dr. George Engelmann, after whom this species was named, was a physician and botanist of St. Louis, who made a notable study of the cacti. His collection of dried plant specimens (herbarium) was the foundation of that of the great Missouri Botanical Garden.

JUMPING CHOLLA or TEDDY-BEAR CACTUS
OPUNTIA BIGELOVII   *Plate 174*

At first sight the chollas do not resemble the prickly-pears enough to be placed in the same genus (*Opuntia*). Examination of the branching stem of a cholla will reveal that it is in joints, though these are more or less cylindrical instead of flat. The arrangement of spines and barbed bristles is the same in both and the flowers have essentially the same structure (see *O. engelmannii*). The petals are a greenish yellow. The spines are so numerous as to conceal the form of the branches and to impart a whitish color to the whole plant; they turn brown as they age, and many of the older joints may die and become discolored. The fruits are small and unarmed.

Jumping cholla is abundant on desert slopes from Nevada to southern California and southward through Arizona into northern Mexico and Baja California. It flowers from February to May. The formidable array of sharp spines, barbed near the tip, are as dangerous as they look. The cactus does not really jump, but the joints are easily detached and may cause painful wounds. The naturalist E. C. Jaeger writes that cactus wrens nest in the branches and pack-rats carry the joints to their runways.

CHOLLA
OPUNTIA TETRACANTHA   *Plate 168*

This cholla is a loosely branched shrub about three feet tall. The spines are enclosed in papery sheaths; there are usually about four in a cluster. The flowers are scarlet. The fruit is tinged with the same color; it is about an inch long.

O. tetracantha is a rare cactus, known only in southern Arizona. It flowers in May.

DEERHORN CHOLLA
OPUNTIA VERSICOLOR   *Plate 175*

Deerhorn cholla is a shrub from six to twelve feet tall, or taller. The dark-colored spines are invested in papery sheaths; there are generally three or four in a cluster and the clusters are close together. The joints of the stem tend to be purplish. The flowers vary in color; they may be red, yellow, or purplish. The fruit is fleshy; it may remain on the plant for more than a year.

Deerhorn cholla is a common cactus in Arizona and northern Mexico. It flowers in May.

171 **BARREL CACTUS** ECHINOCACTUS VIRIDESCENS

172 **HEDGEHOG CACTUS** ECHINOCEREUS TRIGLOCHIDIATUS

173 **HEDGEHOG CACTUS** ECHINOCEREUS ENGELMANNII

174 **JUMPING CHOLLA** OPUNTIA BIGELOVII

175 **DEERHORN CHOLLA** OPUNTIA VERSICOLOR

SAGUARO or GIANT CACTUS
CARNEGIEA GIGANTEA *Plate 170*

Saguaro is the largest cactus in the United States and one of the largest in the world. Specimens are known almost fifty feet tall. The stem is strongly ribbed, with short spines in tufts along the ribs. Branches may occur singly or in circles. The flowers appear at the summits of the upper branches. Each has about twenty-five white petals at the rim of the funnel-shaped receptacle; the blunt sepals pass gradually into the petals. The fruit (*pitahaya*) is an egg-shaped berry with red pulp.

The giant cactus grows on dry slopes and desert flats in southwestern Arizona, northern Mexico, and southeastern California. It flowers in May and June. It is the state flower of Arizona, a spectacular inhabitant of its southwestern deserts. The flowers open at night, remaining open until the following afternoon. A plant may live to a great age—200 years are estimated—and because of its ability to hold water will withstand severe droughts. The Indians (as well as birds and small animals) used the fruits as food, and the woody skeleton as a building material. A butter was made from the seeds, and a beverage from the fermented juice.

BARREL CACTUS
ECHINOCACTUS VIRIDESCENS *Plate 171*

This species has a barrel-shaped or dome-shaped, unbranched stem only about a foot high. It is marked by strong ridges running down from the apex; on these are the spines, in groups, the central spines of each group flattened and slightly curved like swords. The yellow petals are marked by a dark central streak, often red.

E. viridescens occurs on dry hills in scrub and grasslands in southern California and southward into Baja California. The flowers appear in May and June.

HEDGEHOG CACTUS
ECHINOCEREUS TRIGLOCHIDIATUS *Plate 172*

The hedgehog cactus has a nearly cylindrical stem a foot or more tall, with from five to eight strong ribs. Spines are borne in clusters of three to eight at intervals on the ribs. The flowers are scarlet, growing just above the clusters of spines. They remain open at night. The succulent fruit is edible when the spines are removed.

The hedgehog cactus grows in the deserts of Colorado and Utah and thence southward to western Texas, New Mexico, and Arizona. It flowers in May and June. There are a number of other species of *Echinocereus* in our southwestern deserts, all known as hedgehog cactus.

HEDGEHOG CACTUS
ECHINOCEREUS ENGELMANNII *Plate 173*

The stem, not more than a foot tall, is entirely covered with long and short spines. The flowers are a magenta-crimson or sometimes paler. The fruit is red and succulent.

This hedgehog cactus is common on rocky slopes from Utah to southern California and southward to Arizona and Baja California.

160

THE LOOSESTRIFE FAMILY
LYTHRACEAE

The Loosestrife family consists of herbaceous and shrubby plants with flowers in the axils of mostly paired leaves. The flower-parts vary in number. They are seated at the margin of a cuplike receptacle, within which is the single pistil.

PURPLE LOOSESTRIFE
LYTHRUM SALICARIA   *Plate 176*

Purple loosestrife rears its tall spikes of purplish-red flowers to a height of four feet or more. The leaves, in pairs or circles, are lance-shaped, stalkless, indented at the base where they meet the stem. The numerous flowers decorate the upper part of the stem. The most striking feature of the flowers is that the stigma and anthers are at three different levels, and there are three different types of flowers in this respect. In one, the style carries the stigma far beyond the corolla; there is a ring of anthers just at the opening of the corolla; and another ring hidden within it. In a second type, the stigma has the intermediate position, the stamens being longer or shorter than the style. In the third type, the stigma is below the two rings of anthers. This extraordinary arrangement is supposed to further the transfer of pollen to the stigma of another plant (for all the flowers on one plant are of the same type). Darwin, in fact, showed that pollen from short stamens was effective only on the stigma of a short style, and so on. One does not, however, always find all three types growing together.

Purple loosestrife is an invader from Europe, on the whole a welcome one; it grows abundantly in wet meadows, along streams, and around ponds from Newfoundland to Minnesota and southward to Virginia, Ohio, and Missouri, but more commonly in the Atlantic states. It flowers from June to September.

For the origin of the curious English name, see *Lysimachia* in the Primrose family. The plant is also called long purples in England; but this is not the plant Shakespeare meant, in *Hamlet*.

THE MELASTOME FAMILY
MELASTOMATACEAE

The Melastomes are a big tropical family characterized by paired leaves which are ribbed lengthwise and stamens that discharge their pollen through pores in the end of the anther. *Rhexia* is the only genus in North America. There are several other species, found mostly in the southern states.

MEADOW BEAUTY
RHEXIA MARIANA   *Plate 177*

From the creeping stems grow erect, hairy, flowering stems up to two feet tall. These bear pairs of lance-shaped leaves with short stalks, the blades marked by strong ribs running lengthwise (a characteristic of the family). The species is well named for

162

its pretty flowers. There are four sepals on an urn-shaped receptacle, and four pink petals. The eight stamens have anthers sharply bent down; the pollen escapes through a hole at the end. The fruit is a small capsule standing within the enlarged receptacle, which Thoreau compared to a cream-pitcher.

This meadow beauty grows mainly on the coastal plain, in wet sandy or boggy places, from Massachusetts to Florida and Texas, northward in the Mississippi bottom lands to Missouri and Illinois, inland to Kentucky and Indiana. The flowers appear from July to September.

THE EVENING-PRIMROSE FAMILY
ONAGRACEAE

The name is misleading, for these plants are not related to the primroses (*Primula*). The "evening" of the name refers to the habit of some species of *Oenothera* of opening in the evening and closing the following morning. Most species have parts in fours or eights and an inferior ovary. Many species have four stigmas which form a cross in the center of the flower.

FAREWELL-TO-SPRING
CLARKIA AMOENA *Plate 179*

Clarkia is a large genus in the West, thirty-one species being known in California. The petals are mostly pink or red. The genus is named for Captain William Clark, who with Captain Meriwether Lewis led a famous expedition to the Pacific in 1804–1806. (There is also a genus *Lewisia*, the bitter-root.) *C. amoena* grows up to three feet tall or more. The leaves are lance-shaped, with stalks. The flowers are crowded. The corolla varies from pink and lavender to white, mostly with a bright red center.

Farewell-to-spring grows on slopes and bluffs near the California coast, blooming from June to August—hence the common name. The Latin word *amoena* means "charming."

GODETIA
CLARKIA DEFLEXA *Plate 178*

C. deflexa has an erect stem reaching three feet in height. The leaves are lance-shaped, with short stalks. The flower-buds point down (*deflexa*) on the raceme, rising to an erect position as they open. The corolla is lavender, shading to white in the center and flecked with red.

C. deflexa grows in dry clearings in chaparral and woods of the coast ranges of California. It blooms from April to June.

FAREWELL-TO-SPRING
CLARKIA GRACILIS *Plate 180*

This farewell-to-spring grows up to three feet tall and is more or less silvery, with hairs lying flat. The leaves are narrow. The flower-cluster droops at the tip before the

177 **MEADOW BEAUTY** RHEXIA MARIANA

178 **GODETIA** CLARKIA DEFLEXA

179 **FAREWELL TO-SPRING** CLARKIA AMOENA

**FAREWELL-
TO-SPRING**

ARKIA GRACILIS

flowers are open. The corolla varies from pink to lavender, sometimes with a scarlet spot in the center.

C. gracilis grows in woods in the foothills from Washington to California. It flowers from April to July.

FAREWELL-TO-SPRING
CLARKIA BOTTAE   *Plate 181*

This is another of the "farewells-to-spring," sometimes placed in a separate genus, *Godetia*. This type of *Clarkia* has four broad, fan-shaped petals, pink or red. *C. bottae* grows up to eighteen inches tall. The leaves are lance-shaped, sometimes narrowly so. The flower-cluster droops before the flowers open, gradually straightening and displaying the flowers. The lavender-pink corolla has a white center. There are two sets of four stamens, the outer with blue pollen, the inner with cream-colored pollen. The capsule is more or less four-angled.

C. bottae grows near the coast in Monterey County, California. It blooms from May to July.

CLARKIA
CLARKIA UNGUICULATA   *Plate 184*

The stem of *C. unguiculata* may exceed three feet in height. It and the lance-shaped or ovate leaves are smooth and gray-green. The petals, unlike the broad fan-shaped petals of the godetia type, have a diamond-shaped blade on a long stalk (*unguiculus*, in Latin, is a "little nail" or "claw," to which this stalk is compared). The corolla varies from lavender to salmon-pink and red-purple.

C. unguiculata is a common plant of dry slopes in the coast ranges of California. It flowers in May and June.

FAREWELL-TO-SPRING
CLARKIA CYLINDRICA   *Plate 185*

The branched stem of this godetia rarely reaches two feet in height. The leaves are lance-shaped, with short stalks. The corolla is pinkish-lavender shading to white, often with purplish flecks, and bright red-purple in the center.

C. cylindrica grows in dry places of grasslands and foothills in the coastal region of California.

PRIMROSE-WILLOW
JUSSIAEA PERUVIANA   *Plate 182*

Primrose-willow (neither a primrose nor a willow) has a bristly stem from three to twelve feet tall or even more. The leaves are ovate or lance-shaped. The yellow flowers spring from the axils of the leaves.

Primrose-willow is a plant of swamps and stream-edges from North Carolina to Florida. It flowers from spring to autumn, and all the year in the Everglades. The

181 **FAREWELL-TO-SPRING** CLARKIA BOTTAE   *182* **PRIMROSE-WILLOW** JUSSIAEA PERUVIANA

183 **DESERT-PRIMROSE** OENOTHERA DELTOIDES   *184* **CLARKIA** CLARKIA UNGUICULATA

181

182

183

184

name *Jussiaea* is derived from that of the great French botanist of the eighteenth century, Antoine Laurent de Jussieu, who wrote a famous work on the genera of plants, arranging them in a more natural system than that of Linnaeus.

DESERT-PRIMROSE or DEVIL'S-LANTERN
OENOTHERA DELTOIDES   *Plate 183*

This species of *Oenothera* grows from six inches to about a foot tall. The leaves, which are rather narrow and more or less toothed, are attached singly. The large, fragrant, white flowers terminate the stems. All the flower parts except the ovary, which is inferior, are seated at the end of a long tubular receptacle; the ovary is below the hollow part of this structure.

Desert-primrose is found commonly in deserts from Utah and Arizona to California and Baja California. It blooms from March to May. The flowers open in the evening. There are several varieties, differing in shape of leaves, kind of hairs, and other details. The older, outer stems often curve inward so as to enclose the rest of the plant; this causes the species to be known locally as bird-cages or lion-in-a-cage.

WHITE or SHOWY EVENING-PRIMROSE
OENOTHERA SPECIOSA   *Plate 186*

O. speciosa is a delicate plant a foot or two tall. The leaves are narrowly lance-shaped with wavy or toothed margins. The large flowers spring from the axils of the upper leaves; the buds droop, straightening up as they open.

The white evening-primrose grows in prairies and other open places from Missouri to Kansas and southwestward to Texas and Mexico; it has also spread from gardens in the eastern states. It flowers from May to July.

WHITE EVENING-PRIMROSE
OENOTHERA ALBICAULIS   *Plate 187*

White evening-primrose is about a foot tall, but branches up to three feet long may be on the ground. The leaves, pinnately cleft into narrow lobes, are rather crowded on the stem; the lower ones may be merely lobed or toothed. The flowers grow in a short spike at the summit of the stem; the buds at first droop, straightening as the perianth opens.

White evening-primrose grows on mountain slopes and in dry plains from Minnesota to Alberta and southward through the mountains to Texas and into Mexico. It blooms from March to August, depending on latitude.

EVENING-PRIMROSE
OENOTHERA CLAVAEFORMIS   *Plate 189*

This evening-primrose is an annual about a foot tall, with an unbranched stem or with several growing from the same base. The leaves are mostly at the base, ovate and more or less toothed. The white flowers are in narrow clusters. The style is tipped by a disclike stigma, not the four-branched stigma characteristic of some other groups of this large genus. The capsule, which is less than an inch long, broadens upward from a narrow base: it is club-shaped ("clavaeformis").

O. clavaeformis grows in sandy open places and deserts in western Nevada and California. It flowers from March to May.

FIREWEED or WILLOW-HERB
EPILOBIUM ANGUSTIFOLIUM   *Plate 188*

Fireweed may reach six feet in height. The leaves vary from narrowly lance-shaped to ovate, attached singly. The rose-purple flowers grow on short stalks along the upper part of the stem. The perianth crowns a long tubular receptacle, in which is the inferior ovary. The four sepals are bent sharply downward.

Fireweed is so called from its prevalence in burned land, but it also grows in clearings and other places, throughout the northern forest and southward to Maryland, North Carolina (in the mountains), northern Illinois, South Dakota, New Mexico, and California; also in Europe and Asia. It flowers from June to September. As might be expected from its wide range, it is extremely variable, and has been divided into several varieties. In England it is called also apple-pie, cat's-eyes, ranting-widow, and other things. It followed the industrial revolution in invading streamsides, roadsides, and railsides, and more recently covered bombed areas of London with its brilliant flames. The name willow-herb refers to the likeness of its leaves to those of willow.

THE PARSLEY FAMILY
UMBELLIFERAE

The Parsley family has small flowers in umbels which are generally compound; that is, the stalks which radiate from the summit of the flowering stem bear not single flowers but small umbels. The flowers are often numerous. The receptacle containing the inferior ovary is crowned by five small sepals, five petals, five stamens, and two styles. The fruit is an oval or narrow pod, usually ribbed lengthwise. The leaves also are characteristic: each is usually divided and the segments often themselves divided, all on a stalk that sheathes the stem from which it grows.

This is a common family in temperate regions. In it are such well-known herbs as anise, dill, coriander, and caraway, besides celery, parsley, parsnip, and carrot; also the poisonous "hemlock" (not the tree!) whose juice the Athenians of ancient times used to execute criminals; and other common weeds so deadly that everyone should be able to recognize the family and treat it with caution.

WATER-HEMLOCK or SPOTTED COWBANE
CICUTA MACULATA   *Plate 190*

Since *Cicuta maculata* is one of our most poisonous wildflowers—children have died by nibbling the leaves or the tubers—its characteristics are important. The plant

185 **FAREWELL-TO-SPRING** CLARKIA CYLINDRICA

186 **WHITE or SHOWY EVENING-PRIMROSE** OENOTHERA SPECIOSA

is tall, often reaching six or seven feet. The stem may or may not be spotted ("maculate") or streaked with purple. The leaves are pinnately divided, the segments subdivided into narrow, pointed, sharp-toothed segments, which are not close together. The flowers are white. There is generally no circle of bracts beneath the flower-cluster. The fruit is elliptical in outline, with rounded (not sharp) ribs.

Water-hemlock grows in meadows and prairies, especially in ditches along fence-rows and other wet places, from Quebec to Manitoba and southward to Florida, Tennessee, Missouri, and Texas. Another poisonous species, *C. bulbifera*, extends from Newfoundland to British Columbia and southward to Virginia, Illinois, Minnesota, Nebraska, Montana, and Oregon. Both these species have tuberous roots, and *C. bulbifera* has tiny bulbs in the axils of the leaves.

QUEEN-ANNE'S-LACE or WILD CARROT
DAUCUS CAROTA   *Plate 191*

The bristly stem of Queen-Anne's-lace may reach five feet or more in height. The leaves are finely divided into a multitude of small segments. The flowers are borne in a wide flat cluster. They are white, except that the central flower is often a dark red-purple. After flowering, the stalks cup to form a "bird's nest," in which the fruits mature. The ribs of the fruit bear rows of sharp spines.

This native of the Old World is now a weed throughout North America, often troublesome in gardens and pastures but nonetheless a delight along the roadsides. In the photograph it is shown with other roadside weeds, chicory and fleabane.

The cultivated carrot is a relative of *Daucus carota*.

THE DOGWOOD FAMILY
CORNACEAE

Most plants of the Dogwood family are trees and shrubs. They have small flowers with parts in fours or fives and an inferior ovary. The flowers are in loose clusters (cymes) or in close heads; the heads are in several species surrounded by petal-like bracts. The ovary typically develops into a stone-fruit.

BUNCHBERRY or DWARF CORNEL
CORNUS CANADENSIS   *Plate 192*

Bunchberry is somewhat woody but so small that it takes its place among the wildflowers. Its visible stems grow from a rhizome. The erect stem rises about six inches tall, with usually six leaves near the summit. The leaves are characteristic of most species of *Cornus*, ovate, pointed, with prominent veins attached to the midvein below the middle and curving toward the tip. The "flower" proves on examination to be a cluster (head) of small greenish or yellowish flowers; this is surrounded by four conspicuous white (or pink) bracts, which may be mistaken for the petals of one flower; they act as bud-scales, enclosing the flower-cluster, before expanding and becoming petal-like. The flowers are on a plan of four.

171

WHITE EVENING-PRIMROSE

OENOTHERA ALBICAULIS

188
FIREWEED
EPILOBIUM ANGUSTIFOLIUM

189
EVENING-PRIMROSE
OENOTHERA CLAVAEFORMIS

Bunchberry is a plant of the forest floor, flourishing in acid soil and bogs, and retreating to the deep woods and mountains before the growth of cities. It occurs from Greenland to Alaska and southward to Maryland, Ohio, Minnesota, South Dakota, New Mexico, and California; also in eastern Asia. It flowers from May to July.

The fruits are eaten by the natives of far-northern lands. They are said to have the somewhat unfortunate property of increasing the appetite.

THE SHINLEAF FAMILY
PYROLACEAE

The Shinleaf family is related to the Heath family. Some genera are evergreen; some lack green color altogether. All are plants of coniferous forests of the Northern Hemisphere.

INDIAN-PIPE or CORPSE-PLANT
MONOTROPA UNIFLORA
Plate 193

Indian-pipe grows like a slightly dirty white ghost in the deep shade of the forest. Having no green color, it lives as a fungus does by getting food from the dead leaves and other litter of the forest floor (the roots are associated with certain moldlike fungi in this business). From the cluster of roots spring several stems, having scales instead of leaves, about six inches tall; each bears one drooping flower at its tip. The calyx is composed of several scales, which soon fall. The four or five petals are rather thick, blunt at the end. As the fruit matures the flower-stalk straightens and stands erect. The whole plant turns black as it ages or if it is picked.

Monotropa uniflora grows in the leaf-mold of woods throughout North America; also in eastern Asia. Its flowers open from June to September. There is another species with pink or tan flowers, several flowers to a stem.

M. uniflora is said to have furnished the Indians with a healing eye-lotion.

SHINLEAF
PYROLA ELLIPTICA
Plate 194

Shinleaf is a small evergreen herb growing from a rhizome. The leaves all arise from one point at the base of the erect stem. They are fairly long-stalked, with rather dull green elliptic blades. The stem bears only flowers, several in a raceme. Each flower hangs from its stalk, a small, round bell of five concave, white petals, almost separate from each other. There are ten stamens and a long projecting style which curves slightly upward at the tip.

P. elliptica grows in woods from Newfoundland to British Columbia and southward to Pennsylvania and West Virginia, Indiana, Iowa, South Dakota, and New Mexico. The flowers appear from June to August.

There are a number of other species of *Pyrola*, growing in much the same sort of places and having a similar range; some extend south into California. They are some-

174

times called wintergreen, but the true wintergreen is in the genus *Gaultheria* in the Heath family. The name shinleaf is apparently derived from the use of the leaves by early settlers as "shin-plasters" to heal bruises and other injuries.

THE HEATH FAMILY
ERICACEAE

The *Ericaceae* are mainly shrubs and trees, growing in both temperate and tropical regions. Many are evergreen, with thick, tough leaves. The flowers have joined petals, forming a bell-shaped or a flaring corolla. The stamens shed their pollen through pores. Our species are mostly characteristic of acid soils and bogs. The azaleas, rhododendrons, laurels, and heathers are well-known *Ericaceae*. The blueberries, huckleberries, and cranberries are in a closely related family.

PINK-HEATHER
PHYLLODOCE EMPETRIFORMIS   *Plate 195*

Pink-heather is a much-branched shrub less than two feet tall. The stems are covered with numerous narrow, thick, blunt leaves about half an inch long. The fragrant, deep-pink flowers are in small groups at the ends of the branches.

Pink-heather is abundant in high meadows just above the limit of trees in the western mountains, from Wyoming to British Columbia and southward to California. It flowers from June to August. True heather is *Calluna*, in the same family, which has no species native in North America.

SHEEP-LAUREL or LAMBKILL
KALMIA ANGUSTIFOLIA   *Plate 196*

Sheep-laurel is a more slender edition of mountain-laurel, with similar but deeper-colored flowers. The leaves (*folia*) are narrow (*angusti-*), with blunt ends, and are generally in pairs or threes. The flower-clusters grow from the axils of leaves of the previous season.

Sheep-laurel grows in a variety of situations, wet and dry, from Labrador to Manitoba and southward to South Carolina and farther in the mountains, and in Tennessee and Michigan. It blooms from June to August. The English names refer to the poisonous qualities of its foliage, which have killed sheep and lambs that browsed it. The genus *Kalmia* is named for Per Kalm, one of Linnaeus' students, who was among the first European botanists to search North America for its wild plants.

MOUNTAIN-LAUREL
KALMIA LATIFOLIA   *Plate 198*

This, the state flower of Connecticut, is a handsome evergreen shrub, the leaves singly attached, smooth and glossy, and elliptical but pointed at each end. The stems

175

190 **WATER-HEMLOCK** CICUTA MACULATA

191 **QUEEN-ANNE'S-LACE** DAUCUS CAROTA

192 **BUNCHBERRY** CORNUS CANADENSIS

are crooked, tough, much branched, sometimes forming almost impenetrable tangles. The pink-and-white flowers grow in broad clusters which may cover the whole bush. The ten anthers are held in pouches in the corolla, and as the flower opens the stalks of the stamens are bent outward, under tension; a touch in the center of the flowers dislodges them, and they spring up, dusting the intruding object with pollen.

In spite of the name, mountain-laurel flourishes on the coastal plain as well as in the mountains, in a great variety of situations, from swampy thickets to rocky hilltops and mountain slopes, from New Brunswick to Ontario, southward to Florida, and along the coast to Louisiana.

This is no relation to the laurel (*Laurus nobilis*) with which the old Greeks crowned winners at their games.

WESTERN AZALEA
RHODODENDRON OCCIDENTALE   *Plate 197*

The western azalea is a straggling shrub reaching a height of ten feet or sometimes more. The leaves are thin and light green, and elliptic, or ovate with the broad end between middle and tip. The petals are white or pinkish, the uppermost having a yellow spot.

R. occidentale grows along streams and in moist woods in the mountains of Oregon and California. It flowers from April to August. It is poisonous to cattle.

PINXTER-FLOWER or WILD AZALEA
RHODODENDRON NUDIFLORUM   *Plate 200*

The pinxter-flower is a shrub up to ten feet tall (but usually less). The leaves are oblong or elliptic, sharp-pointed; they appear only after the flowers are in full bloom —whence the *nudiflorum* or "naked-flowering" part of the name. The sweet-smelling flowers grow in clusters at the ends of the branches, often in great profusion. The corolla is generally a pale pink, but in different forms of the species it varies from white to purplish.

Pinxter-flower grows in swamps, along streams, even in dry woods, from Massachusetts to Ohio and southward to South Carolina and Tennessee. It flowers from March to May.

"Pinxter" is derived, through Gothic and Dutch, from the Greek word for Pentecost (Whitsuntide), the seventh Sunday after Easter, but in most parts of its range it flowers long before Whitsuntide. It has also been called wild honeysuckle, but the use of this name is to be discouraged, since the plant is no relation to the true honeysuckles (*Lonicera*).

DEERBERRY
POLYCODIUM STAMINEUM   *Plate 199*

Deerberry is a shrub growing up to ten feet tall, with many branches. The leaves are ovate or oblong. The greenish-white, pink-tinged flower-clusters hang from the

177

193 **INDIAN-PIPE** MONOTROPA UNIFLORA   *194* **SHINLEAF** PYROLA ELLIPTICA

195 **PINK-HEATHER** PHYLLODOCE EMPETRIFORMIS   *196* **SHEEP-LAUREL** KALMIA ANGUSTIFOLIA

193

194

195

196

ends of their stalks. The fruit is a juicy but rather thick-skinned, greenish or purplish berry.

Deerberry grows in dry woods from Massachusetts to Kansas and southward to Florida and Louisiana. It flowers from July to September. It is closely related to the blueberries and indeed by some botanists is included in the blueberry genus (*Vaccinium*); but its berries are not palatable.

POINTLEAF MANZANITA
ARCTOSTAPHYLOS PUNGENS
Plate 201

This manzanita is a small shrub a foot or two tall, with crooked stems which make dense thickets. The leaves, borne singly, are small, thick, elliptical, evergreen, tipped with a small sharp point. The white flowers are in clusters at the ends of the branches.

Pointleaf manzanita occurs at high altitudes (up to 8,000 feet above sea level) in the mountainous parts of the Southwest, from Utah to southern California and southward into Mexico. It flowers in March and April. Members of the Heath family are not generally expected in this region; most of them, like the bearberry, *Arctostaphylos uva-ursi*, are at home in a cooler, more boggy environment. The name manzanita means "little apple," and refers to the fruits. These stone-fruits, with a rather dry, mealy flesh, played an important part in the life of the Indians.

THE PRIMROSE FAMILY
PRIMULACEAE

The Primrose family has its parts mostly in fives, with its petals joined at the base. One peculiarity that often serves to identify it is that each stamen stands opposite the center of a petal, instead of the more usual position opposite the junction of two petals.

The family includes, besides the primroses, shooting-stars, cyclamen, pimpernel, and a number of common wildflowers.

SAMODIA
SAMOLUS EBRACTEATUS
Plate 202

Samodia grows a foot or two tall, with small ovate leaves (the broadest part outward) attached singly on the lower part of the stem. The white or pink flowers are arranged along the upper part of the stem. Each has a cuplike base partly joined to the ovary.

S. ebracteatus is found in pinelands and prairies and on the edges of salt marshes on the coastal plain in Florida and westward to Nevada, New Mexico, and Texas. The flowers are seen from December to May, or until August in the western parts of the range.

SHOOTING-STAR
DODECATHEON VIVIPARUM   *Plate 203*

This western shooting-star has a basal tuft of leaves up to ten inches long, mostly lance-shaped with the narrow end down, minutely notched along the margin. The flowering stem may be eighteen inches tall. Both stem and leaves grow from a rhizome. The flowers hang from curved stalks attached close together at the top of the stem. The magenta petals are sharply bent back, so that they point upward. The dark stamens form a cone around the style, the small stigma just projecting.

D. viviparum is common in wet meadows in the mountains from Montana to Alaska and southward to Oregon.

Also shown in the photograph is a yellow violet, *Viola glabella*.

GARDEN LOOSESTRIFE
LYSIMACHIA VULGARIS   *Plate 204*

Garden loosestrife grows three feet tall or more, an erect stem bearing lance-shaped or ovate leaves in pairs or circles on very short stalks. The handsome flowers are crowded at the summit. The flowers are large for this genus, about an inch across. The petals are bright yellow.

L. vulgaris is a native of the Old World, escaped from cultivation in the New, and is now found in roadside thickets and wet places from Quebec and Ontario southward to Maryland and Illinois. It flowers from June to September. In England it has been called yellow loosestrife since 1548; also herbe-willow or willow-herb.

FOUR-LEAVED LOOSESTRIFE
LYSIMACHIA QUADRIFOLIA   *Plate 205*

This loosestrife grows two feet tall or more. The stem is unbranched and bears leaves in circles, usually four or five at each level. The leaves vary from lance-shaped to ovate; they have almost no stalks. The flowers are on long, very thin stalks growing from the axils of leaves, usually the same number of flowers as leaves at any level of the stem. The joined, pointed petals form small yellow stars.

L. quadrifolia grows in open woods, either dry or moist, from Maine to Wisconsin and southward to Georgia, Alabama, and Illinois. It flowers from May to August.

The curious name loosestrife is a mistranslation of *Lysimachia*, which was a plant so named by Greek and Roman authors in honor of Lysimachos, a king in ancient Greece. Several legends derive from his name. To "loose" strife means to dissolve or end it. The name was given to both yellow and red flowers; see purple loosestrife.

SWAMP-CANDLES or YELLOW LOOSESTRIFE
LYSIMACHIA TERRESTRIS   *Plate 206*

This loosestrife is distinguished from other common species by having all its flowers at the summit of the stem, which reaches a height of about three feet. The leaves are

181

200
PINXTER-FLOWER
RHODODENDRON NUDIFLORUM

201
POINTLEAF MANZANITA
ARCTOSTAPHYLOS PUNGENS

202
SAMODIA
SAMOLUS EBRACTEATUS

203
SHOOTING-STAR
DODECATHEON VIVIPARUM

198
MOUNTAIN-LAUREL
KALMIA LATIFOLIA

199
DEERBERRY
POLYCODIUM STAMINEUM

200

201

202

203

lance-shaped and mostly paired. The five yellow petals are generally spotted with dark brown.

L. terrestris justifies its English name by growing in swamps and wet meadows from Newfoundland to Manitoba and southward to Georgia, Kentucky, and Iowa. The flowers open from June to August.

THE LEADWORT FAMILY
PLUMBAGINACEAE

The Leadwort family is characterized by five joined petals, five stamens which stand opposite the centers of the petals (instead of opposite their junctions, the more usual position), and a pistil with five styles.

SEA-LAVENDER or MARSH-ROSEMARY
LIMONIUM SINUATUM
Plate 208

Sea-lavender is no relation to lavender or to rosemary (both in the Mint family) but bears a superficial resemblance, which accounts for its names. The leaves are in a group at the ground; they are pinnately lobed. The flowering stem grows a foot or more tall; it is edged with "wings," which run into narrow, leaflike appendages. The plant is roughly hairy. The five sepals form a blue or white cup; the five petals are yellowish.

Sea-lavender came from the Mediterranean and now grows on beaches and in salt marshes here and there along the California coast. It flowers from June to October. The same English names are applied to a similar species, *L. nashii*, which grows along the Atlantic coast from Newfoundland to Florida and thence along the Gulf coast to northeastern Mexico.

THE GENTIAN FAMILY
GENTIANACEAE

The *Gentianaceae* are a family of mostly herbaceous plants growing in temperate regions the world over. The flowers have parts in fours or fives, the petals joined, the ovary with one chamber containing many ovules.

CANCHALAGUA
CENTAURIUM VENUSTUM
Plate 209

Canchalagua is an annual about a foot tall with a branched stem bearing pairs of ovate or oblong leaves. The flowers are at the ends of the branches. There are five joined sepals with ridges or keels, and five rose-colored petals, white (with red spots) in the center and joined at the base. The stamens become twisted after the pollen is shed.

204 **GARDEN LOOSESTRIFE** LYSIMACHIA VULGARIS

205 **FOUR-LEAVED LOOSESTRIFE** LYSIMACHIA QUADRIFOLIA   *206* **SWAMP-CANDLES** LYSIMACHIA TERRESTRIS

Canchalagua grows in chaparral, grassy slopes, and open dry places in southern California and in the foothills of the Sierra Nevada. It flowers from May to August. Other centauries range across North America.

LARGE-FLOWERED SABATIA
SABATIA GRANDIFLORA   *Plate 207*

This *Sabatia* has a stem up to four feet tall. The leaves are paired, very narrow, not more than four inches long. The calyx is a cup with five short, narrow teeth. The corolla is of five rose or magenta petals joined only at the extreme base, with a yellow "eye," often up to two inches across.

The large-flowered sabatia grows in the everglades and pinelands of southern Florida, flowering all the year. It seems strange that such a handsome flower has not found a place in gardens nor even been given an English name!

ROSE-PINK
SABATIA CAMPESTRIS   *Plate 210*

Sabatia campestris has a stem up to eighteen inches tall, usually branched, bearing pairs of ovate leaves. The flowers are on long leafless stalks at the ends of the branches. The calyx has five projecting flaps or "wings," and five teeth. The corolla consists of five lilac petals joined at the base, in the center of which the yellow stamens (about ten) make a pleasing contrast.

S. campestris is found in moist prairies and woodlands from Iowa to Kansas and southward to Louisiana and Texas. It flowers from June to August. Other species of *Sabatia* are called marsh-pink. They inhabit fresh or salt marshes along the Atlantic Coast. The name of the genus commemorates Liberato Sabbati, an Italian botanist.

THE DOGBANE FAMILY
APOCYNACEAE

The Dogbane family resembles the milkweeds in having milky juice. The flower parts are in fives, the petals joined to form a cup. There are two ovaries which share a single style and stigma, but form in fruit two narrow follicles.

DOGBANE
APOCYNUM ANDROSAEMIFOLIUM   *Plate 211*

This pink-flowered dogbane has a repeatedly forking stem, which forms a bush three feet or more tall. The leaves are paired, ovate, mostly smooth, often drooping on their slender stalks. The small flowers hang from slim stalks in a loose cluster. The pointed tips of the petals curl outward.

Pink dogbane is found in thickets and at the margins of woods, also in fields and waste places, practically throughout North America (except in the extreme south). It flowers from May to August.

207 **LARGE-FLOWERED SABATIA** SABATIA GRANDIFLORA

208 **SEA-LAVENDER** LIMONIUM SINUATUM   209 **CANCHALAGUA** CENTAURIUM VENUSTUM

210

211

212

213

THE MILKWEED FAMILY
ASCLEPIADACEAE

The milkweeds are known not only for their milky juice (which *Asclepias tuberosa* lacks) but for their curious flower structure. The five petals bear appendages which compose a "corona"; in the milkweeds proper (*Asclepias*) and some other genera, this has the form of five cups, often with curious little horns projecting. The two ovaries have two styles but only one stigma (in this resembling those of the dogbanes); and the five stamens are joined by their anthers to the stigma in an extraordinary way, so that an insect alighting on the stigma is compelled—if it can free itself—to carry the pollen away on its legs. Each flower can form two follicles from its two ovaries.

CLIMBING-MILKWEED
FUNASTRUM HETEROPHYLLUM
Plate 212

Climbing-milkweed is a perennial twining vine which clambers among shrubs and trees; the stems may twist themselves into thick ropes. The leaves are narrow, sharp-pointed, and paired. The flowers grow in clusters at the tips of the branches. They form five-pointed stars, colored brownish with a light margin and supporting a crown of five erect lobes. Stamens and pistil are much like those of a true milkweed (*Asclepias*).

F. heterophyllum occurs among other plants in deserts from western Texas to California and Mexico. It flowers from April to September.

BUTTERFLY-WEED or PLEURISY-ROOT
ASCLEPIAS TUBEROSA
Plate 213

This milkweed makes a branching, often rather sprawling bush two or three feet tall, growing from a tough rhizome deep in the soil. Some of the many leaves are in pairs and some are single. The whole plant is rough and hairy. The brilliant orange flowers crown the stems in one or more wide clusters.

Butterfly-weed is widely distributed in dry open places from New Hampshire to Minnesota and Colorado and southward to Florida, Texas, and Arizona. It flowers from June to September.

The flowers are visited by multitudes of butterflies, which probably accounts for its name, though some say the name is due to the bright hue of the flowers. The Indians used the rhizome ("root") as a cure for various maladies, and indeed used the whole plant in several ways. The early settlers continued their faith in it as a cure for pleurisy, and it was mentioned as such by Jane Colden, the first woman botanist of America. Linnaeus named the genus for the Greek god of healing, whom the Romans called Aesculapius.

210 **ROSE-PINK** SABATIA CAMPESTRIS   *211* **DOGBANE** APOCYNUM ANDROSAEMIFOLIUM

212 **CLIMBING-MILKWEED** FUNASTRUM HETEROPHYLLUM   *213* **BUTTERFLY-WEED** ASCLEPIAS TUBEROSA

4

OMMON MILKWEED

CLEPIAS SYRIACA

215

HEDGE BINDWEED

CONVOLVULUS SEPIUM

216

DODDER

CUSCUTA DENTICULATA

COMMON MILKWEED
ASCLEPIAS SYRIACA

Plate 214

The erect, rather downy stems may rise to a height of six feet, though about four is more common. They grow from a rhizome. The leaves are short-stalked, oblong or nearly ovate, with many characteristic veins running parallel from the midrib to the margins; they are light green, downy on the lower side. The flowers are in clusters that grow from the axils of the leaves. The petals are pinkish-lavender or purplish, bent sharply down, with the corona of hoods standing erect. From each hood a curved horn projects toward the stigma. The flowers are sweetly fragrant. The woolly follicles are covered with small projections—"warts." When they open, the silky hairs of the emerging seeds form a familiar and beautiful sight.

This milkweed grows along roadsides and in fields, prairies, and dry open places from New Brunswick to Saskatchewan and southward to Georgia, Tennessee, Missouri, and Nebraska. It flowers from June to August.

Linnaeus named the species under the impression that it came from Syria; it is, however, a native of America. The young shoots are said to make tasty greens. The "silk" of the seeds has been used in many ways. The milky juice protects the flowers from the visits of ants, whose feet puncture the skin of the stem and become entangled in the sticky white sap. Shown in the photograph is the pod of *A. syriaca*.

THE MORNING-GLORY FAMILY
CONVOLVULACEAE

Most of the *Convolvulaceae* are vines, the common morning-glory being fairly typical. The flower-parts are in fours or fives, the petals being joined to form a funnel or tube. The ovary generally has two chambers, each containing two ovules.

HEDGE BINDWEED
CONVOLVULUS SEPIUM

Plate 215

Hedge bindweed creeps over the ground or twines about any support that is available. Each leaf has a long stalk and a more or less heart-shaped blade. The flowers grow on usually long stalks that spring from the axils of leaves. There are two broad bracts at the base of the flower which may be mistaken for sepals; the sepals are concealed by them. The corolla, either white or pink, has the funnel shape familiar in the cultivated morning-glories.

Hedge bindweed grows in thickets and among other weeds in waste places and along roadsides (*sepium* means "of hedges") throughout North America, except in the Southwest. It is found also in Europe and Asia. It is often a troublesome weed, though not so hard to eradicate as *C. arvensis,* an immigrant from Europe with smaller flowers and no bracts. An interesting feature of the corolla is that it is twisted in the bud and once again as it withers.

217 **MOON-FLOWER** CALONYCTION ACULEATUM   *218* **IPOMOPSIS** IPOMOPSIS TENUIFOLIA

219 **GILIA** GILIA CAPITATA   *220* **JACOB'S-LADDER** POLEMONIUM CONFERTUM

217

218

219

220

DODDER
CUSCUTA DENTICULATA

Plate 216

The numerous species of *Cuscuta* are parasites, extracting nourishment from other plants upon which they climb. Their twining stems are usually yellow or orange and bear no leaves. They send small suckers into the plants on which they feed. The small, bell-shaped, white corolla has five scales alternating with its lobes. *C. denticulata* is distinguished from other species of *Cuscuta* by such characteristics as the shape of sepals and capsule.

C. denticulata grows on shrubs in the deserts of Utah, Arizona, and California. The flowers are seen from May to October. Some authorities place the dodders in a family of their own, the *Cuscutaceae*.

MOON-FLOWER
CALONYCTION ACULEATUM

Plate 217

Moon-flower is a twining vine. The leaf-blades vary from ovate to round, sometimes being lobed, and are often six inches long. The flowers grow from the axils of leaves. The corolla may be five or six inches long, flaring into a disc six or eight inches across; it is white, fragrant, and opens at night.

Moon-flower is found in southern Florida and thence to Louisiana. It is a "fire-weed." The botanist J. K. Small wrote: "The growth of vines over burned areas, especially in hammocks, is prodigious." It flowers all the year round.

THE PHLOX FAMILY
POLEMONIACEAE

The Phlox family usually has five narrow sepals and a corolla formed of a tube or funnel flaring into five lobes. There are generally five stamens, partly joined with the corolla. It is distinguished from other families with similar characteristics by its pistil: the ovary has three chambers, and the style bears usually three narrow stigmas. The fruit is a small capsule. The family occurs in all temperate parts of the world and furnishes many well-known garden and wildflowers in North America. The genera and species are most numerous in California (160 species, many subspecies) .

IPOMOPSIS
IPOMOPSIS TENUIFOLIA

Plate 218

Ipomopsis tenuifolia is an almost shrubby perennial, about a foot tall, bearing many very narrow leaves (some pinnately cleft). The flowers are in terminal clusters. The sepals have a strong, green midrib flanked by almost transparent membranes; they also bear short, white hairs. The corolla forms a tube three times as long as the calyx, spreading at the mouth into five square-ended lobes; it is bright red with yellow marks at the base of the lobes. The five long stamens project, as does the three-branched style.

194

This species grows on dry slopes in the mountains of southern California and northern Baja California. Flowering-time is from March to May. The square-ended lobes of the corolla distinguish it from the widely distributed and extremely variable *I. aggregata*. Both species are by some botanists included in the very large western genus *Gilia*.

JACOB'S-LADDER
POLEMONIUM CONFERTUM   *Plate 220*

This Jacob's-ladder of the Rocky Mountains differs from its eastern relatives in having its flowers in a close head rather than a coiled cluster. The plant is about six inches tall. The leaves are mostly at the base, divided pinnately into many small, round segments (the narrower segments of *P. reptans* in the East make the rungs of "Jacob's ladder"). The flowers have a bell-shaped corolla of five blue petals, joined only by their lower halves.

P. confertum is found among rocks at high altitudes from Wyoming to New Mexico, and in Oregon and California. It blooms from June to September.

GILIA
GILIA CAPITATA   *Plate 219*

This species of *Gilia* is extremely variable. The plant in the photograph belongs to the subspecies *chamissonis,* which grows up to two feet tall or more. The stems branch near the base, bearing many small glands. Most of the leaves are at the base, pinnately divided and subdivided. The leaves on the stem are also pinnately divided, into very narrow segments. The flowers are crowded in heads at the tips of the branches. The color is blue or violet. The five anthers are white.

The subspecies grows along the coast of California, flowering from May to July. Other subspecies grow in the coast ranges, on open slopes or in the forest.

BIRD'S-EYES
GILIA TRICOLOR   *Plate 224*

This species of *Gilia* is a branching annual up to eighteen inches tall. The leaves are pinnately divided into narrow segments, which are often again divided. The flowers grow in small clusters at the tips of the branches. The color is variable. The tube of the corolla is generally yellow or orange. Just where it spreads into the lobes, there are five pairs of spots of a deep brown-purple color (sometimes so close together as to form a dark band). The "limb" of the corolla—that is, the flaring part—varies from white to deep violet, often passing through a pinkish stage as it matures. The anthers are at first white but are blue when mature.

Bird's-eyes grows in open grassy places in the coast ranges, the central valley, and the Sierra foothills of California. The period of bloom is March and April. *Gilia* (named for an Italian botanist of the eighteenth century) is a large genus in western

221
PHLOX
PHLOX CAESPITOSA

222
PRICKLY-PHLOX
LEPTODACTYLON CALIFORNICUM

and southwestern North America (one species extending east to Florida) and in temperate South America. "Tricolor" seems inadequate as an epithet for this particular many-colored gem. At the top of the photograph is a flower of baby-blue-eyes.

PRICKLY-PHLOX
LEPTODACTYLON CALIFORNICUM   *Plate 222*

Prickly-phlox is a much-branched shrub about three feet tall, with woolly stems. The leaves are palmately lobed, the lobes sharp-pointed. In their axils grow bunches of smaller, prickly leaves, which remain there after the older leaves have fallen. The rose or lavender flowers are like those of phlox.

Prickly-phlox grows in dry places in southern California, flowering from March to June.

PHLOX
PHLOX CAESPITOSA   *Plate 221*

Phlox caespitosa forms clumps only about three inches high, with many short branches. The leaves are very narrow and crowded on the branches. The tube of the corolla emerges from the five-toothed calyx and flares into five flat, violet-blue lobes, somewhat whitish on the edges.

P. caespitosa is found among rocks on high mountains from Montana to British Columbia and southward to Colorado and California. It flowers from April to August or in some places even later.

PHLOX
PHLOX PILOSA   *Plate 223*

Phlox pilosa grows some two feet tall, the several stems bearing pairs of narrow, sharp-pointed leaves. The whole plant is more or less hairy. The flowers are at the summits of the stems. From the calyx, which has five narrow teeth, emerges the long, narrow tube of the corolla, flaring at the end into five flat lobes, colored pink or violet.

This species of phlox grows in various situations—in woods and fields and on prairies—from Connecticut to Ontario and Manitoba and southward to Florida and Texas. It flowers from April to July. It is highly variable in hairiness, shape of leaves, and other minor characteristics.

MUSTANG-CLOVER
LINANTHUS MONTANUS   *Plate 225*

Mustang-clover is an annual, having mostly unbranched stems up to two feet tall. The paired leaves are cleft into from five to eleven very narrow, sharp-pointed, bristly parts about an inch long. The stalkless flowers grow in heads. The sepals are narrow, sharp, and bristly. The corolla, a tube about an inch long, flares into five pink lobes with a dark red or purple spot at the base of each and a yellow "throat" (where the tube begins to flare).

223

224

225

226

Mustang-clover grows in dry, rocky places quite high in the foothills of the Sierra Nevada in California. It flowers from May to August. *Linanthus* means "flax-flower," but the resemblance, at least in this species, is not close. Nor is it much like a true clover (*Trifolium*).

THE WATERLEAF FAMILY
HYDROPHYLLACEAE

The Waterleaf family resembles the Borage family in its inflorescence, this being usually a coiled false raceme; many species are rough, bristly, like the borages. The sepals, petals, and stamens are in fives, radially symmetric. The ovary has one chamber, the ovules being in two rows and the style often bearing two stigmas.

WILD-HELIOTROPE
PHACELIA TANACETIFOLIA   *Plate 226*

The name is scarcely distinctive, for several quite unrelated plants are called wild-heliotrope. This one is an annual growing two feet tall or taller. The leaves, attached singly, are pinnately divided into lance-shaped segments, themselves toothed or lobed or often again divided. The whole plant may be roughish or merely hairy. The almost stalkless flowers grow in conspicuous, coiled clusters which terminate the branches. The sepals are very narrow and bristly. The corolla forms an open blue funnel from which the long stamens project.

Wild-heliotrope grows in open places in many sorts of situations from Nevada to California and southward to Arizona and Baja California. It flowers from March to May. *Phacelia* is a large genus in the West (eighty-seven species in California alone), with a few species in the East and South. The name wild-heliotrope refers to the appearance of the inflorescence, which recalls that of the true heliotropes (in the Borage family). The tongue-twisting epithet *tanacetifolia* means "tansy-leaf" (the common herb tansy is *Tanacetum*); the resemblance is not close.

FIVE-SPOT
NEMOPHILA MACULATA   *Plate 227*

Five-spot forms several stems, up to a foot long, which tend to lie on the ground with the tips growing upward. The leaves are paired, oblong, hairy. The flowers grow from the axils. The corolla forms a white bowl, each lobe marked with a purple blotch—whence the names, both English and Latin (*maculata* means "spotted"). ·

N. maculata grows in grasslands and on the slopes of the Sierra Nevada in California. It flowers from April to July.

BABY-BLUE-EYES
NEMOPHILA MENZIESII   *Plate 228*

Baby-blue-eyes is a rather succulent, branching plant which sprawls among other plants, the stems up to a foot long. The leaves are mostly paired, pinnately divided into

223 **PHLOX** PHLOX PILOSA   *224* **BIRD'S-EYES** GILIA TRICOLOR

225 **MUSTANG-CLOVER** LINANTHUS MONTANUS   *226* **WILD-HELIOTROPE** PHACELIA TANACETIFOLIA

toothed segments, beset with stiff hairs which lie flat. The flowers grow from the axils of leaves. The corolla is about an inch across, with five joined petals that make a five-pointed cup colored bright blue with a white center.

N. menziesii grows in moist grassy and brushy places in the coast ranges and foothills of the Sierra Nevada nearly throughout California. It blooms from February to June. It is quite variable in the degree of division of the leaves, in the color of the corolla, and in other characteristics. The name *Nemophila* means, in Greek, "glade-loving." The species, like many other western species, was named for Archibald Menzies of Scotland, the first botanist to visit the Pacific Coast (1792–1794).

THE BORAGE FAMILY
BORAGINACEAE

The *Boraginaceae* are generally roughly hairy plants. The flowers, which are commonly small, have parts in fives, except that the ovary is four-lobed and develops into four nutlets. The flowers are arranged in false racemes, coiled at the tip.

BLUEBELLS
MERTENSIA VIRIDIS
Plate 229

M. viridis has slender stems not much more than a foot tall. The lower leaves have blunt-ended blades on stalks; the upper ones are lance-shaped or elliptic, without stalks. The blue flowers grow in coiled clusters. The corolla is less than half an inch long.

M. viridis is a species of high altitudes and grows in the mountains from Wyoming to Idaho and south to Colorado, flowering from June to August.

BLUEBELLS or LANGUID-LADY
MERTENSIA CILIATA
Plate 230

This species of bluebells has a stem nearly two feet tall, bearing single oval or elliptic or lance-shaped leaves, the lower ones with stalks. The flowers are in a drooping coil at the summit. The corolla forms a hanging bell, at first pink, turning blue as it opens.

M. ciliata is common along streams in the mountains from Wyoming to Nevada and southward to New Mexico. It flowers from June to August. These bluebells are no relation to English bluebells (Lily family) or Scottish bluebells (Bluebell family).

FORGET-ME-NOT
MYOSOTIS SCORPIOIDES
Plate 231

Forget-me-not is a plant of wet places, often growing with its feet in the water, its stems spreading and branching. The leaves are lance-shaped or oblong and narrow, attached singly. The flowers grow alternately to right and to left along a stem that

227 **FIVE-SPOT** NEMOPHILA MACULATA

228 **BABY-BLUE-EYES** NEMOPHILA MENZIESII

229 **BLUEBELLS** MERTENSIA VIRIDIS

230
BLUEBELLS
MERTENSIA CILIATA

231
FORGET-ME-NOT
MYOSOTIS SCORPIOIDES

coils at the tip where the unopened buds are. The blue petals are joined to form a short tube which flares into five round, flat lobes; at the center is a bright yellow "eye." The fruit consists of four minute, one-seeded nuts.

M. scorpioides is a species naturalized from Europe, now found from Newfoundland to Ontario and southward to Georgia and Louisiana; also on the Pacific Coast; and in Europe and Asia. It flowers from May to August. The very similar *M. verna* is a North American native.

THE VERVAIN FAMILY
VERBENACEAE

The Vervain family is mainly a tropical group, represented in temperate regions principally by the genus *Verbena*. It is closely related to the Mint family, but differs in having an ovary that is not deeply four-lobed. The corolla is a tube which flares into five nearly equal lobes. There are usually four stamens.

SHRUB-VERBENA
LANTANA CAMARA
Plate 232

Shrub-verbena has prickly stems which reach a height of five feet. The leaves are paired, with ovate or elliptic, toothed, veiny blades on short stalks. The flowers are in very short spikes. The corolla is a narrow tube flaring abruptly into five broad lobes which are unequal in size. These are folded in the bud so as to make a four-cornered object. When it opens, the corolla is pale yellow or pink; as it ages, it turns orange or red. The ovary becomes a more or less succulent stone-fruit.

These decorative shrubs grow in sandy soil on the coastal plain from Georgia to Texas. They flower from spring to autumn; or, in Florida, all the year. Other species of *Lantana* are natives of the West Indies, Mexico, and Central and South America; several, including *L. camara,* are familiar in cultivation.

BLUE VERVAIN
VERBENA HASTATA
Plate 233

Blue vervain is a tall weed, up to four feet in height, with lance-shaped, toothed leaves; the lower leaves may have pointed lobes at the base ("hasta" is a spear). The stem is much branched in its upper part, each branch ending in a long, pointed spike of flowers. Only a few flowers, in a ring, are open at any time on each spike; but the petals are of a violet-blue so intense that the plant makes a good showing.

This species is often seen in fields, especially moist fields, and in other open, moist places, even in swamps; it grows practically throughout southern Canada and the United States, flowering from July to September.

"Vervain" was an adaptation of the Latin *verbena,* which was the name given to a European plant much used in sacred rites; apparently sometimes a name given to any branches carried in such rites. The European *V. officinalis* was also celebrated as a cure-all.

203

MOSS-VERBENA
VERBENA TENUISECTA

Plate 235

This vervain is inclined to sprawl on the ground. Its paired leaves are pinnately cleft or divided into a number of narrow lobes, these being often again cleft. The flowers are in spikes which tend to be flat-topped. The color is white, pink, or purple.

Moss-verbena is found in waste places, along roadsides, and in woods on the coastal plain from Georgia to Florida and Louisiana. It flowers from March to October; or, in Florida, throughout the year.

VERVAIN
VERBENA TAMPENSIS

Plate 236

This vervain is a branched herb with stems up to two feet long. The leaves are paired, lance-shaped or elliptic, and coarsely toothed (leaves of some other plant are seen in the photograph). The lavender-pink flowers are in spikes, which terminate the branches; the arrangement of the flowers makes the spikes flat-topped.

V. tampensis grows in sandy soil in the hammocks of southern Florida, flowering from December to June.

FALSE VERVAIN or BRAZILIAN-TEA
STACHYTARPHETA JAMAICENSIS

Plate 234

This is a shrub, the spreading branches reaching five feet in length. The leaves are ovate or elliptical, with teeth at the margin. The flowers grow in long rattail-like branches, only a few opening at one time; the base of each flower is immersed in a curious cavity in the thick stem. The corolla is a slender tube which flares into five almost equal violet lobes—the whole only about a quarter of an inch across.

Stachytarpheta is a plant of the Florida pinelands, sand-dunes, and keys (also of the West Indies and South and Central America). The flowers open from December to June.

THE MINT FAMILY
LABIATAE

Many plants of the mint family form essential oils which give them strong aromatic odors and tastes; the mints themselves are but one genus of this large group. The family is often recognized by the paired leaves growing on square stems (but there are exceptions). The flowers have a two-lipped corolla (there are exceptions to this too), with two or four stamens and a deeply four-lobed ovary, which becomes four nutlets. Many of our medicinal and culinary herbs belong to this family: oregano, basil, savory, sage, thyme, marjoram, and many others, besides spearmint, peppermint, and the variety that yields menthol.

233

234

235

236

237

238

239

240

HORSE-MINT
MONARDA CLINOPODIOIDES   *Plate 237*

This species is usually about a foot tall. The stem is downy. The leaves are sharply toothed. The flowers are in a head at the top of the stem and also in several dense clusters that surround the stem below the top, where pairs of leaves are attached. Each head or cluster is surrounded by many bracts which are ovate and taper sharply to a long spinelike end. The corolla is white or pale pink.

M. clinopodioides grows in dry soil in Kansas, Oklahoma, and Texas, blooming in June.

WILD BERGAMOT
MONARDA FISTULOSA   *Plate 238*

Wild bergamot sometimes grows to five feet in height but is generally about four feet tall. Its stem is usually unbranched, more or less hairy, bearing pairs of light green leaves which have lance-shaped or ovate blades on short stalks. The whole plant has a strong, minty smell. The flowers are in an ample head at the summit of the stem, with additional clusters often present in the axils of leaves just below. Each head is surrounded by pointed bracts, which may be tinged with pink. The narrow curved corolla of each flower is a bright lavender or even pink.

M. fistulosa is a familiar and handsome plant which grows in masses along roadsides and the borders of woods from Quebec to British Columbia and southward to Georgia, Alabama, Texas, and northern Mexico.

BEE-BALM or OSWEGO-TEA
MONARDA DIDYMA   *Plate 245*

Bee-balm has a stem three or four feet tall, bearing paired leaves and, at its summit, a head of bright red flowers. The leaves have dark green, ovate, toothed blades on stalks; they are hairy on the lower side. Around the head of flowers are several pointed bracts, which are red at the base or throughout. The corolla is narrow, curved, two-lipped, and much like that of wild bergamot in structure. The pure red color is typical, but similar species are known with pink or magenta-purple flowers.

Bee-balm is found in rich woods from New York to Michigan and southward, in the mountains, to Georgia and Tennessee; elsewhere it is cultivated and sometimes runs wild. The flowering period is July and August.

Like other red flowers, bee-balm is visited by hummingbirds, whose long tongues can penetrate the narrow, curved corolla and sip the nectar at its base. The Indians are said to have made a tea from the flowers.

PENNYROYAL
PYCNOTHYMUS RIGIDUS   *Plate 239*

This pennyroyal is a hairy shrub sometimes reaching two feet in height, but often low and spreading. The leaves are small and narrow. The pinkish-lavender flowers are in dense clusters at the ends of the branches.

233 **BLUE VERVAIN** VERBENA HASTATA   *234* **FALSE VERVAIN** STACHYTARPHETA JAMAICENSIS

235 **MOSS-VERBENA** VERBENA TENUISECTA   *236* **VERVAIN** VERBENA TAMPENSIS

       237 **HORSE-MINT** MONARDA CLINOPODIOIDES   *238* **WILD BERGAMOT** MONARDA FISTULOSA

       239 **PENNYROYAL** PYCNOTHYMUS RIGIDUS   *210* **SELF-HEAL** PRUNELLA VULGARIS

P. rigidus grows in the pinelands of Florida, flowering all the year. A tea is made from the leaves. True pennyroyal is a European herb, *Mentha pulegium,* long celebrated for many medicinal qualities and used also in puddings, whence the old English name of pudding-herb. "Pennyroyal" is, by devious etymological pathways, a corruption of *pulegium,* which in turn is derived from *pulex,* Latin for "flea"; the plant (or some plant like it) was thought to banish fleas!

SELF-HEAL
PRUNELLA VULGARIS   *Plate 240*

Prunella grows a foot or two tall, usually with several stems rising from one base. The leaves vary from lance-shaped to ovate or oblong; the plant may be hairy or smooth. The flowers are crowded with conspicuous bracts in a thick spike at the summit of each stem. The corolla varies from blue to violet (or even white). It is markedly two-lipped, the upper lip like a hood, the lower three-lobed.

Self-heal grows in grassy places, waste places, clearings, along roadsides, etc., throughout North America, often becoming a weed in gardens. It flowers from May to October. It is extremely variable, and the many varieties and forms have received names.

The botanical name was originally spelled *Brunella.* According to the herbalists it was so named by the Germans, who prescribed it as a remedy for "Bruen" (quinsy). The universal healing properties once ascribed to this herb are not borne out by modern science. This is one species of the mint family without a strong aromatic odor.

WILD THYME
THYMUS SERPYLLUM   *Plate 241*

Wild thyme is a creeping plant, the stems extending about a foot, bearing small, paired, ovate leaves. The ends of the stems rise and carry the spikes of small lavender-pink or purplish flowers. The flower is two-lipped. The corolla has two lobes above and three below.

Wild thyme comes from Europe, where there are many species. Here it is cultivated and has escaped into old fields and woodlands from Quebec to Ontario and south to North Carolina, Ohio, and Indiana; it is also found in Oregon. It flowers from June to September. This aromatic herb has long been known for various medicinal properties. According to the naturalist and poet Grigson, a tea made of wild thyme was drunk by Scots to prevent bad dreams, and the smell of the plant was supposed to confer strength and courage (which, certainly, few Highlanders lacked). The thyme used in cooking is another species, *T. vulgaris.*

LYRE-LEAVED SAGE
SALVIA LYRATA   *Plate 242*

This sage grows up to two feet tall, with a hairy stem. The leaves are mostly at the base and have the shape called "lyrate" by the botanist; that is, pinnately cleft,

241 **WILD THYME** THYMUS SERPYLLUM

242 **LYRE-LEAVED SAGE** SALVIA LYRATA

243 **WOOLLY-BLUE-CURLS** TRICHOSTEMA LANATUM

244 **WESTERN JIMSON-WEED** DATURA METELOIDES

245 **BEE-BALM** MONARDA DIDYMA

246 **PURPLE NIGHTSHADE** SOLANUM ELAEAGNIFOLIUM

with a large terminal lobe. (The resemblance between this shape and the musical instrument called a lyre seems extremely farfetched if not entirely mistaken.) The flowers are in circles with bare intervals of stem between. The violet corolla is markedly two-lipped, with a hooded, two-lobed upper lip and a spreading, three-lobed lower lip about an inch long. There are only two stamens, and they have a peculiar form: the anther is crescent-shaped, with pollen on the upper end of the crescent.

Lyre-leaved sage is found in woodlands and various other situations from Connecticut to Missouri and southward to Florida and Texas; it is especially abundant in Florida. It flowers from March to June. The genus *Salvia* is an extraordinary one, consisting of more than 800 known species, mainly native in South America. The brilliant red flowers of *S. splendens* are familiar in our gardens and parks. *S. officinalis*, of Europe, furnishes the herb for culinary use. These sages must not be confused with the "purple sage" of western plains and mountains, which belongs to a genus of the Daisy family; the only thing the two kinds of "sage" have in common is their aromatic foliage.

WOOLLY-BLUE-CURLS or ROMERO
TRICHOSTEMA LANATUM   *Plate 243*

This is a shrub up to five feet tall, with many branches. The very narrow leaves are woolly (*lanate*) on the lower surface. The flowers grow in tall spikes composed of small, dense clusters in the axils of bracts, partly immersed in the long woolly hairs. The corolla is pinkish in bud, blue when open.

Woolly-blue-curls grows on the dry slopes of the coast ranges in the southern half of California. It flowers from May to August. Several other species grow in the Pacific states, and one, *T. dichotomum*, from Maine to Michigan and south to North Carolina and Missouri. They are all known as blue-curls from the prominent curved, blue stamens.

A flower-head of tidy-tips intrudes into the lower part of the photograph.

THE POTATO FAMILY
SOLANACEAE

The Potato family is characterized by flower-parts in fives, the petals being united, and an ovary that contains numerous ovules in two chambers. The fruit is a berry or capsule. The family is known for the number of species that contain poisonous alkaloids: strychnine, atropine, nicotine, and others.

WESTERN JIMSON-WEED or THORNAPPLE
DATURA METELOIDES   *Plate 244*

The western Jimson-weed is a coarse, widely branching herb two or three feet tall. The leaves have ovate blades on stalks; they are coarsely but shallowly toothed. The flowers grow in forks of the stem (a very unusual arrangement). They are large trum-

212

247
MONKEY-FLOWER
MIMULUS GUTTATUS

248
INDIAN PAINTBRUSH
CASTILLEIA LANATA

pets; the calyx is a five-toothed cylinder, from which emerges the flaring tube of the corolla, which may be eight inches across its spreading, pointed lobes. The color is white tinged with violet. There are five stamens and a two-chambered pistil, which becomes a spiny capsule.

D. meteloides occurs in dry, open ground from Utah to southern California and southward into Mexico. The flowers are seen all summer, from April to October. Like the eastern Jimson-weed, this species is narcotic and poisonous. It is used in medicine, and Indians have used it to induce visions; there are records of deaths of persons and animals from eating parts of the plants.

PURPLE NIGHTSHADE
SOLANUM ELAEAGNIFOLIUM   *Plate 246*

Purple nightshade grows about three feet tall. The stem and leaves are covered with white hairs, each hair being branched, starlike; there are also usually sharp, yellowish prickles. The leaves, singly attached, are oblong or lance-shaped, with wavy margins. The corolla is bright purple, contrasting with the five bright yellow stamens, which do not quite come together around the style. The ovary forms a berry.

S. elaeagnifolium grows in deserts and along roadsides from Missouri to California and southward, flowering from April to August. Like many other species of the family, it contains a poisonous alkaloid. Another purple nightshade, *S. xanti*, has similar flowers but no spines on the leaves or stem. It occurs in Arizona, California, and Baja California.

THE SNAPDRAGON FAMILY
SCROPHULARIACEAE

The flowers of the Snapdragon family have five joined sepals and five petals which are joined to make a generally two-lipped corolla (in a few species flaring into four or five nearly equal lobes). Most species have two or four stamens, but a few have five. The pistil forms a capsule with many small seeds in its two chambers. This is a large family, familiar in gardens (snapdragons, foxgloves, beard-tongues, and others) as well as in the wild.

MONKEY-FLOWER
MIMULUS GUTTATUS   *Plate 247*

This species of monkey-flower has hollow stems that may partly recline on the ground and put out roots at the points where leaves are attached; or they may reach a height of three feet or more. The leaves are in pairs and ovate, often with a few teeth or sharp lobes near the base. The calyx is strongly angled. The corolla is two-lipped, the upper lip two-lobed, the lower with three lobes and a ridge or "palate" that closes the opening. The petals are bright yellow, variously spotted with red.

This is one of the commonest western species of *Mimulus*, growing in wet places from Alaska to Mexico and often cultivated farther east. *Mimulus* is a large genus,

214

with seventy-seven species listed on the West Coast, and several in the East; the flowers are mostly blue or purple or yellow. The name means "little clown" (compare "mimic") in reference to the amusing "face" made by the corolla seen face-on. All the species are known by the same English name. *M. guttatus* is cultivated in England and has run wild there. The other flower in the photograph is bitter cress.

PINK MONKEY-FLOWER
MIMULUS LEWISII   *Plate 252*

The stem of *M. lewisii* varies from one to two feet tall; it is somewhat downy and clammy. The leaves are paired and lance-shaped or ovate. The flowers grow singly from their axils. Each has a five-angled, five-toothed calyx and a rose-pink corolla with five nearly equal lobes; the lowest lobe is notched, bears yellow hairs, and is yellow at the base. The opening of the corolla is not closed as it is in some other species of *Mimulus*.

Pink monkey-flower is abundant in wet meadows high in the mountains, from Montana to British Columbia and southward to Utah and California. It flowers from June to August.

INDIAN PAINTBRUSH
CASTILLEIA LANATA   *Plate 248*

C. lanata is about eighteen inches tall. The stem is covered with a close white wool (*lanata* means "woolly"). The leaves are narrowly lance-shaped with gradually tapering tips. The bracts are undivided, rather broad and blunt, and of a dusky pink or red color.

This is a plant of dry ground, mostly in mountains, from Wyoming to Texas and Arizona. It flowers from February (in Arizona) to July.

SEASIDE PAINTED-CUP
CASTILLEIA LATIFOLIA   *Plate 253*

Among the numerous and confusing species of *Castilleia*, the seaside painted-cup is distinguished by its rather broad leaves and bracts which are round at the end and hairy on the outer side; each bract has two lobes on the sides, narrower than the central part. The slim yellowish flowers project beyond the bracts.

C. latifolia grows along the California coast south of San Francisco. It flowers from February to September. A closely related species, *C. mendocinensis*, extends along the coast northward.

INDIAN PAINTBRUSH
CASTILLEIA RUPICOLA   *Plate 256*

C. rupicola has many downy stems in a tuft, rising to a height of six or eight inches. The leaves, which are borne singly, are cleft into from three to seven narrow lobes, arranged more or less palmately. The bracts in the spike of flowers are similarly cleft, but the lobes are a bright scarlet. These lobes are what one sees and takes for flowers; the actual flowers are insignificant.

C. rupicola adorns cliffs and rocky slopes at high altitudes with masses of scarlet bloom. It was discovered by C. V. Piper, an authority on western plants, in 1888 on Mt. Rainier—where the photograph shown in this book was made. It flowers in July and August.

SCARLET BUGLER
PENSTEMON CENTRANTHIFOLIUS   *Plate 257*

Scarlet bugler grows up to three feet tall. The stem bears pairs of gray-green, lance-shaped leaves, mostly without stalks; the upper ones have basal "ears" which "clasp" the stem. The flowers grow in a narrow but loose cluster, the individual groups springing from the axils of bracts and all tending toward the same side of the stem. The joined petals form a scarlet trumpet about an inch long, with five small teeth at the end. As in other penstemons, there are five stamens of which the lowest has no anther. In many species this sterile stamen has a "beard" of hairs; in *P. centranthifolius* this is lacking. The fruit is a small, pointed capsule.

Scarlet bugler grows in dry places, chiefly in disturbed soil, in the coast ranges of California (commoner southward) and in Baja California. It flowers from April to July. A very similar species, occurring from Utah to California on dry rocky slopes, is *P. eatoni*. It is not gray-green, and the lowest stamen may be bearded.

Penstemon is a large genus in the West, fifty-eight species being listed for California alone. Several are cultivated in rock gardens. Many of the species are difficult to distinguish.

CRIMSON BEARD-TONGUE
PENSTEMON RUPICOLA   *Plate 249*

Crimson beard-tongue has stems that lie on the surface of the ground, often forming mats. The leaves, which are in pairs, are round or ovate, slightly scalloped on the edges, and with a whitish bloom. They are only about half an inch long. The flowering stems rise erect to a height of about four inches, bearing relatively large crimson flowers (nearly two inches long). The anthers are hairy, but the sterile stamen has no "beard." The corolla is markedly two-lipped, the opening mouthlike.

Crimson beard-tongue is a plant of cliffs and other rocky places (*rupicola* means "rock-inhabiting") mostly at high altitudes in the Cascade Mountains of Washington. It flowers from May to August, depending on altitude.

BEARD-TONGUE
PENSTEMON HETEROPHYLLUS   *Plate 251*

This penstemon has stems up to eighteen inches tall, growing in clumps and more or less woody. The leaves are very narrow and grow usually in bunches. The flowers

249

250

251

252

253

251

251 A

255

249 CRIMSON BEARD-TONGUE
PENSTEMON RUPICOLA

250 MULLEIN
VERBASCUM THAPSUS

251 BEARD-TONGUE
PENSTEMON HETEROPHYLLUS

252 PINK MONKEY-FLOWER
MIMULUS LEWISII

253 SEASIDE PAINTED-CUP
CASTILLEIA LATIFOLIA

254 LITTLE-RED-ELEPHANT
PEDICULARIS GROENLANDICA

254 A BEARD-TONGUE
PENSTEMON CANESCENS

255 LILAC BEARD-TONGUE
PENSTEMON DAVIDSONII

grow in the narrow but loose cluster characteristic of the penstemons. Each has a rose corolla tipped with five blue lobes. The sterile stamen has no "beard."

P. heterophyllus grows on dry hillsides in the coast ranges of California, flowering from April to July.

BEARD-TONGUE
PENSTEMON CANESCENS   *Plate 254 A*

This penstemon grows up to three feet tall. The stem is downy or sometimes hairy, and the leaves are ovate or lance-shaped, round or indented at the base. The violet or purplish corolla enlarges suddenly above a narrow tube, the two upper lobes erect, the lower lip extending forward. The sterile stamen is bearded.

P. canescens grows in open woods and thickets, mostly in uplands, from Pennsylvania to Indiana and southward to Georgia and Alabama. It flowers from May to July.

LILAC BEARD-TONGUE
PENSTEMON DAVIDSONII   *Plate 255*

This beard-tongue, like *P. rupicola*, grows lying on the ground, forming mats. The leaves are oval, or widest and blunt at the tips, about half an inch long. Only the flowering stalks stand erect, each bearing a close cluster of lilac-pink flowers. The flower-stalks and sepals bear minute, gland-tipped hairs.

Lilac beard-tongue grows on rocks high in the mountains from western Washington to California. It flowers from June to August.

MULLEIN
VERBASCUM THAPSUS   *Plate 250*

Common mullein appears first as a rosette of broad, overlapping leaves close to the ground, all covered with dense white wool (agreeable to the bare feet of small persons). Through a magnifier, each hair of a leaf is seen to be branched, like a miniature tree. The second year the flowering stem rises from the center of the rosette, sometimes more than six feet tall, often branched. The small yellow flowers would make an attractive showing if more than two or three were open at one time.

Mullein is a native of Europe, but now grows throughout North America, in all sorts of open places, especially in rocky and sterile soil, even exposed to the burning sun of the dry canyons of Arizona.

It is called in England Aaron's-rod, also Adam's-flannel, poor-man's-blanket, etc. "Mullein" is related to the Latin *mollis*, "soft." "Aaron's-rod" refers to supposed magical powers of the tall stem, which was reputed to ward off wild beasts and other dangers.

The tall spikes often stand, gaunt dried sticks, through the winter along roadsides and in rocky fields.

256 **INDIAN PAINTBRUSH** CASTILLEIA RUPICOLA   *257* **SCARLET BUGLER** PENSTEMON CENTRANTHIFOLIUS

258 **OWL'S-CLOVER** ORTHOCARPUS PURPURASCENS   *259* **CHINESE-HOUSES** COLLINSIA HETEROPHYLLA

256

257

258

259

LITTLE-RED-ELEPHANT
PEDICULARIS GROENLANDICA

Plate 254

The reason for the English name is at once evident from a glance at the flowers. The upper lip of the corolla is extended in a long, narrow, red proboscis which curls upward; the two lateral lobes of the lip give an amusing imitation of an elephant's large ears. The lower lip is completely hidden. The reddish flowers are on a stem that extends far above the leaves. The leaves are pinnately cleft or divided into narrow lobes or segments.

The little-red-elephant grows in moist meadows, chiefly in coniferous forests, from Greenland to British Columbia and southward in the mountains to Colorado and California. It flowers from June to August. Eastern species, as *P. canadensis*, have flowers densely massed in a spike or head, and a small beak on the tip of the corolla instead of an elephant's trunk. They are called lousewort, from the old English belief that cattle that grazed on them became infested with lice (as they probably did). The Latin name, from *pediculus*, "louse," refers to the same superstition. They are also known as wood betony.

OWL'S-CLOVER or PAINT-BRUSH
ORTHOCARPUS PURPURASCENS

Plate 258

Owl's-clover is an annual growing a foot or more tall. The stem, which is generally branched as in the photograph, bears many pinnately cleft leaves with narrow lobes. The flowers are in a dense spike at the summit of each branch, each in the axil of a palmately lobed bract, which is greenish at the base and rose-crimson toward the tips of the lobes. The whole forms a dense crimson mass.

Owl's-clover grows in open places in the central valley and the coast ranges of California; and south and southeastward to Arizona and northern Mexico. It flowers from March to May. It may grow mixed with gold-fields (Daisy family) and lupines (Bean family), forming brilliant floral fields.

CHINESE-HOUSES or INNOCENCE
COLLINSIA HETEROPHYLLA

Plate 259

The peculiarity of the genus *Collinsia* is in its corolla, which has five lobes but only four visible lobes. The petals are joined part-way to form a tube (in many species bulging on the upper side). At the end of the tube the upper lip, formed as usual of two lobes, stands erect. The lower lip extends forward, composed of three lobes; but the central lobe is folded and entirely concealed by the lobes on either side, which are contiguous. In *C. heterophylla* the upper lip is white (or nearly so) and the lower lip violet. The stamens and pistil are concealed within the folded and invisible lobe of the lower lip.

C. heterophylla is common in shady places, often on rocky ground, through most of California west of the Sierra Nevada, and into Baja California. It flowers from March to June. *Collinsia* is a genus of many species, with petals of many different colors. Two species occur in the East, of which the commonest, *C. verna*, has a white upper corolla-lip and blue lower lip; it is called blue-eyed-Mary. The name innocence is shared by a common species of bluets, in the Bedstraw family.

THE BLADDERWORT FAMILY
LENTIBULARIACEAE

The bladderworts are small plants which grow in water or mud, only their flowering stems standing up above the surface. Their leaves consist of many threadlike divisions, on which are the little bladders that give them the name; these trap minute insects. The leaves may be immersed partly or wholly in water, or they may creep beneath the soft soil. The family also includes the butterworts (*Pinguicula*), which catch insects on sticky leaves.

HORNED BLADDERWORT
UTRICULARIA CORNUTA   *Plate 260*

U. cornuta grows on wet soil, its leaves mostly underground. Its stem rises about a foot above the surface, bearing a few yellow flowers in a narrow cluster. The calyx is two-lipped, with one lobe above and one below. The corolla also is two-lipped, the upper lip having two lobes; the lower, three. The opening is closed by a ridge or "palate" on the lower lip. From the base of the corolla a long hollow tube or "spur" —the "horn"—extends downward. The ovary has one chamber, which contains several ovules.

The horned bladderwort grows at the edges of pools and in bogs from Newfoundland to Minnesota and southward to Florida and Texas. The flowers appear from June to September.

THE ACANTHUS FAMILY
ACANTHACEAE

The Acanthus family is largely tropical. The flower-parts are typically in fives, except the stamens, which are generally two or four. The petals are joined and usually form a two-lipped corolla (*Ruellia* is exceptional in this).

RUELLIA
RUELLIA HUMILIS   *Plate 261*

Ruellia humilis (which seems not to have acquired an English name) is a branching plant about two feet tall with paired, oblong or ovate, stalkless leaves. The stem is often hairy, and the leaves generally bear long hairs in a fringe at their margins. The flowers grow in small clusters in the axils of the leaves. The calyx ends in five teeth

260

261

262

263

so narrow as to be hairlike, with fringes of hairs like those on the leaves. The corolla is a tube one or two inches long, expanding into five lobes which add a half-inch to its length; the color is blue.

R. humilis grows in all sorts of places, chiefly open and dry, from Pennsylvania to Nebraska and southward to Florida and Texas. It flowers from May to August, or later in the South. It is extremely variable in size of corolla, shape of leaves, and hairiness, and on such characteristics has been divided into several varieties.

THE BEDSTRAW FAMILY
RUBIACEAE

The Bedstraw family is a very large family in the tropics. The species of the United States are mostly herbaceous (one is a shrub) with leaves paired or in circles. The flower-parts number from three to five. The petals are joined and radially symmetric. The ovary is inferior.

LADY'S or YELLOW BEDSTRAW
GALIUM VERUM
Plate 262

Lady's bedstraw grows about three feet tall, bearing at intervals circles of six or eight short, narrow, stiff, and rather rough leaves. The flowers are tiny but very numerous, crowded in a tall cluster at the summit of the stem. Each flower has four yellow petals and four stamens. They are honey-scented, and the dried herbage has the smell of hay.

Lady's bedstraw is a native of Europe, now established in dry fields and along roadsides from Newfoundland to Ontario and North Dakota; and southward to Virginia, Ohio, Missouri, and Kansas. It flowers from June to August. In its native countries it often forms wide, sweet-smelling mats. Many superstitions gathered round it in northern Europe, especially connected with childbirth. According to medieval legend, the Virgin lay upon it at the Nativity; whence the later version of the name, "Our Lady's bedstraw." The plant has had many other uses: curdling milk in cheesemaking, as a source of a red dye, coagulating blood, and as an astringent to repel fleas in bed. *Galium* is a large genus with many native American species—mostly small weeds with inconspicuous flowers. White bedstraw, also sweet-smelling, is *G. septentrionale.*

BLUETS or QUAKER-LADIES
HOUSTONIA CAERULEA
Plate 263

These tiny plants grow only about six inches tall and are often much shorter. The flowering stems arise in tufts from slender rhizomes, with a rosette of tiny leaves at the base, and even smaller leaves in pairs on the stems. Each stem ends in a single flower. The corolla is a narrow tube expanding into four pointed, horizontal lobes; these are blue (or sometimes white) with a yellow center.

0 **HORNED BLADDERWORT** UTRICULARIA CORNUTA   *261* **RUELLIA** RUELLIA HUMILIS

2 **LADY'S OR YELLOW BEDSTRAW** GALIUM VERUM   *263* **BLUETS** HOUSTONIA CAERULEA

264

265

266

267

268

269

270

271

Bluets adorn many a field, meadow, and open slope from Nova Scotia to Wisconsin and southward to Georgia, Alabama, and Missouri. They flower in early spring, from April to June. One variety extends high in the mountains of New England. The flowers are of two kinds: one with short stamens far down in the tube of the corolla and a style that projects from it; in the other the position of these parts is reversed. (See purple loosestrife, *Lythrum salicaria*.)

THE HONEYSUCKLE FAMILY
CAPRIFOLIACEAE

The *Caprifoliaceae* are mostly shrubs and vines with paired leaves. In some species the flowers also are in pairs and even partly joined in each pair. The flower-parts are mostly in fives. The petals are joined, making a tubular corolla which usually flares at the end. The ovary is inferior. It forms a berry or stone-fruit.

TWIN-FLOWER
LINNAEA BOREALIS
Plate 264

Twin-flower has a slender, creeping stem from which arise erect branches about six inches tall. The leaves are evergreen and ovate with a few blunt teeth and short stalks. At the summit of each of these branches are two forks, from each of which hangs a small, fragrant, pink or white flower (about half an inch long).

Linnaea grows all round the pole (wherever plants can grow) and south in North America to Maryland, Pennsylvania, Indiana, South Dakota, Colorado, and northern California. It flowers from June to August.

The name commemorates Carl Linnaeus, the celebrated Swedish naturalist from whom we date our method of naming genera and species, and who invented the first usable system of classification of plants. He liked to be painted with a sprig of twin-flower in his hand.

BUSH HONEYSUCKLE
DIERVILLA LONICERA
Plate 265

Most of our honeysuckles are vines; *Diervilla* is a small shrub with ovate, toothed, stalked leaves. The flower-stalks spring mostly from the axils of the upper leaves, each bearing usually three flowers. The corolla is at first yellow but turns red as it ages.

Bush honeysuckle grows in dry woods and clearings, often among rocks, from Newfoundland to Manitoba and southward to Delaware, North Carolina (in the mountains), Illinois, and Iowa. It flowers from June to August.

JAPANESE HONEYSUCKLE
LONICERA JAPONICA
Plate 266

Japanese honeysuckle creeps on the ground, rooting frequently and forming mats, or clambers and twines over fences, other plants, and any other objects available. Its

264 **TWIN-FLOWER** LINNAEA BOREALIS   265 **BUSH HONEYSUCKLE** DIERVILLA LONICERA
266 **JAPANESE HONEYSUCKLE** LONICERA JAPONICA   267 **TRUMPET OR CORAL HONEYSUCKLE** LONICERA SEMPERVIRENS
268 **GREAT BLUE LOBELIA** LOBELIA SIPHILITICA   269 **CARDINAL-FLOWER** LOBELIA CARDINALIS
270 **HAREBELL** CAMPANULA ROTUNDIFOLIA   271 **BELLFLOWER** CAMPANULA RAPUNCULOIDES

stem is slender but very tough. The leaves are oblong or ovate, often pinnately lobed, downy or smooth. The yellowish flowers are usually in pairs on short stalks which grow from the axils of leaves. The flower is very sweet-smelling. The fruit is a black berry.

Japanese honeysuckle, coming from eastern Asia, has become a pernicious weed from Massachusetts to Kansas and southward to Florida and Texas. Especially in eastern and southeastern states it clambers over trees, strangling and destroying entire groves. It is cultivated in the West, where it apparently does not escape. It is planted also in the East, as a ground cover and to hold embankments; because it so easily becomes a weed, such a use of the plant is dangerous. It flowers all summer; but masses of the vine often bear no flowers or fruit.

TRUMPET or CORAL HONEYSUCKLE
LONICERA SEMPERVIRENS
Plate 267

Like other honeysuckles, trumpet honeysuckle is a twining plant which supports itself on other plants or inanimate objects. The leaves, in pairs, are elliptical or oblong and tend to be white on the lower surface. The pair just under the flowers meet around the stem to form an oblong disc; sometimes two pairs take this form. The red flowers are generally in pairs, the pairs in clusters which hang at the ends of a branch. The fruit is a red berry.

Trumpet honeysuckle is found in woods and thickets from Massachusetts to Nebraska and southward to Florida and Texas. It is often cultivated, and plants in the northern part of this range are probably "escapes" from cultivation. It flowers from March to July.

THE BLUEBELL FAMILY
CAMPANULACEAE

This family is divided into two subfamilies: the bluebells and the lobelias. Both have milky juice in many species, and singly attached, undivided leaves. In both, the flower-parts are in fives, the petals joined. The bluebells have a radially symmetric corolla and five separate stamens. The lobelias have a bilaterally symmetric corolla split on the upper side; through the split emerge the five joined stamens, which form a tube around the style. In both subfamilies the ovary is inferior.

GREAT BLUE LOBELIA
LOBELIA SIPHILITICA
Plate 268

The great blue lobelia may reach a height of four feet but is commonly about half that size. The stem forms offshoots from its base, which send up new stems the next summer. The ovate or lance-shaped leaves are toothed at the margins. The showy flowers are usually densely arranged along the upper part of the stem, but are looser in the midwestern variety illustrated. The corolla is two-lipped; the lower lip has three large pointed lobes extending downward, colored blue or purplish, generally white at the top; the upper lip has two relatively small erect blue lobes. The stamen-

272
SPANISH-NEEDLES
BIDENS ARISTOSA

273
WILD ASTER
ASTER PATENS

274
BLANKET-FLOWER
GAILLARDIA PULCHELLA

tube and style arch through the split in the tube of the corolla and appear just between or above the lobes of the upper lip.

This lobelia inhabits low woods, swamps, roadside ditches, and wet grassy places from New England to Manitoba and southward to Virginia, the mountains of North Carolina, and Alabama, Louisiana, and Texas. It flowers in August and September. The Latin name refers to supposed curative properties.

CARDINAL-FLOWER
LOBELIA CARDINALIS   *Plate 269*

Cardinal-flower is one of the most striking of wildflowers for both the shape and color of its flowers. These grow in a narrow cluster, rising sometimes four or five feet above the ground, though usually the plant is not so tall. Each flower has a deep-red, two-lipped corolla of five joined petals; this resembles that of the great blue lobelia in the arrangement of its parts. The long tube of the stamens has a brush or "beard" of short hairs at the tip. The style and the stigma (its branches folded together) emerge through this tube after the pollen has been shed. The leaves are lance-shaped and toothed.

Cardinal-flower flaunts its red flowers at the margins of rivers and in damp meadows and swamps from Quebec to Minnesota and southward to Florida and Texas. A similar species, with narrower leaves and shorter stamens, grows in California and Mexico, extending eastward to Missouri and Texas. Only a few species of *Lobelia* grow in North America. Many more grow in South America, some being shrubs or even trees.

The name refers to the color of the vestments of the Roman Catholic cardinal.

HAREBELL
CAMPANULA ROTUNDIFOLIA   *Plate 270*

The harebell has a very slender, branched stem about a foot tall, or taller. At first sight the epithet *rotundifolia* ("round-leafed") seems strangely inappropriate, for the leaves on the stem are very narrow, almost hairlike. But at the base one may find small leaves with round or oval blades on stalks. The bell-shaped blue flowers hang singly from the tips of the branches.

The harebell grows in northern latitudes all around the world, on cliffs, in other rocky places, even in meadows, from sea level up to more than 6,000 feet above. It flowers from June to September. This is the "bluebells of Scotland," but not the English bluebell (Lily family) nor the Virginia-bluebell (Borage family). *C. rotundifolia* has naturally acquired many other names in its wide dispersion; among the English names are fairy-bells, ding-dongs, fairy-thimbles, and granny's-tears. According to the English poet and naturalist Grigson, the "hare" of harebell is a witch animal.

BELLFLOWER
CAMPANULA RAPUNCULOIDES

Plate 271

Bellflower grows to a height of three feet or more. The lower leaves have heart-shaped blades on long stalks; the upper ones have ovate blades with short stalks or none. The flowers grow along the upper part of the stem, each drooping slightly. The five joined petals form the dark-blue bell, which has five teeth at its rim.

This bellflower is an immigrant from Europe, now found growing along roadsides and in thickets and other places from Newfoundland to North Dakota and southward to Maryland, Ohio, Illinois, and Missouri. It flowers from July to September.

THE DAISY FAMILY
COMPOSITAE

The Daisy or Composite family is the largest family of flowering plants, and one of the most distinctive. Its flowers are individually small, but they grow in large clusters—heads—which are often mistaken for single flowers. In the "flower" of a daisy, for instance, each of the white "rays," which may be taken for a petal, is a flower: a "ray-flower." The yellow center of the flower-head, the "disc," is occupied by "disc-flowers," which are tubular, usually with a five-toothed corolla, five stamens, and an inferior ovary. At the base of the corolla there is in many species (not in the common white daisy) a circle, or pair, of scales, hairs, spines, or bristles, called the "pappus"; this is considered to represent the calyx.

Many species of this family, as ironweeds and thistles, lack the rays. Others, as dandelion, have all their flowers raylike in appearance.

The "seeds" of sunflower, dandelion, and other composites are really achenes, each composed of the receptacle containing the inferior ovary with its one seed.

BLANKET-FLOWER or FIREWHEEL
GAILLARDIA PULCHELLA

Plate 274

Gaillardia pulchella is an annual about a foot tall. The stem bears many leaves, attached singly. The lower leaves may be pinnately cleft; the upper ones are mostly lance-shaped. Large flower-heads terminate the erect branches. The rays are red with yellow tips, or wholly red. The disc is yellow but turns red as the anthers emerge. Several small scales make up the pappus.

This is the species from which the garden gaillardias have mostly been developed. It occurs wild from Nebraska to Colorado, southward to Louisiana and Arizona, flowering from May to September. In many other parts of North America, from California to Florida and northward, it may be found as an "escape" from cultivation.

BLANKET-FLOWER
GAILLARDIA PINNATIFIDA

Plate 296

This blanket-flower grows on a branching stem a foot or more tall. The leaves, which are attached singly, are cleft pinnately into narrow lobes ("pinnatifida"); or

275 **BLACK-EYED-SUSAN**	*276* **DESERT-DANDELION**	*277* **PAPER-FLOWER**
RUDBECKIA SEROTINA	MALACOTHRIX CALIFORNICA	PSILOSTROPHE COOPERI
278 **GOLDEN-YARROW**	*279* **STAR-THISTLE**	*280* **BAHIA**
ERIOPHYLLUM CONFERTIFLORUM	CENTAUREA MACULOSA	BAHIA ABSINTHIFOLIA
281 **MILK-THISTLE**	*282* **DESERT-MARIGOLD**	*283* **TALL TICKSEED**
SILYBUM MARIANUM	BAILEYA PLENIRADIATA	COREOPSIS TRIPTERIS

275

276

277

278

279

280

281

282

283

some of the leaves are very narrow and not lobed. The flower-heads terminate long leafless branches. The rays are yellow and three-lobed at the end. The orange disc is convex. A few bristle-tipped scales make up the pappus. The achenes are covered with long white hairs.

This blanket-flower grows on plains and low hills from Colorado to Texas, New Mexico, and Arizona. The flowers are seen from May to October. Several other species of *Gaillardia* occur in the Southwest.

TALL TICKSEED
COREOPSIS TRIPTERIS   *Plate 283*

Tall tickseed earns its name by sometimes attaining a height of ten feet; but three feet is more usual. The erect stems grow from a rhizome, which also sends out runners. The larger leaves have three or five narrow segments at the tip of a long stalk; those on the upper parts of the stem are not divided. The stem is branched above, each branch bearing a flower-head. The genus *Coreopsis* (with its close relative *Bidens*, beggar-ticks) is distinguished by its involucre—the circle of bracts around the flower-head. This is composed of bracts of two kinds. In *C. tripteris* the outer are narrow and spread widely; the inner are both broader and longer, overlapping around the base of the flowers of the head. The rays are bright yellow, toothed at the end. The disc is a darker yellow, becoming brown or purplish. The pappus may consist of two small spines with upward-pointing teeth on their sides, or of a few bristles; or it may be lacking.

Tall tickseed is found along the edges of woods and roadsides, and in various other situations, from Massachusetts and southern Ontario to Wisconsin, and southward and southwestward to Florida and Texas. Through much of this range, especially in the northeast, it has escaped from cultivation.

The genus owes its English and botanical names to the fancied resemblance of its "seed" (really its achene) to a tick. This is more marked in some species than in others. Several species are common in gardens. Some species form beautiful roadside masses in Kansas and other western and southwestern states.

SPANISH-NEEDLES or TICKSEED-SUNFLOWER
BIDENS ARISTOSA   *Plate 272*

Spanish-needles is an annual (or perhaps perennial) with stems up to four feet tall but usually less. The leaves are pinnately divided into narrow, toothed segments— and these may be subdivided. The flower-heads terminate the branches. The involucre (like that of a *Coreopsis*) is composed of two kinds of bracts: the outer of very narrow, green bracts; the inner, of broader and more delicate bracts. The bright yellow rays are pointed, scarcely toothed. The pappus is composed of two spines (still present on the achene), with teeth or barbs on their sides, which may point upward or downward.

Spanish-needles grow in open fields, especially in slight depressions where water may run, from Delaware to Minnesota and southward to Virginia, Louisiana, and

Texas; and is occasionally found in the northeastern states. In the midwest it often forms carpets of gold in low fields, and is valued for the dark, distinctively flavored honey that bees make from its nectar. Its flowering period is from August to October. *Bidens* means "two-teeth," in reference to the pappus. It is a large genus; most of the species are much less handsome than this.

SHEPHERD'S-NEEDLE
BIDENS LEUCANTHA   *Plate 291*

Shepherd's-needle has a stem which may be three or four feet tall, its leaves mostly paired and pinnately divided into ovate or lance-shaped, toothed segments. As in *Coreopsis,* the flower-heads of *Bidens* have an involucre composed of two unlike kinds of bracts: the outer ones of *B. leucantha* are narrow, short, and spreading; the inner ones, broader and pressed together. The pappus consists of from two to four barbed spines, which are present on the mature achene.

B. leucantha grows in all sorts of places, especially along roadsides and on waste ground, on the coastal plain in Florida, and less abundantly in Georgia and Alabama. It flowers all the year round. It is exceptional in this genus in having white rays; most species have yellow rays, or none. Because of their barbed spines the flat achenes of this and other species of *Bidens* are caught by clothing and by the hair of animals, often in great numbers, earning them the name of beggar-ticks or Spanish-needles. Many species are weeds with inconspicuous flowers; but some make golden carpets in fields (see *B. aristosa*).

WILD ASTER
ASTER PATENS   *Plate 273*

Aster patens has a rather rough stem, up to three feet tall, usually unbranched except near the top. The leaves are distinctive, being oblong, blunt, and without stalks; the blades have two basal lobes that "clasp" the stem (i.e., project on either side of it). The flower-heads terminate the branches. The clear blue rays number about twenty-five.

A. patens grows in dry woods and sometimes in thickets and open places from Maine to Minnesota and southward to Florida and Texas. It flowers from August to October.

The great genus *Aster* has many species in the eastern United States, whose identification depends usually on minute characteristics. Even most botanists cannot name all of them. The above species, however, is easy to distinguish.

FLEABANE or WILD DAISY
ERIGERON SP.*   *Plate 284*

The genus *Erigeron* is an enormous one; California alone has forty-six species; Arizona lists twenty-three; and other western states contribute their quotas; the eastern states also have a few. In appearance an *Erigeron* is much like an *Aster.* The principal distinction is in the bracts of the involucre, which in this genus are in a single circle. The rays are mostly blue, lavender, or white; the disc, usually yellow. The pappus is composed of fine bristles.

Identification of a plant in this group is impossible without a complete and carefully collected specimen in hand.

*Species unknown.

MOUNTAIN-DAISY
ERIGERON CALLIANTHEMUS   *Plate 285*

Mountain-daisy has a downy stem some two feet tall, bearing leaves singly. The leaves at the base are stalked, their blades widest near the end; those on the stem have no stalks and are lance-shaped. There is often but one flower-head at the summit; or there may be several, on short branches. The numerous rays (fifty to seventy) are rose-lavender or purplish, the disc yellow; the whole head is more than an inch across.

Mountain-daisy is abundant in high mountain meadows from Wyoming to Alberta and British Columbia and southward to New Mexico and California. It flowers in July and August. It is treated by some botanists as a subspecies of the extremely variable *E. peregrinus*.

SEASIDE-DAISY
ERIGERON GLAUCUS   *Plate 302*

The hairy and sticky stem of seaside-daisy starts by leaning and then curves upward to as much as a foot or more. It and a rosette of rather thick leaves grow from a crown at ground-level or from an offset. There are leaves on the stems also. The flower-heads are at the tips of branches; they may be nearly two inches across. The bracts around the head—the involucre—are all equal and in one circle. This distinguishes *Erigeron* from *Aster*. There are about a hundred lavender rays. The pappus is composed of fine hairs.

Seaside-daisy grows on beaches, sand dunes, and bluffs along the west coast from southern Oregon to southern California, and in the Santa Barbara Islands. It flowers from April to August. The rather succulent leaves are characteristic of many beach plants.

DAISY FLEABANE
ERIGERON PHILADELPHICUS   *Plate 306*

E. philadelphicus is usually about three feet tall. The stem is softly hairy. The leaves, mostly at the base, are oblong and toothed; there are a few smaller leaves on the stem, "clasping" the stem between their projecting lobes. The stem branches several times near the summit, the branches bearing the flower-heads at their tips. There are a hundred or more narrow rays, varying from white to pink or lavender. The pappus is of slender, white bristles.

234

284 **FLEABANE** ERIGERON *sp.*

285 **MOUNTAIN-DAISY** ERIGERON CALLIANTHEM

286

287

288

289

290

291

292

293

294

The daisy fleabane is a common species of fields, roadsides, meadows, etc., from Labrador to British Columbia and southward to Florida, Texas, and California. It flowers from April to August. The epithet *philadelphicus* obviously does not mean that it grows only in Philadelphia, but only that it was first named there. A similar species, robin's-plantain (*E. pulchellus*), has fewer rays, often only one head to a stem, and leaves that do not "clasp."

HAWKWEED
HIERACIUM CUSICKII   *Plate 290*

This western species grows up to three feet tall. The basal leaves and those on the lower part of the stem are long and narrow. Higher on the stem they are smaller. Stem and leaves are beset with long, rather stiff hairs, and the bracts bear blackish hairs tipped with glands. The flowers are a bright yellow.

H. cusickii is found in dry open places from Wyoming to British Columbia and southward to Utah and Oregon. The flowering season is from June to August.

DEVIL'S-PAINTBRUSH
HIERACIUM AURANTIACUM   *Plate 293*

Devil's-paintbrush grows two feet tall or more from spreading runners. The leaves are mostly at the base of the stems; they are elliptical or lance-shaped with the broadest part toward the tip. The whole plant is covered with coarse hairs. The almost or entirely leafless stems branch near the top, the many short branches ending in the flower-heads. The bracts of the involucre are narrow, sharp-pointed, and covered with black hairs. The flowers are orange. The pappus is a rather dirty white.

Devil's-paintbrush comes from Europe and is now a pernicious (if handsome) weed in fields and waste places through the northeastern part of the United States (Newfoundland to Minnesota, southward to Virginia, Illinois, and Iowa); also in western Washington and Oregon. It flowers from June to August. Other species of *Hieracium* from Europe, equally unwelcome, are *H. pratense* and *H. floribundum*, both known as king-devil. They resemble *H. aurantiacum* but have yellow flowers. The numerous species of *Hieracium* are also called hawkweed, which is a translation into English of the Latin name of the genus, this having been derived from the Greek word for a hawk. An ancient superstition held that hawks swooped on the leaves of these plants, the juice thus obtained sharpening their eyesight.

BLACK-EYED-SUSAN or NIGGER-HEAD
RUDBECKIA SEROTINA   *Plate 275*

The stem of black-eyed-Susan may be three feet tall. There is a tuft of leaves at the base, these narrow with the widest part toward the tip. There are also leaves of various sizes and shapes on the stem. The whole plant is more or less bristly. The flower-heads terminate the stems. The bright yellow rays are often bent downward about the middle. The conical center is not really black but a purplish brown. There is no pappus.

286 **PINCUSHION-FLOWER**   287 **YARROW**   288 **GROUNDSEL**
   CHAENACTIS GLABRIUSCULA   ACHILLEA LANULOSA   SENECIO LONGILOBUS

     289 **COBWEB THISTLE**   290 **HAWKWEED**   291 **SHEPHERD'S-NEEDLE**
        CIRSIUM OCCIDENTALE   HIERACIUM CUSICKII   BIDENS LEUCANTHA

          292 **THISTLE**   293 **DEVIL'S-PAINTBRUSH**   294 **DESERT ZINNIA**
             CIRSIUM ACAULE   HIERACIUM AURANTIACUM   ZINNIA PUMILA

R. serotina grows in fields, roadsides, open waste places, etc., throughout the eastern half of North America. It flowers from June to October. It is a very common and beautiful weed, which originated on the Great Plains and has spread eastward. A similar but less aggressive species also called black-eyed-Susan may be distinguished by its broader, more ovate basal leaves; this is *R. hirta*. It occurs from Massachusetts to Illinois and southward to Georgia and Alabama.

GROUNDSEL
SENECIO LONGILOBUS   *Plate 288*

This groundsel is a bush three feet tall or more. The leaves are singly attached and pinnately divided, except the very narrow uppermost ones. The whole plant is white with dense wool, at least when young. The yellow flower-heads terminate the many branches. The pappus is composed of many soft white hairs.

S. longilobus grows in deserts, grasslands, and dry woodlands from southern Utah and western Texas to Colorado and Arizona; and in northern Mexico. It flowers from May to November. It is very abundant in the grasslands of southern New Mexico and Arizona. It has proven poisonous to cattle. However, it is used medicinally by the Indians.

DESERT-DANDELION
MALACOTHRIX CALIFORNICA   *Plate 276*

Desert-dandelion has a cluster of woolly leaves at the ground, each leaf cleft pinnately into very narrow lobes. From this tuft rises a leafless stem about a foot tall, bearing one fragrant flower-head. The head, like that of the true dandelion (*Taraxacum*), consists entirely of pale yellow flowers of the ray type, i.e., with the corolla expanded on one side into a flat, long, petal-like body. The pappus is composed of white bristles, two of which do not fall but are found on the achene.

Desert-dandelion grows in dry sandy places in the central valley and coast ranges of the southern half of California. It flowers from March to May.

PAPER-FLOWER
PSILOSTROPHE COOPERI   *Plate 277*

Paper-flower is a shrub a foot or two tall. The stems are covered with white wool. The leaves also may be woolly; they are very narrow and an inch or two long. The flower-heads terminate the numerous short branches. The rays of each head are few, broad, bright yellow, and notched at the end; they fade to straw color as they age, becoming papery in texture. The pappus is composed of scales.

This species of paper-flower is found in desert mountains and rocky slopes from Utah to California and southward to New Mexico, Arizona, and probably Mexico. It often flowers twice in the year, once after the spring rains and again after the summer rains. At these times the rounded plants are literally covered with bloom. *Psilostrophe* is one of the many genera of *Compositae* that cover the arid landscapes of the Southwest with gold at certain seasons.

295
DESERT-MARIGOLD
BAILEYA MULTIRADIATA

296
BLANKET-FLOWER
GAILLARDIA PINNATIFIDA

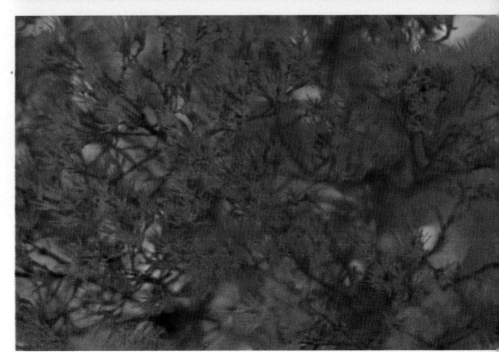

297
RABBIT-BRUSH
CHRYSOTHAMNUS NAUSEOSUS

GOLDEN-YARROW
ERIOPHYLLUM CONFERTIFLORUM   *Plate 278*

Golden-yarrow is a small shrub, a foot or two tall, the base woody but the many leafy branches herbaceous and covered with white wool. The leaves are only an inch or two long, pinnately lobed, white and woolly on the under surface. The yellow flower-heads are numerous at the tips of the branches. There are in each head from four to six broad rays and a small disc; such a head may easily be mistaken for a single flower with from four to six petals. From five to twelve minute scales make up the pappus.

Golden-yarrow is found on brushy slopes, ascending to high altitudes, in the coast ranges and Sierra Nevada foothills nearly throughout California and in Baja California. It flowers from April to August. The general appearance and the character of the flower-heads recall yarrow (*Achillea*).

BAHIA
BAHIA ABSINTHIFOLIA   *Plate 280*

B. absinthifolia is a tall plant whitened with minute hairs. The leaf-blades are palmately divided into three or five narrow segments, which are subdivided or lobed (except in a common Arizona variety). The yellow flower-heads terminate long, leafless branches. The pappus consists of small scales.

B. absinthifolia is found in the deserts from Texas to Arizona and southward into Mexico. It flowers from April to October.

DESERT-MARIGOLD
BAILEYA PLENIRADIATA   *Plate 282*

The desert-marigold has a number of stems attaining eighteen inches in height, each bearing one flower-head. The leaves are mostly narrow; the lower ones are pinnately lobed. Both stems and leaves are more or less woolly, with tangled white hairs. In the flower-head there are from twenty to forty golden rays, each blunt and notched at the tip. There are many disc-flowers, opening in succession from the margin in, as is clearly shown by the photograph. There is no pappus.

Desert-marigold is common in dry soil from Utah to California and southward to Texas and northern Mexico. It flowers from October to November.

DESERT-MARIGOLD
BAILEYA MULTIRADIATA   *Plate 295*

This desert-marigold grows about a foot tall. The stem bears leaves, pinnately cleft or not, only on its lower half. The plant is covered with white wool. The yellow flower-heads terminate the branches. Each has twenty or more large rays, which as they age become white and papery and are bent downward. There is no pappus.

Desert-marigold is very common in sandy plains from western Texas and Utah to southern California and southward to northern Mexico. It flowers from March to October. It is not related to the marigolds of our gardens.

240

298
THISTLE
CIRSIUM DISCOLOR

299
WING-STEM
ACTINOMERIS ALTERNIFOLIA

MILK-THISTLE
SILYBUM MARIANUM

Plate 281

Milk-thistle is an annual or biennial plant reaching six feet in height. The leaves have wavy or lobed margins with sharp yellow spines; the bases clasp the stem. A single flower-head terminates the stem. The bracts are broadbased; their spiny tips point outward; their edges also bear spines. The purple flowers are narrow, like those of the thistles (*Cirsium*). The pappus is composed of shining white hairs joined at the base.

This is a common weed which came from the Mediterranean and is now naturalized in the Pacific states and occasionally found elsewhere in this country. It flowers from May to July.

STAR-THISTLE
CENTAUREA MACULOSA

Plate 279

The bushy stem of *C. maculosa* is about three feet tall. The leaves are pinnately divided into very narrow lobes, except a few of the uppermost. The bracts of the involucre are oval, with a dark triangular tip, which bears slender projections along its sides. The flowers are rose or purplish or white, in form like those of *C. jacea*.

Like most other species of *Centaurea*, *C. maculosa* is European in origin, having established itself as a weed from Quebec to British Columbia and southward; it is said to be still spreading. The flowers are seen from June to October. Another species, *C. cyanus*, is cultivated under the name of bachelor's-buttons and is often found growing wild. In England this is called cornflower, having been generally found as a weed in cornfields ("corn" in English is "grain," usually wheat); it is now becoming rare there. Other names for it are bluebottle, blue-buttons, knotweed, miller's-delight, and witches'-thimble. It used to serve as a medicine for fevers, wounds, plague, and poison; probably ineffectively.

COBWEB THISTLE
CIRSIUM OCCIDENTALE

Plate 289

This western thistle grows up to three feet tall, or more. The leaves of the rosette formed the first season are lance-shaped (tapering inward) and more or less lobed, with prickly edges. The leaves on the stem are sharply toothed, the teeth ending in spines. The whole plant is beset with long hairs, which form a web or, sometimes, tufts of wool. The flower-heads occur singly at the tips of the stems. The flowers are purplish-red. The bracts of the involucre are very narrow and end in strong spines.

Cobweb thistle occurs on coastal dunes and in open grassy or brushy places in California. Flowering is from April to July.

THISTLE
CIRSIUM ACAULE

Plate 292

This thistle is usually without a visible stem (*acaule* means "stemless") but may have a stem a foot tall. The leaves are quite covered on the under surface with cobwebby

300 **WYETHIA** WYETHIA ELATA

301 **SNAKEWEED** GUTIERREZIA SAROTHRAE

302 **SEASIDE-DAISY** ERIGERON GLAUCUS

303 **TANSY** TANACETUM VULGARE

304 **TIDY-TIPS** LAYIA PLATYGLOSSA

white hairs. They are more or less pinnately lobed, the lobes bearing sharp spines. The outer bracts of the flower-head may also be spine-tipped, but the inner ones have no such armament. The numerous slender flowers are white or white tinged with pink or lavender.

C. acaule is common in damp meadows from the Rocky Mountains to California. It flowers from June to August.

THISTLE
CIRSIUM DISCOLOR   *Plate 298*

The stem of this thistle rises from a rosette of leaves which are green on the upper side, white with wool underneath (*discolor* signifies "differing in color") and deeply cleft pinnately. The flowering stem grows in the second year, up to ten feet tall (but usually less). The leaves on the stem are much like those at the base but smaller, pinnately divided into very narrow segments tipped with spines; there are leaves of this kind just beneath each flower-head. The red-purple flowers are very narrow, all of the tubular type usually called disc-flowers. The pappus is the soft white thistle-down.

C. discolor is a common thistle in fields, thickets, and various other situations from Quebec to Manitoba and southward to Georgia, Tennessee, and Missouri. It flowers from July to October.

PINCUSHION-FLOWER
CHAENACTIS GLABRIUSCULA   *Plate 286*

This is an annual with branched stems, a foot tall or taller. The small leaves, which are attached singly, are pinnately cleft, the lobes of some of them again cleft into narrow lobes. The yellow flower-heads flare like a top. They have no proper rays, but the outer flowers have somewhat larger corolla-lobes. The pappus is composed of four or five scales nearly as long as the corolla.

The species consists of numerous varieties differing in degree of branching, presence or absence of wool, size of flower-heads, characteristics of pappus, and other details. They grow in grassy and sandy places and chaparral in the central valley and coast ranges of California. The flowering period is from March to July.

YARROW
ACHILLEA LANULOSA   *Plate 287*

Yarrow is a perennial a foot or two tall, generally considered a weed when it is found in gardens and roadsides. The stem is woolly ("lanulose") and bears leaves which are pinnately divided or "dissected" into innumerable small, narrow segments. The plant is strongly aromatic. The flowers grow in numerous heads which have short, blunt, white rays and white disc-flowers. (Sometimes both rays and disc are pink.)

The species of this genus are confused and confusing, not to be accurately identified without microscopic study of certain internal details. *A. lanulosa* is a native species which grows practically throughout North America in open places and light shade. It flowers from June to August. An almost identical species, *A. millefolium*, has been introduced from the Old World and has become a weed in many parts of North America, especially in the East. The name of the genus is said to refer to healing powers discovered by the classic Greek hero Achilles.

DESERT or WILD ZINNIA
ZINNIA PUMILA
Plate 294

Wild zinnia is a branching herb which forms a clump about six inches high. The leaves are very narrow, with a strong midrib, and come in pairs. The flower-heads bear usually from four to six white or pale yellow rays which turn downward; they do not wither and fall as the achenes develop. The small disc projects as a cone.

This species is a desert plant, occurring from Texas to southern Arizona and northern Mexico. The flowers are seen in April and October. The garden zinnias are derived from a Mexican species, *Z. elegans*.

RABBIT-BRUSH
CHRYSOTHAMNUS NAUSEOSUS
Plate 297

The extremely variable species *C. nauseosus* consists of shrubs generally three or four feet tall, some varieties taller, some shorter. The leaves are very narrow, inconspicuous. The stems and leaves are gray-green, the stems being more or less covered with white wool. The yellow flower-heads terminate the numerous branches. They are tall and narrow, surrounded by overlapping bracts in many circles. There are no ray flowers. The photograph shows the flower-heads as seen from above, each consisting of several tubular flowers whose tips diverge. The pappus consists of bristles.

The many varieties of rabbit-brush occur in alkaline flats and on rocky slopes from North Dakota to British Columbia and southward to California and northern Mexico. It flowers in late summer and autumn. It has also been called rubber-brush; the latex yields a good quantity of rubber, which is, however, not economically available. The herbage has a resinous odor and a very bitter taste. The flowers are fragrant and often occur in great masses, making a fine show in dry places.

WING-STEM
ACTINOMERIS ALTERNIFOLIA
Plate 299

Wing-stem reaches a height of six feet or even more. The leaves, which are mostly singly attached, are narrow and lance-shaped; and the edges of each leaf seem to run down on the stem as two "wings." The plant is somewhat rough and hairy. The flower-heads are clustered at the top of the stem and on branches that grow from the axils of the upper leaves. The species is easily recognizable from the somewhat moplike appearance of the heads: the yellow rays are directed downward, and the disc-flowers at maturity project in all directions. (This characteristic distinguishes wing-stem from the closely related crownbeard, genus *Verbesina*.) The achenes are flat and usually edged with thin wings, which pass upward into small spines—the pappus.

Wing-stem grows in woodlands and wooded waste places, usually where the soil is damp, from New York to Iowa and southward to Florida and Louisiana. It flowers from August to October.

WYETHIA
WYETHIA ELATA   *Plate 300*

The stems of *Wyethia elata* grow from a large root, reaching a height of three feet or more. The numerous leaves are lance-shaped or ovate. The whole plant is coarsely hairy. Both rays and yellow disc-flowers are fertile. The pappus consists of several scales, which may still be seen on the fruits.

W. elata grows on dry open slopes in the foothills of the Sierra Nevada in central California. It flowers from June to August.

SNAKEWEED
GUTIERREZIA SAROTHRAE   *Plate 301*

Snakeweed is shrubby, but woody only at the base, reaching a height of about a foot. The leaves are very narrow, almost needlelike, an inch or two long. The flower-heads are crowded at the ends of short branches. There are only a few golden-yellow flowers in a head (from six to sixteen). A few scales compose the pappus.

Snakeweed occurs in deserts and dry woodlands and grasslands from Montana southward and southwestward to New Mexico, Arizona, and southern California; and in northern Mexico. Its presence in livestock ranges usually indicates overgrazing, with the destruction of the forage grasses.

TANSY
TANACETUM VULGARE   *Plate 303*

Tansy grows up to three feet tall. The leaves are pinnately divided and the segments again toothed or divided so that the general appearance is almost fernlike. The foliage is strongly aromatic. The numerous yellow flowers are in buttonlike heads, with or without a few short rays at the margins.

Common tansy is an old-world herb brought to American gardens by early settlers (to whom it had sovereign medicinal virtues) and now frequently found growing wild along roadsides and in fields and waste places throughout North America. It flowers from July to October. In England it is also called—among other names—bitter-buttons, scented fern, and stinking Willie; the taste is bitter and the scent or stink (as one may react to it) pronounced. Tea made from tansy leaves has been used for a remedy against almost any ailment. The leaves themselves, called tansies, were also used in medieval medicine. It was even recommended to lay one leaf on the navel to promote childbearing. The oil, however, is poisonous. The name is connected with a Greek word meaning "long," in reference presumably to the long-lasting flowers.

305
OX-EYE DAISY
CHRYSANTHEMUM LEUCANTHEMUM

306
DAISY FLEABANE
ERIGERON PHILADELPHICUS

TIDY-TIPS
LAYIA PLATYGLOSSA   *Plate 304*

Tidy-tips is an annual with succulent stems from four inches to a foot long, which lie on the ground or bend down. The leaves are toothed or pinnately lobed and hairy. The flower-heads are about an inch across. The yellow rays are fan-shaped, the outer margin of each having three white lobes. The pappus is a circle of many fine bristles, white or tan, in one variety covered with side-branches like a feather.

Tidy-tips occurs in grassy open places through most of lowland California. It flowers from March to June and contributes to the astonishing displays of massed flowers that transform the slopes of California hills. *Layia* includes fifteen species, all native to California, and only two of these are known outside that state.

In the photograph a lupine (*Lupinus bicolor*) may also be seen.

OX-EYE DAISY
CHRYSANTHEMUM LEUCANTHEMUM   *Plate 305*

The stem of ox-eye daisy is two or three feet tall; it is rarely branched, except near the summit. The leaves are of various shapes, the lower with more or less oval blades on long stalks, the upper narrower and without stalks, all quite irregularly toothed or lobed. The flower-heads terminate short branches at the top, which bear no leaves for some distance down. There are twenty or thirty white rays and a yellow disc.

Ox-eye daisy is a native of Europe and Asia, now a common weed in fields and along roadsides from Labrador to British Columbia and southward to Florida, Kentucky, and Kansas; and it is found elsewhere less commonly. It flowers from May to October. A well-known American botanist, Fernald, called this familiar plant "a pernicious but beautiful weed." The older English name is moon daisy or moon-flower. Another name is dunder or thunder daisy, for, since it blooms in midsummer, it was associated with St. John and thought effective in keeping away lightning. For this purpose it was hung indoors in Europe. German names for it are Johanneskraut, Gewitterblume, etc. It will come as a surprise to many that this is a species of *Chrysanthemum*. Our garden forms, however, are derived from oriental species. *Chrysanthemum* means "golden flower" and *leucanthemum* means "white flower"; this species has both.

Mixed with the daisies in the photograph are plants of devil's-paintbrush, *Hieracium aurantiacum*.

INDEX

Abronia umbellata, 76, *pl.* 58
Abutilon theophrasti, 143, *pl.* 151
Acanthaceae, 221
Acanthus family, 221
Achillea lanulosa, 244, *pl.* 287
Actinomeris alternifolia, 245, *pl.* 299
Adenostoma fasciculatum, 122, *pl.* 121
Air-plant (*see* Wild pineapple)
Aizoaceae, 91
Alismataceae, 58
Allium schoenoprasum, 44, *pl.* 11
Alum-root (*see* Coral-bells)
Amaryllidaceae, 47
Amole (*see* Soap-plant)
Anemone, rue-, 82, *pl.* 66
    tree-, 114, *pl.* 107
Anemone hudsoniana, 82, *pl.* 62
Anemonella thalictroides, 82, *pl.* 66
Annonaceae, 88
Apache-plume, 122, *pl.* 120
Apocynaceae, 186
Apocynum androsaemifolium, 186, *pl.* 211
Aquilegia caerulea, 80, *pl.* 67
    canadensis, 77, *pl.* 74
    chrysantha, 80, *pl.* 73
    formosa, 80, *pl.* 71
    pubescens, 80, *pl.* 60
Araceae, 59
Arctostaphylos pungens, 180, *pl.* 201
Argemone alba, 104, *pl.* 92
    platyceras, 104, *pl.* 94
Arisaema triphyllum, 59, *pl.* 37
Arrowleaf family, 58
Arum family, 59
Asclepiadaceae, 189
Asclepias syriaca, 192, *pl.* 214
    tuberosa, 189, *pl.* 213
Ascyrum tetrapetalum, 147, *pl.* 157
Asimina reticulata, 88, *pl.* 76
    speciosa, 88, *pl.* 75
Aster, wild, 233, *pl.* 273
Aster patens, 233, *pl.* 273
Atamasco-lily (*see* Easter-lily)
Avalanche-lily, 45, *pl.* 19
Azalea, western, 177, *pl.* 197
    wild, 177, *pl.* 200

Baby-blue-eyes, 199, *pl.* 228
Bahia, 240, *pl.* 280
Bahia absinthifolia, 240, *pl.* 280
Baileya multiradiata, 240, *pl.* 295
    pleniradiata, 240, *pl.* 282
Balsaminaceae, 142
Barrel cactus, 160, *pl.* 171
Bean family, 123
Beard-tongue (*P. canescens*), 218, *pl.* 254A
    (*P. heterophyllus*), 216, *pl.* 251
    crimson, 216, *pl.* 249
    lilac, 218, *pl.* 255
Bear-grass, 41, *pl.* 8
Bedstraw, lady's, 223, *pl.* 262
Bedstraw family, 223
Bee-balm, 208, *pl.* 245
Bellflower, 230, *pl.* 271
Bellwort, 39, *pl.* 6
Bergamot, wild, 208, *pl.* 238
Bidens aristosa, 232, *pl.* 272
    leucantha, 233, *pl.* 291
Bindweed, hedge, 192, *pl.* 215
Bird's-eyes, 195, *pl*, 224
Bird's-foot trefoil, 132, *pl.* 133
Bitter cress, 105, *pl.* 96
Black-eyed Susan, 237, *pl.* 275
Black mustard, 108, *pl.* 101
Bladder campion, 96, *pl.* 84
Bladder-pod, 105, *pl.* 98
Bladderwort, horned, 221, *pl.* 260
Bladderwort family, 221
Blanket-flower (*G. pinnatifida*), 230, *pl.* 296

(*G. pulchella*), 230, *pl.* 274
Blazing-star, 156, *pl.* 167
Bloodroot, 101, *pl.* 91
Bloomeria crocea, 47, *pl.* 22
Bluebell family, 227
Bluebells (*M. ciliata*), 201, *pl.* 230
    (*M. viridis*), 201, *pl.* 229
Blue columbine, 80, *pl.* 67
Blue-dicks, 49, *pl.* 24
Blue-eyed-grass, 53, *pl.* 27
Bluets, 223, *pl.* 263
Blue vervain, 203, *pl.* 233
Bog orchis, 67, *pl.* 46
Borage family, 201
Boraginaceae, 201
Brassica nigra, 108, *pl.* 101
Brazilian-tea (*see* False vervain)
Brodiaea, 49, *pl.* 23
Brodiaea coronaria, 49, *pl.* 23
    pulchella, 49, *pl.* 24
Bromeliaceae, 56
Broom, Spanish, 135, *pl.* 139
Buckwheat, climbing, 73, *pl.* 54
    desert-, 71, *pl.* 52
    wild, 71, *pl.* 55
Bugler, scarlet, 216, *pl.* 257
Bunchberry, 171, *pl.* 192
Bur-reed, 62, *pl.* 39
Bur-reed family, 62
Bush honeysuckle, 226, *pl.* 265
Bush lupine, 129, *pl.* 131
Buttercup, swamp, 77, *pl.* 70
    tall, 77, *pl.* 59
Buttercup family, 76
Butterfly-weed, 189, *pl.* 213
Brodiaea, 49, *pl.* 23

Cactaceae, 156
Cactus, barrel, 160, *pl.* 171
    hedgehog (*E. engelmanii*), 160, *pl.* 173
    hedgehog (*E. triglochidiatus*), 160, *pl.* 172
Cactus family, 156
California campion, 96, *pl.* 85
California columbine, 80, *pl.* 60
Calochortus albus, 41, *pl.* 9
    venustus, 41, *pl.* 15
Calonyction aculeatum, 194, *pl.* 217
Calopogon tuberosus, 67, *pl.* 44
Caltha leptosepala, 85, *pl.* 68
    palustris, 88, *pl.* 72
Campanula rapunculoides, 230, *pl.* 271
    rotundifolia, 229, *pl.* 270
Campanulaceae, 227
Campion, bladder, 96, *pl.* 84
    California, 96, *pl.* 85
Canada mayflower, 44, *pl.* 10
Canchalagua, 184, *pl.* 209
Candlewood (*see* Ocotillo)
Caper family, 99
Capparidaceae, 99
Caprifoliaceae, 226
Cardamine cordifolia, 105, *pl.* 96
Cardinal-flower, 229, *pl.* 269
Cardinal-spear, 123, *pl.* 124
Carnegiea gigantea, 160, *pl.* 170
Carolina-poppy, 104, *pl.* 92
Carpenteria californica, 114, *pl.* 107
Carpet-weed family, 91
Caryophyllaceae, 96
Cassia aspera, 125, *pl.* 126
    fasciculata, 125, *pl.* 141
Castilleia lanata, 215, *pl.* 248
    latifolia, 215, *pl.* 253
    rupicola, 215, *pl.* 256
Cat-claw, 123, *pl.* 125
Centaurea maculosa, 242, *pl.* 279
Centaurium venustum, 184, *pl.* 209
Centrosema virginianum, 132, *pl.* 134
Cerastium oreophilum, 96, *pl.* 86
Cercidium microphyllum, 128, *pl.* 128
Chaenactis glabriuscula, 244, *pl.* 286

Chamise (*see* Greasewood)
Chickweed, great, 99, *pl.* 87
    mountain, 96, *pl.* 86
Chinese-houses, 220, *pl.* 259
Chives, 44, *pl.* 11
Chlorogalum pomeridianum, 39, *pl.* 5
Cholla, 157, *pl.* 168
    deerhorn, 157, *pl.* 175
    jumping, 157, *pl.* 174
Chorizanthe, 73, *pl.* 56
Chorizanthe fimbriata, 73, *pl.* 56
Chrysanthemum leucanthemum, 248, *pl.* 305
Chrysothamnus nauseosus, 245, *pl.* 297
Cicuta maculata, 169, *pl.* 190
Cinquefoil, shrubby, 117, *pl.* 122
    three-toothed, 117, *pl.* 113
Cirsium acaule, 242, *pl.* 292
    discolor, 244, *pl.* 298
    occidentale, 242, *pl.* 289
Cistaceae, 147
Clammyweed, 99, *pl.* 88
Clamshell orchid, 67, *pl.* 48
Clarkia, 166, *pl.* 184
Clarkia amoena, 163, *pl.* 179
    bottae, 166, *pl.* 181
    cylindrica, 166, *pl.* 185
    deflexa, 163, *pl.* 178
    gracilis, 163, *pl.* 180
    unguiculata, 166, *pl.* 184
Claytonia lanceolata, 93, *pl.* 82
    virginica, 93, *pl.* 83
Clematis, marsh, 85, *pl.* 65
Clematis crispa, 85, *pl.* 65
Clethra alnifolia, 70, *pl.* 50
Clethraceae, 70
Cliff-rose, 123, *pl.* 123
Climbing buckwheat, 73, *pl.* 54
Climbing-milkweed, 189, *pl.* 212
Clover, mustang-, 197, *pl.* 225
    rabbit-foot, 134, *pl.* 135A
    red, 134, *pl.* 136
    white sweet-, 129, *pl.* 132
Coachwhip (*see* Ocotillo)
Cobweb thistle, 242, *pl.* 289
Cocoa family, 145
Collinsia heterophylla, 220, *pl.* 259
Columbine, 77, *pl.* 74
    blue, 80, *pl.* 67
    California, 80, *pl.* 60
    golden, 80, *pl.* 73
    mountain, 80, *pl.* 71
Commelina communis, 56, *pl.* 32
Commelinaceae, 53
Common blue violet, 151, *pl.* 161
Common milkweed, 192, *pl.* 214
Compositae, 230
Convolvulaceae, 192
Convolvulus sepium, 192, *pl.* 215
Coral-bean (*see* Cardinal-spear)
Coral-bells, 116, *pl.* 110
Coral honeysuckle (*see* Trumpet honeysuckle)
Corallorhiza mertensiana, 64, *pl.* 40
Coral-root, 64, *pl.* 40
Coreopsis tripteris, 232, *pl.* 283
Cornaceae, 171
Cornus canadensis, 171, *pl.* 192
Corpse-plant (*see* Indian-pipe)
Corydalis, pink, 99, *pl.* 90
Corydalis sempervirens, 99, *pl.* 90
Cowania mexicana, 123, *pl.* 123
Cow-horn orchid, 64, *pl.* 42
Crane's-bill (*G. cowenii*), 140, *pl.* 146
    (*G. maculatum*) (*see* Wild geranium)
Crassulaceae, 110
Cream-cups, 101, *pl.* 89
Cress, bitter, 105, *pl.* 96
    yellow, 108, *pl.* 99
Crimson beard-tongue, 216, *pl.* 249
Crinkleroot, 108, *pl.* 100
Crow-poison (*see* Osceola's-plume)
Cruciferae, 104

Cuscuta denticulata, 194, pl. 216
Cyperaceae, 36
Cypripedium acaule, 65, pl. 45
  calceolus, 65, pl. 47
Cyrtopodium punctatum, 64, pl. 42

Daffodil family, 47
Daisy, mountain, 234, pl. 285
  ox-eye, 248, pl. 305
  seaside-, 234, pl. 302
Daisy family, 230
Daisy fleabane, 234, pl. 306
Dalea spinosa, 134, pl. 137
  wislizenii, 128, pl. 127
Dandelion, desert-, 238, pl. 276
Datura meteloides, 212, pl. 244
Daucus carota, 171, pl. 191
Dayflower, 56, pl. 32
Deerberry, 177, pl. 199
Deerhorn cholla, 157, pl. 175
Delicate Ionopsis, 64, pl. 41
Delphinium glareosum, 85, pl. 64
Dentaria diphylla, 108, pl. 100
Desert-buckwheat, 71, pl. 52
Desert-dandelion, 238, pl. 276
Desert-mallow (see Globe-mallow)
Desert-marigold (B. multiradiata), 240,
  pl. 295
  (B. pleniradiata), 240, pl. 282
Desert-primrose, 168, pl. 183
Desert zinnia, 245, pl. 294
Desmodium canadense, 128, pl. 129
Devil's-lantern (see Desert-primrose)
Devil's-paintbrush, 237, pl. 293
Dichromena colorata, 36, pl. 1
Diervilla lonicera, 226, pl. 265
Dock, 71, pl. 51
Dodder, 194, pl. 216
Dodecatheon viviparum, 181, pl. 203
Dog-apple (see Pawpaw)
Dogbane, 186, pl. 211
Dogbane family, 186
Dogwood family, 171
Dudleya saxosa, 111, pl. 105
Dwarf cornel (see Bunchberry)

Early meadow-rue, 83, pl. 63
Early saxifrage, 114, pl. 111
Easter-lily, 49, pl. 25
Echinocactus viridescens, 160, pl. 171
Echinocereus englemannii, 160, pl. 173
  triglochidiatus, 160, pl. 172
Eichhornia crassipes, 58, pl. 35
Epidendrum cochleatum, 67, pl. 48
Epilobium angustifolium, 169, pl. 188
Ericaceae, 175
Erigeron callianthemus, 234, pl. 285
  glaucus, 234, pl. 302
  philadelphicus, 234, pl. 306
  species unknown, 233, pl. 284
Eriogonum crocatum, 71, pl. 55
  deflexum, 71, pl. 52
Eriophyllum confertiflorum, 240, pl. 278
Erysimum cheiranthoides, 105, pl. 97
Erythrina herbacea, 123, pl. 124
Erythronium americanum, 45, pl. 18
  montanum, 45, pl. 19
  pallidum, 47, pl. 20
Euphorbia heterophylla, 140, pl. 148
Euphorbiaceae, 140
Evening-primrose, 168, pl. 189
Evening-primrose, white (O. albicaulis),
  168, pl. 187
  white (O. speciosa), 168, pl. 186
Evening-primrose family, 163
Everlasting-pea (see Vetchling)

Fairy-lantern, 41, pl. 9
Fallugia paradoxa, 122, pl. 120
False buckwheat (see Climbing
  buckwheat)
False vervain, 205, pl. 234
Farewell-to-spring (C. amoena), 163, pl.
  179
  (C. bottae), 166, pl. 181
  (C. cylindrica), 166, pl. 185
  (C. gracilis), 163, pl. 180

Fiddler's-spurge (see Fire-on-the-
  mountain)
Field lily, 38, pl. 3
Fire-on-the-mountain, 140, pl. 148
Fireweed, 169, pl. 188
Firewheel (see Blanket-flower, G.
  pulchella)
Five-spot, 199, pl. 227
Flag, blue (I. hexagona), 52, pl. 26
  blue (I. versicolor), 52, pl. 28
  southern blue, 53, pl. 29
Flag-pawpaw, 88, pl. 75
Flannel-bush, 145, pl. 155
Flax, wild, 135, pl. 143
Flax family, 135
Fleabane, 233, pl. 284
  daisy, 234, pl. 306
Foamflower (T. cordifolia), 111, pl. 109
  (T. unifoliata). 111, pl. 106
Forget-me-not, 201, pl. 231
Fouquieria splendens, 148, pl. 160
Fouquieriaceae, 148
Four-leaved loosestrife, 181, pl. 205
Four-o'clock, 76, pl. 57
Four-o'clock family, 76
Fragaria virginiana, 122, pl. 118
Fremontia californica, 145, pl. 155
Funastrum heterophyllum, 189, pl. 212

Gaillardia pinnatifida, 230, pl. 296
  pulchella, 230, pl. 274
Galactia wrightii, 134, pl. 138
Galium verum, 223, pl. 262
Garden loosestrife, 181, pl. 204
Gentian family, 184
Gentianaceae, 184
Geraniaceae, 137
Geranium, wild, 140, pl. 147
Geranium cowenii, 140, pl. 146
  maculatum, 140, pl. 147
Geranium family, 137
Giant cactus (see Saguaro)
Gilia, 195, pl. 219
Gilia capitata, 195, pl. 219
  tricolor, 195, pl. 224
Globe-lily (see Fairy-lantern)
Globe-mallow, 145, pl. 154
Godetia, 163, pl. 178
Golden-club, 62, pl. 38
Golden-columbine, 80, pl. 73
Golden-stars, 47, pl. 22
Golden-yarrow, 240, pl. 278
Grass-pink, 67, pl. 44
Greasewood, 122, pl. 121
Great blue lobelia, 227, pl. 268
Great chickweed, 99, pl. 87
Groundsel, 238, pl. 288
Gutierrezia sarothrae, 246, pl. 301

Habenaria dilatata, 67, pl. 46
  saccata, 67, pl. 43
Hairy vetch, 132, pl. 135
Harebell, 229, pl. 270
Hawkweed, 237, pl. 290
Heath family, 175
Heather, pink-, 175, pl. 195
Hedge bindweed, 192, pl. 215
Hedgehog cactus (E. engelmannii), 160,
  pl. 173
  (E. triglochidiatus), 160, pl. 172
Helianthemum corymbosum, 148, pl.
  158
  scoparium var. aldersonii, 148, pl. 159
Heliotrope, wild-, 199, pl. 226
Hemlock, water-, 169, pl. 190
Hepatica nobilis, 83, pl. 61
Heuchera sanguinea, 116, pl. 110
Hieracium aurantiacum, 237, pl. 293
  cusickii, 237, pl. 290
Honeysuckle, bush, 226, pl. 265
  Japanese, 226, pl. 266
  trumpet, 227, pl. 267
Honeysuckle family, 226
Horned bladderwort, 221, pl. 260
Horse-mint, 208, pl. 237
Houstonia caerulea, 223, pl. 263
Hyacinth, water-, 58, pl. 35
Hydrophyllaceae, 199

Hymenocallis occidentalis, 47, pl. 21
Hypericaceae, 147
Hypericum perforatum, 147, pl. 156

Ice-plant, 93, pl. 81
Impatiens capensis, 142, pl. 149
Indian paintbrush (C. lanata), 215, pl.
  248
  (C. rupicola), 215, pl. 256
Indian-pipe, 174, pl. 193
Indian turnip (see Jack-in-the-pulpit)
Indigo-bush, 128, pl. 127
Innocence (see Chinese-houses)
Ionopsis, delicate, 64, pl. 41
Ionopsis utricularioides, 64, pl. 41
Ipomopsis, 194, pl. 218
Ipomopsis tenuifolia, 194, pl. 218
Iridaceae, 52
Iris, 53, pl. 30
Iris family, 52
Iris hexagona, 52, pl. 26
  missouriensis, 53, pl. 30
  versicolor, 52, pl. 28
  virginica, 53, pl. 29

Jack-in-the-pulpit, 59, pl. 37
Jacob's-ladder, 195, pl. 220
Japanese honeysuckle, 226, pl. 266
Jewelweed, 142, pl. 149
Jimson-weed, western, 212, pl. 244
Jumping cholla, 157, pl. 174
Jussiaea peruviana, 166, pl. 182

Kalmia angustifolia, 175, pl. 196
  latifolia, 175, pl. 198
Kosteletzkya virginica, 145, pl. 153

Labiatae, 205
Lady's bedstraw, 223, pl. 262
Lady's-slipper, pink, 65, pl. 45
  yellow, 65, pl. 47
Lambkill (see Sheep-laurel)
Languid lady (see Bluebells, M. ciliata)
Lantana camara, 203, pl. 232
Large-flowered sabatia, 186, pl. 207
Large-flowered trillium, 44, pl. 12
Larkspur, 85, pl. 64
Lathyrus latifolius, 128, pl. 130
Laurel, mountain-, 175, pl. 198
  sheep-, 175, pl. 196
Lavatera assurgentiflora, 143, pl. 150
Lavender, sea-, 184, pl. 208
Layia platyglossa, 248, pl. 304
Leadwort family, 184
Leather-flower (see Marsh clematis)
Leguminosae, 123
Lentibulariaceae, 221
Leptodactylon californicum, 197, pl. 222
Lesquerella kingii, 105, pl. 98
Lilac beard-tongue, 218, pl. 255
Liliaceae, 36
Lilium canadense, 38, pl. 3
  columbianum, 38, pl. 16
  philadelphicum, 38, pl. 17
Lily, avalanche-, 45, pl. 19
  Easter-, 49, pl. 25
  field, 38, pl. 3
  mariposa-, 41, pl. 15
  spider-, 47, pl. 21
  western, 38, pl. 16
  wood, 38, pl. 17
Lily family, 36
Limonium sinuatum, 184, pl. 208
Linaceae, 135
Linanthus montanus, 197, pl. 225
Linnaea borealis, 226, pl. 264
Linum lewisii, 135, pl. 143
Little-red-elephant, 220, pl. 254
Live-forever, 111, pl. 105
Live-forever family, 110
Liverleaf, 83, pl. 61
Lizard-tail, 70, pl. 49
Lizard-tail family, 70
Loasa family, 156
Loasaceae, 156
Lobelia, great blue, 227, pl. 268

Lobelia cardinalis, 229, *pl.* 269
  siphilitica, 227, *pl.* 268
Loco-weed, 135, *pl.* 142
Lonicera japonica, 226, *pl.* 266
  sempervirens, 227, *pl.* 267
Loosestrife, four-leaved, 181, *pl.* 205
  garden, 181, *pl.* 204
  purple, 162, *pl.* 176
Loosestrife family, 162
Lotus, 90, *pl.* 77
Lotus scoparius, 132, *pl.* 133
Lupine, bush, 129, *pl.* 131
  sky-blue, 129, *pl.* 140
Lupinus arboreus, 129, *pl.* 131
  cumulicola, 129, *pl.* 140
Lyre-leaved sage, 209, *pl.* 242
Lysimachia quadrifolia, 181, *pl.* 205
  terrestris, 181, *pl.* 206
  vulgaris, 181, *pl.* 204
Lythraceae, 162
Lythrum salicaria, 162, *pl.* 176

Maianthemum canadense, 44, *pl.* 10
Malacothrix californica, 238, *pl.* 276
Mallow, globe-, 145, *pl.* 154
  musk, 143, *pl.* 152
  seashore-, 145, *pl.* 153
  tree-, 143, *pl.* 150
Mallow family, 142
Malva moschata, 143, *pl.* 152
Malva-rosa (*see* Tree-mallow)
Malvaceae, 142
Manzanita, pointleaf, 180, *pl.* 201
Marigold, desert- (*B. multiradiata*), 240, *pl.* 295
  desert- (*B. pleniradiata*), 240, *pl.* 282
Mariposa-lily, 41, *pl.* 15
Marsh clematis, 85, *pl.* 65
Marsh-marigold, 88, *pl.* 72
  white, 85, *pl.* 68
Marsh-rosemary (*see* Sea-lavender)
Mayflower, Canada, 44, *pl.* 10
Meadow beauty, 162, *pl.* 177
Meadow-rue, early, 83, *pl.* 63
  tall, 83, *pl.* 69
Meadowsweet, 116, *pl.* 115
Melastomataceae, 162
Melastome family, 162
Melilotus alba, 129, *pl.* 132
Mentzelia involucrata, 156, *pl.* 167
Merrybells (*see* Bellwort)
Mertensia ciliata, 201, *pl.* 230
  viridis, 201, *pl.* 229
Mesembryanthemum crystallinum, 93, *pl.* 81
Milk-pea, 134, *pl.* 138
Milk-thistle, 242, *pl.* 281
Milkweed, climbing-, 189, *pl.* 212
  common, 192, *pl.* 214
Milkweed family, 189
Mimulus guttatus, 214, *pl.* 247
  lewisii, 215, *pl.* 252
Mint, horse-, 208, *pl.* 237
Mint family, 205
Mirabilis froebelii, 76, *pl.* 57
Mitella diphylla, 116, *pl.* 112
Miterwort, 116, *pl.* 112
Moccasin-flower (*see* Pink lady's-slipper)
Monarda clinopodioides, 208, *pl.* 237
  didyma, 208, *pl.* 245
  fistulosa, 208, *pl.* 238
Monkey-flower, 214, *pl.* 247
  pink, 215, *pl.* 252
Monotropa uniflora, 174, *pl.* 193
Moon-flower, 194, *pl.* 217
Morning-glory family, 192
Moss-verbena, 205, *pl.* 235
Mossy stonecrop, 110, *pl.* 103
Mountain chickweed, 96, *pl.* 86
Mountain columbine, 80, *pl.* 71
Mountain-daisy, 234, *pl.* 285
Mountain-laurel, 175, *pl.* 198
Mountain saxifrage, 114, *pl.* 108
Mullein, 218, *pl.* 250
Musk mallow, 143, *pl.* 152
Mustang-clover, 197, *pl.* 225
Mustard, black, 108, *pl.* 101
Mustard family, 104
Myosotis scorpioides, 201, *pl.* 231

Nelumbo lutea, 90, *pl.* 77
Nemophila maculata, 199, *pl.* 227
  menziesii, 199, *pl.* 228
Nigger-head (*see* Black-eyed Susan)
Nightshade, purple, 214, *pl.* 246
Nootka rose, 119, *pl.* 117
Nuphar advena, 91, *pl.* 79
Nyctaginaceae, 76
Nymphaea odorata, 90, *pl.* 78
Nymphaeaceae, 90

Ocotillo, 148, *pl.* 160
Ocotillo family, 148
Oenothera albicaulis, 168, *pl.* 187
  clavaeformis, 168, *pl.* 189
  deltoides, 168, *pl.* 183
  speciosa, 168, *pl.* 186
Onagraceae, 163
Opuntia bigelovii, 157, *pl.* 174
  engelmannii, 156, *pl.* 169
  tetracantha, 157, *pl.* 168
  versicolor, 157, *pl.* 175
Orchid, clamshell, 67, *pl.* 48
  cow-horn, 64, *pl.* 42
Orchid family, 64
Orchidaceae, 64
Orchis, bog, 67, *pl.* 46
  rein (*H. saccata*), 67, *pl.* 43
Ornithogalum umbellatum, 36, *pl.* 2
Orontium aquaticum, 62, *pl.* 38
Orthocarpus purpurascens, 220, *pl.* 258
Osceola's-plume, 39, *pl.* 4
Oswego-tea (*see* Bee-balm)
Our-Lord's-candle, 41, *pl.* 7
Owl's-clover, 220, *pl.* 258
Oxalidaceae, 137
Oxalis family, 137
Oxalis stricta, 137, *pl.* 145
  violacea, 137, *pl.* 144
Ox-eye daisy, 248, *pl.* 305
Oxytropis splendens, 135, *pl.* 142

Paint-brush (*see* Owl's-clover)
Paintbrush, devil's-, 237, *pl.* 293
  Indian (*C. lanata*), 215, *pl.* 248
  Indian (*C. rupicola*), 215, *pl.* 256
Painted-cup, seaside, 215, *pl.* 253
Pale dogtooth-violet, 47, *pl.* 20
Palo verde, 128, *pl.* 128
Papaver californicum, 101, *pl.* 93
Papaveraceae, 99
Paper-flower, 238, *pl.* 277
Parsley family, 169
Partridge-pea (*C. aspera*), 125, *pl.* 126
  (*C. fasciculata*), 125, *pl.* 141
Pasque-flower, 82, *pl.* 62
Pawpaw, 88, *pl.* 76
Pawpaw, flag-, 88, *pl.* 75
Pawpaw family, 88
Pea, milk-, 134, *pl.* 138
  partridge- (*C. aspera*), 125, *pl.* 126
  partridge- (*C. fasciculata*), 125, *pl.* 141
  spurred-butterfly-, 132, *pl.* 134
Pear, prickly-, 157, *pl.* 169
Pedicularis groenlandica, 220, *pl.* 254
Pennyroyal, 208, *pl.* 239
Penstemon canescens, 218, *pl.* 254A
  centranthifolius, 216, *pl.* 257
  davidsonii, 218, *pl.* 255
  heterophyllus, 216, *pl.* 251
  rupicola, 216, *pl.* 249
Phacelia tanacetifolia, 199, *pl.* 226
Phlox (*P. caespitosa*), 197, *pl.* 221
  (*P. pilosa*), 197, *pl.* 223
  prickly-, 197, *pl.* 222
Phlox caespitosa, 197, *pl.* 221
  pilosa, 197, *pl.* 223
Phlox family, 194
Phyllodoce empetriformis, 175, *pl.* 195
Phytolacca americana, 91, *pl.* 80
Phytolaccaceae, 91
Pickerel-weed, 59, *pl.* 36
Pickerel-weed family, 58
Pie-marker (*see* Velvet-leaf)
Pincushion-flower, 244, *pl.* 286
Pineapple, wild, 58, *pl.* 33
Pineapple family, 56
Pink, grass-, 67, *pl.* 44

rose-, 186, *pl.* 210
swamp-, 67, *pl.* 44
Pink corydalis, 99, *pl.* 90
Pink family, 96
Pink-heather, 175, *pl.* 195
Pink lady's-slipper, 65, *pl.* 45
Pink monkey-flower, 215, *pl.* 252
Pinkweed (*see* Smartweed)
Pinxter-flower, 177, *pl.* 200
Pitcher-plant, 110, *pl.* 102
Pitcher-plant family, 108
Platystemon californicus, 101, *pl.* 89
Pleurisy-root (*see* Butterfly-weed)
Plumbaginaceae, 184
Pointleaf manzanita, 180, *pl.* 201
Pokeweed, 91, *pl.* 80
Pokeweed family, 91
Polanisia trachysperma, 99, *pl.* 88
Polemoniaceae, 194
Polemonium confertum, 195, *pl.* 220
Polycodium stamineum, 177, *pl.* 199
Polygonaceae, 71
Polygonatum biflorum, 45, *pl.* 13
Polygonum pensylvanicum, 73, *pl.* 53
  scandens, 73, *pl.* 54
Pond-lily, yellow, 91, *pl.* 79
Ponil (*see* Apache-plume)
Pontederia cordata, 59, *pl.* 36
Pontederiaceae, 58
Poppy, Carolina-, 104, *pl.* 92
  prickly-, 104, *pl.* 94
  red, 101, *pl.* 93
Poppy family, 99
Portulacaceae, 93
Potato, swamp-, 58, *pl.* 34
Potato family, 212
Potentilla, 117, *pl.* 116
Potentilla flabellifolia, 117, *pl.* 116
  fruticosa, 117, *pl.* 122
  tridentata, 117, *pl.* 113
Prickly-pear, 156, *pl.* 169
Prickly-phlox, 197, *pl.* 222
Prickly-poppy, 104, *pl.* 94
Primrose, desert-, 168, *pl.* 183
Primrose family, 180
Primrose-willow, 166, *pl.* 182
Primulaceae, 180
Prunella vulgaris, 209, *pl.* 240
Psilostrophe cooperi, 238, *pl.* 277
Purple loosestrife, 162, *pl.* 176
Purple nightshade, 214, *pl.* 246
Purslane family, 93
Pycnothymus rigidus, 208, *pl.* 239
Pyrola elliptica, 174, *pl.* 194
Pyrolaceae, 174

Quaker-ladies (*see* Bluets)
Queen-Anne's-lace, 171, *pl.* 191
Quixote-plant (*see* Our-Lord's-candle)

Rabbit-brush, 245, *pl.* 297
Rabbit-foot clover, 134, *pl.* 135A
Radish, 105, *pl.* 95
Ranunculaceae, 76
Ranunculus acris, 77, *pl.* 59
  septentrionalis, 77, *pl.* 70
Raphanus sativus, 105, *pl.* 95
Red clover, 134, *pl.* 136
Red poppy, 101, *pl.* 93
Rein orchis (*H. dilatata*) (*see* Bog orchis)
  (*H. saccata*), 67, *pl.* 43
Rhexia mariana, 162, *pl.* 177
Rhododendron nudiflorum, 177, *pl.* 200
  occidentale, 177, *pl.* 197
Rock-harlequin (*see* Pink corydalis)
Rockrose (*H. corymbosum*), 148, *pl.* 158
  (*H. scoparium* var. *aldersonii*), 148, *pl.* 159
Rockrose family, 147
Romero (*see* Woolly-blue-curls)
Rorippa islandica, 108, *pl.* 99
Rosa carolina, 119, *pl.* 119
  gymnocarpa, 119, *pl.* 114
  nutkana, 119, *pl.* 117
Rosaceae, 116
Rose, cliff-, 123, *pl.* 123
  Nootka, 119, *pl.* 117
  wild (*R. carolina*), 119, *pl.* 119

wild (*R. gymnocarpa*), 119, *pl.* 114
Rose family, 116
Rose-pink, 186, *pl.* 210
Rosemary, marsh-, 184, *pl.* 208
Rubiaceae, 223
Rudbeckia serotina, 237, *pl.* 275
Rue-anemone, 82, *pl.* 66
Ruellia, 221, *pl.* 261
Ruellia humilis, 221, *pl.* 261
Rumex hastatulus, 71, *pl.* 51

Sàbatia, large-flowered, 186, *pl.* 207
Sabatia campestris, 186, *pl.* 210
   grandiflora, 186, *pl.* 207
Sacred-bean (*see* Lotus)
Sage, lyre-leaved, 209, *pl.* 242
Sagittaria graminea, 58, *pl.* 34
Saguaro, 160, *pl.* 170
St.-Andrew's-cross (*see* St.-Peter's-wort)
St.-John's-wort, 147, *pl.* 156
St.-John's-wort family, 147
St.-Peter's-wort, 147, *pl.* 157
Salvia lyrata, 209, *pl.* 242
Samodia, 180, *pl.* 202 .
Samolus ebracteatus, 180, *pl.* 202
Sand-verbena, 76, *pl.* 58
Sanguinaria canadensis, 101, *pl.* 91
Sarracenia purpurea, 110, *pl.* 102
Sarraceniaceae, 108
Saururus cernuus, 70, *pl.* 49
Saururaceae, 70
Saxifraga greenei, 114, *pl.* 108
   virginiensis, 114, *pl.* 111
Saxifragaceae, 111
Saxifrage, early, 114, *pl.* 111
   mountain, 114, *pl.* 108
Saxifrage family, 111
Scarlet bugler, 216, *pl.* 257
Schrankia nuttallii, 123, *pl.* 125
Scrophulariaceae, 214
Sea-lavender, 184, *pl.* 208
Seashore-mallow, 145, *pl.* 153
Seaside-daisy, 234, *pl.* 302
Seaside painted-cup, 215, *pl.* 253
Sedge family, 36
Sedum acre, 110, *pl.* 103
   divergens, 110, *pl.* 104
Self-heal, 209, *pl.* 240
Senecio longilobus, 238, *pl.* 288
Senna, dwarf, 125, *pl.* 126
Sensitive-brier (*see* Cat-claw)
Sheep-laurel, 175, *pl.* 196
Shepherd's-needle, 233, *pl.* 291
Shinleaf, 174, *pl.* 194
Shinleaf family, 174
Shooting-star, 181, *pl.* 203
Showy evening-primrose (*see* White evening-primrose, *O. speciosa*)
Shrubby cinquefoil, 117, *pl.* 122
Shrub-verbena, 203, *pl.* 232
Silene cucubalus, 96, *pl.* 84
   laciniata, 96, *pl.* 85
Silybum marianum, 242, *pl.* 281
Sisyrinchium bellum, 53, *pl.* 27
Skeleton-weed (*see* Desert-buckwheat)
Sky-blue lupine, 129, *pl.* 140
Smartweed, 73, *pl.* 53
Smartweed family, 71
Smoke-tree, 134, *pl.* 137
Snakeweed, 246, *pl.* 301
Snapdragon family, 214
Soap-plant, 39, *pl.* 5
Solanaceae, 212
Solanum elaeagnifolium, 214, *pl.* 246
Solomon's-seal, 45, *pl.* 13
Sour-grass (*see* Yellow wood-sorrel)
Southern blue flag, 53, *pl.* 29
Spanish broom, 135, *pl.* 139
Spanish-needles, 232, *pl.* 272
Sparganiaceae, 62
Sparganium androcladum, 62, *pl.* 39
Spartium junceum, 135, *pl.* 139
Spatterdock (*see* Yellow pond-lily)
Sphaeralcea ambigua, 145, *pl.* 154
Spider-lily, 47, *pl.* 21
Spiderwort, 56, *pl.* 31
Spiderwort family, 53
Spiraea latifolia, 116, *pl.* 115
Spotted cowbane (*see* Water-hemlock)

Spring beauty (*C. lanceolata*), 93, *pl.* 82
   (*C. virginica*), 93, *pl.* 83
Spurge, fiddler's-, 140, *pl.* 148
Spurge family, 140
Spurred-butterfly-pea, 132, *pl.* 134
Stachytarpheta jamaicensis, 205, *pl.* 234
Star-of-Bethlehem, 36, *pl.* 2
Star-thistle, 242, *pl.* 279
Stellaria pubera, 99, *pl.* 87
Sterculiaceae, 145
Sticktight, 128, *pl.* 129
Stonecrop, 110, *pl.* 104
   mossy, 110, *pl.* 103
Strawberry, wild, 122, *pl.* 118
Sunflower, tickseed-, 232, *pl.* 272
Swamp buttercup, 77, *pl.* 70
Swamp-candles, 181, *pl.* 206
Swamp-pink, 67, *pl.* 44
Swamp-potato, 58, *pl.* 34
Swamp violet, 153, *pl.* 165
Sweet-clover, white, 129, *pl.* 132
Sweet-pepper-bush, 70, *pl.* 50
Sweet white violet, 153, *pl.* 163

Tall buttercup, 77, *pl.* 59
Tall meadow-rue, 83, *pl.* 69
Tall tickseed, 232, *pl.* 283
Tanacetum vulgare, 246, *pl.* 303
Tansy, 246, *pl.* 303
Teddy-bear cactus (*see* Jumping cholla)
Thalictrum dioicum, 83, *pl.* 63
   polygamum, 83, *pl.* 69
Thistle (*C. acaule*), 242, *pl.* 292
   (*C. discolor*), 244, *pl.* 298
   cobweb, 242, *pl.* 289
   milk-, 242, *pl.* 281
   star-, 242, *pl.* 279
Thornapple (*see* Western jimson-weed)
Three-toothed cinquefoil, 117, *pl.* 113
Thyme, wild, 209, 241
Thymus serpyllum, 209, *pl.* 241
Tiarella cordifolia, 111, *pl.* 109
   unifoliata, 111, *pl.* 106
Tickseed, tall, 232, *pl.* 283
Tickseed-sunflower (*see* Spanish-needles)
Tidy-tips, 248, *pl.* 304
Tillandsia fasciculata, 58, *pl.* 33
Touch-me-not (*see* Jewelweed)
Touch-me-not family, 142
Tradescantia ohiensis, 56, *pl.* 31
Tree-anemone, 114, *pl.* 107
Tree-mallow, 143, *pl.* 150
Trefoil, bird's-foot, 132, *pl.* 133
Trichostema lanatum, 212, *pl.* 243
Trifolium arvense, 134, *pl.* 135A
   pratense, 134, *pl.* 136
Trillium, large-flowered, 44, *pl.* 12
   wood, 45, *pl.* 14
Trillium grandiflorum, 44, *pl.* 12
   viride, 45, *pl.* 14
Trumpet honeysuckle, 227, *pl.* 267
Twin-flower, 226, *pl.* 264

Umbelliferae, 169
Utricularia cornuta, 221, *pl.* 260
Uvularia sessilifolia, 39, *pl.* 6

Velvet-leaf, 143, *pl.* 151
Verbascum thapsus, 218, *pl.* 250
Verbena, moss-, 205, *pl.* 235
   sand-, 76, *pl.* 58
   shrub-, 203, *pl.* 232
Verbena hastata, 203, *pl.* 233
   tampensis, 205, *pl.* 236
   tenuisecta, 205, *pl.* 235
Verbenaceae, 203
Vervain, 205, *pl.* 236
   blue, 203, *pl.* 233
   false, 205, *pl.* 234
Vervain family, 203
Vetch, hairy, 132, *pl.* 135
Vetchling, 128, *pl.* 130
Vicia villosa, 132, *pl.* 135
Viola adunca, 153, *pl.* 166
   blanda, 153, *pl.* 163
   palustris, 153, *pl.* 165
   papilionacea, 151, *pl.* 161

pensylvanica, 153, *pl.* 164
   primulifolia, 151, *pl.* 162
Violaceae, 151
Violet, common blue, 151, *pl.* 161
   pale dogtooth-, 47, *pl.* 20
   swamp, 153, *pl.* 165
   sweet white, 153, *pl.* 163
   western blue, 153, *pl.* 166
   white, 151, *pl.* 162
   yellow, 153, *pl.* 164
   yellow dogtooth-, 45, *pl.* 18
Violet family, 151
Violet wood-sorrel, 137, *pl.* 144

Wallflower, wild, 105, *pl.* 97
Wallpepper (*see* Mossy stonecrop)
Water-hemlock, 169, *pl.* 190
Water-hyacinth, 58, *pl.* 35
Waterleaf family, 199
Water-lily, 90, *pl.* 78
Water-lily family, 90
Western azalea, 177, *pl.* 197
Western blue violet, 153, *pl.* 166
Western jimson-weed, 212, *pl.* 244
Western lily, 38, *pl.* 16
White-alder (*see* Sweet-pepper-bush)
White-alder family, 70
White evening-primrose (*O. albicaulis*), 168, *pl.* 187
   (*O. speciosa*), 168, *pl.* 186
White marsh-marigold, 85, *pl.* 68
White sweet-clover, 129, *pl.* 132
White-tops, 36, *pl.* 1
White violet, 151, *pl.* 162
Wild aster, 233, *pl.* 273
Wild azalea (*see* Pinxter-flower)
Wild bergamot, 208, *pl.* 238
Wild buckwheat, 71, *pl.* 55
Wild carrot (*see* Queen-Anne's-lace)
Wild daisy (*see* Fleabane)
Wild flax, 135, *pl.* 143
Wild geranium (*G. cowenii*) (*see* Crane's-bill)
   (*G. maculatum*), 140, *pl.* 147
Wild-heliotrope, 199, *pl.* 226
Wild lily-of-the-valley (*see* Canada mayflower)
Wild pineapple, 58, *pl.* 33
Wild rose (*R. carolina*), 119, *pl.* 119
   (*R. gymnocarpa*), 119, *pl.* 114
Wild strawberry, 122, *pl.* 118
Wild thyme, 209, *pl.* 241
Wild wallflower, 105, *pl.* 97
Wild zinnia (*see* Desert zinnia)
Willow, primrose-, 166, *pl.* 182
Willow-herb (*see* Fireweed)
Wing-stem, 245, *pl.* 299
Winter vetch (*see* Hairy vetch)
Wood lily, 38, *pl.* 17
Wood-sorrel, violet, 137, *pl.* 144
   yellow, 137, *pl.* 145
Wood trillium, 45, *pl.* 14
Woolly-blue-curls, 212, *pl.* 243
Wormseed-mustard (*see* Wild wallflower)
Wyethia, 246, *pl.* 300
Wyethia elata, 246, *pl.* 300

Xerophyllum tenax, 41, *pl.* 8

Yarrow, 244, *pl.* 287
   golden-, 240, *pl.* 278
Yellow bedstraw (*see* Lady's bedstraw)
Yellow cress, 108, *pl.* 99
Yellow dogtooth-violet, 45, *pl.* 18
Yellow lady's-slipper, 65, *pl.* 47
Yellow loosestrife (*see* Swamp-candles)
Yellow pond-lily, 91, *pl.* 79
Yellow violet, 153, *pl.* 164
Yellow wood-sorrel, 137, *pl.* 145
Yucca whipplei, 41, *pl.* 7

Zephyranthes treatiae, 49, *pl.* 25
Zinnia, desert, 245, *pl.* 294
Zinnia pumila, 245, *pl.* 294
Zygadenus densus, 39, *pl.* 4